Pitt Latin American Series

THE DYNAMICS OF
DOMINATION

STATE, CLASS, AND
SOCIAL REFORM IN MEXICO
1910–1990

Viviane Brachet-Marquez

UNIVERSITY OF PITTSBURGH PRESS

Pittsburgh and London

To the memory of Charles Staehling,
a loving grandfather and teacher
in the art of disagreement.

Library of Congress Cataloging-in-Publication Data

Marquez, Viviane Brachet de.
    The dynamics of domination : state, class, and social reform in
Mexico, 1910–1990 / Viviane Brachet-Marquez.
        p.   cm. — (Pitt Latin American series)
    Includes bibliographical references and index.
    ISBN 0-8229-3780-8 (alk. paper)
    1. Working class—Political activity—Mexico—History—20th
century.   2. Social conflict—Mexico—History—20th century.
3. Mexico—Politics and government—20th century.   4. Mexico—Social
policy. I. Title. II. Series.
    HD8114.M28   1994
    305.5′0972—dc20   93-30949
                                                                              CIP

Published by the University of Pittsburgh Press, Pittsburgh, Pa. 15260
Copyright © 1994, University of Pittsburgh Press
Manufactured in the United States of America
Printed on acid-free paper

A CIP catalogue record for this book is available from the British Library.
Eurospan, London

✳

Contents

Acknowledgments

For many years I have searched for ways to make the analysis of social policy open the doors to a broad understanding of the dynamics of society. Policy links the world of single decisions and organizations to that of institutions and collective action. It also links state to society, although all too often policy in countries such as Mexico is presented as singlehandedly engineered by the state. Lastly, it bridges the past, the present, and the future. This book is an attempt to bring out these potentials.

A previous study of health policy in Mexico and a Fulbright fellowship at Columbia University's Center for Social Policy and Planning in Developing Countries provided the initial impetus for this book. For this early stage of elaboration of the study, I owe thanks to Robert Alford, who tirelessly provided advice on the theoretical framework. During the elaboration of the empirical body of the study, my greatest debt is to my study group in Mexico, which, despite many obstacles, met regularly for two years and helped keep the ideas flowing. In particular, I wish to thank Maria Herrera, Susan Street, Karen Kovacs, and José Antonio Aldrete for their comments on different parts of the manuscript. My special thanks goes to Peter Cleaves for his critical review of the entire manuscript. I also want to thank the anonymous reviewers and my friends and colleagues for their faith, encouragement, criticism, and suggestions. Among them, I wish to mention particularly Charles Perrow, Diane Davis, and Barbara Helfferich.

The Dynamics of

DOMINATION

1

Introduction

Domination, defined as the capacity to impose upon others a course of action, is self-perpetuating to the extent that the dominated are unable to alter their subordinate condition. In capitalist societies, the central form of domination is the unequal apportioning of the economic surplus. This condition, identified by classical Marxism as the basis of class formation, is the specifically economic expression of capitalist domination via market mechanisms. Yet the rate at which different categories of wage earners are remunerated transcends the market. In any given society, the "going rate" is, to a large extent, the outcome of political processes in which actors with opposing class interests confront one another and negotiate legally binding conditions of work, which in turn are backed by the coercive power of the state.[1]

Far from being a given exogenous to class interests, these processes and the rules that govern their course are partly a product of political participation by subordinate classes. Therefore, if we cannot assume, as early Marxists did, that economically defined class relations necessarily lead to class conflict or class-based collective action (Katznelson, 1986:20), neither can we assert that the political context of capitalist societies is independent of class, especially regarding the role of wage earners in shaping these contexts.

Whereas the social democratizing effect of working class struggles has been recognized in the case of developed Western nations (Esping Andersen, 1985; Therborn, 1977), it has generally been underrated or ignored in the case of the capitalist periphery, mainly due to the incipient and fragmented state of the proletariat in these countries. In such contexts, concessions to wage earners have generally been interpreted as the result of state interventions instrumentally oriented toward capitalist development.[2]

Contrary to this trend, this book proposes to rediscover the role of subordinate classes in shaping political mechanisms in Mexico, one of the few countries of the capitalist periphery to have experienced a popular revolution in the twentieth century and, as a result, to have witnessed an early entry of the laboring classes into the political process. In this attempt, I shall steer away from preconceived notions of the nature of the Mexican Revolution (e.g., as a bourgeois or a defeated proletarian revolution). My purpose is to examine the role of the working class in the making of modern Mexico. In order to carry out this task, I must establish the link between labor's limited and issue-specific struggles to improve its economic lot (the narrowly economic aspect of class struggles) and its participation in shaping or modifying the Mexican system of political domination.

In this search, I shall look upon Mexico's political institutions as an outcome of the partial transformation by subordinate classes, through periodic episodes of confrontation followed by temporary settlements, of the forms of capitalist domination that have developed historically in Mexico. Far from remaining a neutral arbiter in such confrontations, the state has played a crucial mediating role by supplying ideological tools to economic and political struggles from below, determining their institutional forms, influencing their settlements, and ensuring the subsequent enforcement of such settlements. I argue that these settlements, in turn, have shaped the structure of the state and the form that political and economic domination have taken in Mexico. In this way, I regard capitalist "rationality," as it has developed in Mexico, as the contingent result of class struggles (Esping Andersen, Friedland, and Wright, 1976:215).

In practice, this means that even in conditions of relatively harsh capitalist exploitation such as those obtaining in Mexico, the state does not unconditionally support capitalist claims on labor,[3] nor do organized groups among the subordinate classes unconditionally submit to the verdict of the state. Which institutional solutions emerge, how much coercion they involve, and how long they last is a function of the historical circumstances in which capitalism has developed in Mexico and of the kinds of class struggles and state interventions that have unfolded. Therefore, though it may be true that the history of capitalism illustrates the submission of dominated classes more often than examples of their capacity to overthrow the oppressor, it is also true, as this book attempts to show, that the oppressed can significantly affect the forms that such domination takes.

Having gained freedom from colonial Spain in 1821 after a decade of warfare that cost close to half of the country's adult male population, Mexico entered the world system of industrial capitalism in the last quarter of the nineteenth century.[4] Under the most repressive dictatorship of its independence, the doors were opened to European and U.S. capital for the exploitation of the country's vast mineral wealth and for the building of its infrastructure (railroads, ports, electrification, etc). It also became more capitalist by intensifying the production of basic agricultural commodities for export, yet without altering the seigneurial relations of production on the land inherited from the colonial hacienda system.

Mexico's twentieth-century history opens with the breakdown of this regime that had made possible a certain form of capitalist development, but had simultaneously perpetuated a rigid form of state power incapable of incorporating the social transformations such development was triggering. After thirty-five years of what has been called *the Pax Porfiriana,* during which a new class structure emerged and Mexico "developed" (in the conventional economic sense of the term), the country became the scene of the first social revolution of the twentieth century. The social composition of the forces that participated in this conflagration and their subsequent contribution to the constitution of a new regime radically transformed the conditions under which different groups in Mexican society—the incipient industrial proletariat, the peasantry, the middle sectors, foreign investors, and the emerging national bourgeoisie—were able to relate to each other and to the newly assembled apparatus of political power.

After the Revolution established what purported to be a more just social order, Mexico went through several dislocations and transformations both in its internal structure and in its relation to foreign investors and the world market. It did so, however, not under the spur of a dynamic entrepreneurial class but ostensibly as a result of a systematic state policies. Under these policies, Mexico became extensively industrialized. Yet, in spite of special claims to more justice and recognition of the part played by the laboring masses in this process of growth, this development was and still is characterized by deep inequalities among the conspicuously rich few, a slim middle sector, and the poor majority.

Despite these deficiencies, Mexico was, for decades, a role model for other fledgling Third World nations set on a course toward "development." Since the 1970s, however, this image has become tarnished. This can be perceived in the downward trend of most conventional economic indicators and in serious sectorial imbalances. Among these, the most visible has been the decline of agriculture, as evidenced by the inability of the poor peasantry to feed themselves or the country and their exodus to the United States or to the three largest cities of Mexico.

Following a brief interlude of oil-supported growth from 1980 to 1982, Mexico was plunged into the deepest and longest economic crisis of its history, manifested by massive capital flight, towering foreign debt, record unemployment, triple-digit inflation, and widespread deindustrialization. This crisis left the employed underpaid and millions unemployed or underemployed, with hardly anyone to turn to but their families and the Virgin of Guadalupe. It also fundamentally transformed the scope and nature of state intervention in society, resulting in a far slimmer and partially decentralized state apparatus. Simultaneously, practically every form of public welfare—in education, health care, housing, transportation, and food—was slashed to pay the mushrooming foreign debt.

In any other Latin American country, such a massive crisis would likely have brought political turmoil and violent regime change. In Mexico, astoundingly, nothing changed in the institutional arrangements that define the scope and limits of state power. Nothing changed, that is, in the formal regime arrangements that ostensibly remained in force as of 1993: the official party still drew the majority of votes (by illegal means, if necessary), and the Salinas administration that took office, right on cue, in December 1988, firmly held the reins of power.

What was happening behind this imposing institutional facade in the late 1980s and early 1990s was from the outset a constant source of speculation among social scientists, journalists, and interested observers. Some focused on the political reactions of the middle classes; others scrutinized indicators of the democratization of public life; still others examined the transformation of central-local political and economic relations.[5] Since signs of clearly identifiable political change have failed to materialize, most commentators seem to have given up on futuristic predictions, concentrating instead on the day-to-day policies handed down by the Salinas administration, be they of "modernization," free trade, or "solidarity," the latest innovation in social policy.

None of these discussions have much to rely on, however, save the observation of immediate events that trigger instant interpretations. Because the entire research effort of the past twenty years has been oriented toward understanding Mexico's political stability and resilience as a function of unilateral state power, few observers are now prepared to link the unexpected social policy innovations undertaken by the Salinas administration to political turmoil in the 1980s.

While this book does not pretend to have all the answers, it does offer new terms in which to understand the deep changes that have taken place in postrevolutionary Mexico. Its fundamental starting point is that such an understanding cannot be gained by making instant causal inferences about political processes merely on the basis of economic change. Neither can such an analysis be guided by the belief in the unbreakability of established bureaucratic mechanisms of state control over subordinate classes.

I center my analysis of postrevolutionary Mexico on the concept of a *pact of domination* that expresses the pressures from below to which the political regime has been subjected at different historical moments. Through this concept, I establish a relationship between periods of political crisis (signifying the partial rupture of institutional mechanisms) and concessions offered by the state in the form of social reforms. These crises constitute the concrete and historically specific conjunctures that render more visible the processes of class struggle that have shaped contemporary Mexico. I propose that the key to understanding the relationship between such crises and reformist state responses lies in analysing the particular episodes of class conflict out of which social reforms have emerged and in the ways such reforms have eventually filtered through the state apparatus to become part of an institutionalized class compromise.

The enigma of Mexican exceptionalism lies in the fact that political crises have repeatedly produced—up through 1993 and probably beyond—class compromises consolidated by social reform rather than violent regime changes as in most other Latin American nations. The answer offered in this study is that Mexico has been saved from the more extreme forms of state repression and exclusion of subordinate classes—exemplified by Argentina and Chile—not by the strength of the state, as is too often assumed, but by its periodic vulnerability, and hence responsiveness, to pressures from below.

SOCIAL REFORMS AND LABOR

In principle, any social group could be selected to substantiate the thesis presented here. In practice, however, our choices are limited by the structure of Mexican political arrangements, which draws institutional lines around three formal groupings: the rural population, as represented by the Confederación Nacional Campesina (CNC—National Peasant Confederation); labor as organized under the Congreso del Trabajo (CT—Labor Congress); and a residual middle sector loosely aggregated between 1943 and 1989 as the Confederación Nacional de Organizaciones Populares (CNOP—National Confederation of Popular Organizations), subsequently transformed into UNE and finally discontinued altogether in 1992.[6]

Although organized labor is not the only actor to have influenced welfare policies, it was nevertheless the most prominent until the 1980s and, as such, the most important one to study. It is also the group that has attracted the largest number of case studies indispensable to the kind of secondary analysis undertaken here. Contrary to the CNC and the CNOP-UNE wings of the official party, the Mexican labor movement owes its origin to its own actions. It was born in the last decades of the nineteenth century, under the combined influence of anarchism and mutualism (Hart, 1978).[7] In its early formative stage, it was strongly influenced by radical foreign groups, particularly the Industrial Workers of the World (IWW).[8] The first great strikes of 1906 in the copper mines of Cananea and in 1908 in the textile works of Rio Blanco formed the prelude to the Revolution.

Despite its relatively small size and extreme fragmentation, labor has played a key role in shaping political institutions from the beginnings of the revolutionary process. As the institutions of the postrevolutionary state were consolidated, labor became the target of governmental actions aimed at both controlling it and using it as a political weapon to control other groups. This process, in turn, led to many transformations in the structure and character of the Mexican working class, both as a result of these actions and as a consequence of its own internal dynamic. At each stage, labor retained limited means of action, always contingent upon its capacity for independent organization and insurgency.

Contrary to the bulk of labor history, this study focuses on workers, not on their leaders. Leaders nevertheless figure prominently in the study insofar as they act as forces mobilizing or demobilizing the rank and file. The theoretical question of whether these leaders are part of the state or part of society does not have to be raised at this point. Inasmuch as state and society are understood here as participants in an interactive process, this distinction is not a necessary one. Whether labor leaders either see themselves as objectively representing the state or the workers in a given situation is not something that can be determined a priori.

It is both impossible and unnecessary to contemplate the sum total or purportedly redistributive social measures implemented since the Revolution in Mexico. More than the development of the welfare state as such, it is labor's direct or indirect agency in triggering social reforms that is the object of this inquiry. Therefore, my research strategy is to identify (1) social welfare policies that were implemented as a consequence of prior labor mobilizations; (2) significant instances of labor mobilization that were not followed by reforms; or (3) social benefits that were bestowed without any prior social agitation by labor. In the first case, positive substantiation of the hypothesis is sought; in the second and third, negative evidence could be uncovered.

Two kinds of state concessions to labor are included in the analysis. The most immediate concessions, but also the easiest to take back via inflation, are wage raises. These closely follow the conventional demand and response model throughout the period considered. Welfare measures, on the other hand, require structural (fiscal, bureaucratic, etc.) changes which are more difficult to achieve but are also more durable. Among these, I have selected three major social reforms targeted at organized labor: social insurance, profit sharing, and public housing. The first was adopted in 1943 and marks a period during which relations between state and labor underwent profound changes. The second was adopted in 1961, at a time when the violent confrontations that had opposed the state to various elements in the labor movements seemed to be over. The last, adopted in 1972, came in the wake of the student uprising of 1968. All three measures have been maintained, despite important budget cuts, since the onset of the debt crisis of the 1980s, while reforms directed at other sectors such as the Mexican Food System (SAM) or food distribution through the Compañía Nacional de Subsistencias Populares (CONASUPO—National Confederation for Popular Subsistence) have been discontinued.

Between wage gains or losses and income transfers in the form of welfare benefits lies the ill-defined and oft-disputed institutional area corresponding to the forms of collective action that labor adopts in its attempts to exert pressure on the state. In some cases (such as the right to organize or to strike), these forms may closely follow the letter of the law but not necessarily the de facto rules that the state attempts to impose. In others, they clearly lie outside the law. In some cases, labor leaders act as the representatives of contestatory pressures, while in others they act in concert with the state in resisting such pressures.

The question may be raised as to why I refer to the state rather than capital as labor's antagonist. At this point, suffice it to say that in Mexico as elsewhere, capital and labor, when left to their own devices, have been unable to settle their differences without stability-threatening social explosions. The state's involvement in the regulation of labor-capital relations can therefore be seen simultaneously as a way of securing its own stability and as a necessary condition for the establishment of a favorable context for capital accumulation.

METHODS

The study is based on the secondary analysis of a multiplicity of sources, on the basis of which a historical narrative is constructed. The narrative I present differs from conventional historical analysis, although it tries to emulate the best qualities of historians: their integration of levels of analysis; their general avoidance of simplistic taxonomies; their renunciation of pseudoscientific empirical generalizations (which is not tantamount to renouncing all comparative inquiry or global explanation); and, most of all, their acceptance of the simple fact that historical events, to occur, require people and unique convergences. Thanks to these qualities, historians are more apt than other social scientists to capture the uneven and contingent character of state-society relations. In addition, the long perspective they adopt gives them insights too often denied other social disciplines. Although historians, until recently, have tended to be implicit rather than explicit builders of explanations, the rise of social history, which has so successfully resurrected the whole texture of social relations, has placed historians in much the same predicament as sociologists: not merely to tell a good story but to offer a broad interpretation within which single hypotheses serve as guiding threads through the overwhelming mass of data. On this terrain, the social historian and the historical sociologist have become virtually indistinguishable.

The end result is not a proof likely to satisfy the canons of "normal" sociology, in the sense given by Thomas Kuhn to "normal science." less ambitiously, this narrative seeks to provide a plausible, that is, a reasonably acceptable, interpretation of the events depicted. In this enterprise, the only practical methodological course is to follow as little method as possible, save the attempt to establish through a narrative the relationship between actions by subordinate groups and reformist measures by the state.

The difficulty in developing such a narrative lies in finding appropriate language to couch this historical process in terms of state *and* class, when the available literature speaks in terms of state *or* class. This amounts to sailing an uncharted course, beset with treacherous statist and classist shoals. Diane Davis sums up this state of theoretical embattlement when she notes that, "caught in allegiance to either world-system theory, state-centered theory or class analysis, many scholars have ignored the centrality of state-class relationships" (1989a:446). In this study, an intermediate language linking state and class is achieved mainly through the concept of a *pact of domination,* developed in the next chapter, which informs the whole analysis. My purpose in exploiting this concept is to link the actions and reactions between state and subordinate actors so as to depict a continuous historical process.

Lastly, we must note that the policy processes analyzed here are not limited to governmental adoptions, as so often appears the case in policy studies (Grindle, 1981). They are studied from the emergence of the issues that lead (or fail to lead) to a governmental decision and followed up through the uneven path of implementation, which often implies rethinking of earlier decision in the context of new political situations. Many policy proposals fail to see the light of day, and many more die prematurely. Yet, they all form part of the process linking the struggles taking place in society to governmental decisions. The social scientist must try to encompass all such social larvae as manifestations of a societal process and as potential events, regardless of the final outcome. Therefore, particular attention is given to the forces that block the emergence of given issues or postpone their resolution. This has been the case, for example, with social insurance, which was ostensibly placed on the government's agenda in the early twenties and was alternatively discussed and shelved for several decades before it was finally adopted in 1943. Even then, the program was so poorly implemented that it did not begin to function on any kind of national scale until the 1960s. In the case of profit sharing, the issue was included in Article 123 of the Constitution of 1917. Nevertheless, it did not appear in worker demands until many decades later (in conjunction, as we shall see, with the negotiations over social insurance) and finally reached the government agenda in 1959, when organized labor was no longer stressing this demand.

Adopted policies must therefore be looked upon as survivors of long lists of unexpressed and rejected proposals. This process of elimination must be considered simultaneously as the result of (1) the structural features of the pact of domination (what some authors call regime); (2) the specific actions or non-actions by potential beneficiaries and their opponents; and (3) the balance of powers among reformist and antireformist "policy currents" within the state—in short, as the resultant of several vectors leading to events that break and reshape structural arrangements.[9]

THE LIMITS OF THE STUDY

The scope of the study is limited in many ways. First, the findings can be generalized only to countries with historical trajectories similar to Mexico's or to those involved in a transition to a stable civilian regime (such as, for example, the fledgling democracies of the southern cone). Nevertheless, the case-study form adopted should not imply a negation of comparability. On the contrary, this case should be considered as a test of a general approach in historical comparative studies, one that stays close to the specificity of each society yet places it within a theoretical framework that goes beyond the single case.

Second, the policies selected all center almost exclusively on the relationship between the state and the urban working class, with the bourgeoisie sometimes influencing state decisions. This illustrates the fact that the pact of domination is not one monolithic agreement (as my discussion in the next chapter makes clear) but a loose set of rules, practices, and prescriptions that apply selectively. The policies whose history we reconstruct tell us little about the agrarian aspects of pact formation or the struggles of particular groups, such as students, women, or ecologists. Without including them, an understanding of the full complexity and internal contradictions of the successive postrevolutionary pacts of domination is not possible. In order to assess better the fruitfulness of this perspective, we would therefore need a wider spectrum of policies dealing with the participation of a wider gamut of actors. Needless to say, such an ambitious goal is impossible for one single study to reach.

Today as before, organized labor in Mexico remains numerically weak and organizationally fragmented (Bizberg, 1984, 1990b). Most analysts consider its bargaining power greatly diminished by the reorientation of the economy toward exports, which has driven down wages and increased unemployment. Apart from isolated insurgent reactions, organized labor has not responded to the austerity measures that have curtailed living standards since 1982.[10] This raises the questions of whether labor's role in the building up of social reforms has come to an end and whether the bases of social protest and political dissent have changed. This study can offer only a tentative and partial answer to this most difficult question.

A third limitation of this study lies in the nature of the data out of which the historical narrative is constructed. This work does not pretend to go back to original sources, but combines in a new way works by historians, sociologists, political scientists, labor specialists, and so on. I am therefore limited to some extent by the biases and lacunae of each individual source of information. In particular, following the top-down bias from which these primary sources generally suffer, the narrative may tend to underestimate the degree of internal strife within the state while overestimating that within labor organizations. Such bias is especially limiting in view of the importance attributed in recent scholarship to internal divisions within the state (Maxfield, 1990; Davis, 1989b). The accuracy of the data may also suffer for two further reasons. First, owing to the secretive nature of Mexican politics, it is difficult to follow internal struggles taking place within state agencies or labor organizations that neither these organizations nor the government have been willing to disclose, even four decades later. Additionally, the closer we come to the present period, the hazier and the hastier available analyses become. Despite such limitations, crises have been recorded, and enough data have been gathered on them to make a plausible case for the hypothesis that guides this analysis.

A fourth limitation may be seen in the relative innocuousness of the policies selected. Health and welfare issues are rarely a top priority in any country, least of all in the Third World. To select issues related to the concerns of the laboring masses for food, shelter, or health is therefore tantamount to looking at the back burners of the government's agenda. Issues in the forefront include oil refinery nationalization, fiscal reform, bank nationalization, entry into the GATT, and the North American Free Trade Agreement. There are several drawbacks to studying the latter issues, however. One is that they almost invariably involve exclusively the bourgeoisie (foreign or national) and the state, leaving dominated classes in the shadows. Although there is little doubt that the 1981 bank nationalization, for example, has had far-reaching consequences for the working class (in particular, capital flight and deindustrialization, followed by deflationary policies that have reduced purchasing power), labor's role in this policy has been practically reduced to massing in Mexico City's Zócalo to offer mandatory support. Focusing on allegedly major issues, therefore, would reinforce the top-down view according to which the state has the working class well in hand, so that little initiative can be expected from below.

Relative political tepidness has its advantages, however. Health and welfare policies require less window dressing and suffer fewer turbulent reverberations from other policy arenas than do macroeconomic policies. After all, they are supposed to be merely technical policies, with little politics of any kind involved, save limited sectorial ones. This relative placidity, in turn, makes it somewhat easier to identify the actors and their interests than would be the case with general economic policies, in which virtually everyone and everything is involved. Nevertheless, the analysis of the policies selected can give us only an imperfect empirical view of the general historical process I call the pact of domination. To correct somewhat this limitation, I contextualize the empirical elements investigated, by incorporating them into a wider spectrum of state activities portrayed as the general policy climate exercising constraints on the possibility of welfare reforms. I also include wage demands and concessions, even though the latter too often vanish under the effect of inflation and devaluation, which are manipulated independently of organized labor. The importance of these processes lies in their permanence, that is, the fact that they continuously require the active participation of labor's leaders and followers and, therefore, necessarily color the outcome of the welfare issues upon which the analysis focuses.

A fifth limitation is the obvious unsuitability of the study for policy evaluation. Has social insurance made a difference to the health of the Mexican population? Have profits been effectively shared, or has the measure remained symbolic in most cases? No attempt has been made to answer such questions, which are the purview of mainstream policy studies, whose chief purpose is "Speaking Truth to Power" (Wildavsky, 1979)—in other words, helping state administrators to staff the machinery.[11] This study can address only tangentially the problems of policy appropriateness, internal design, or efficacy. If I include some aspects of implementation, as, for example, the assignment of resources to state programs after adoption, it is relevant to my purpose only insofar as it is indicative of the state's commitment.[12] The impact of the reforms analyzed upon the living standards of the Mexican population is assumed to be only a partial consequence of this political process. Living standards are the consequence of a host of other conditions that stand outside the theoretical focus of this analysis. Nevertheless, the political visibility of indicators of success or failure in obtaining results and the efforts to inflate those results are important elements in the political battles depicted here.

THE ORGANIZATION OF THE BOOK

The book is divided into six chapters. Chapter 2 situates the study within current theoretical debates, defines key concepts, and lays out the leading hypothesis. The following three chapters present the successive links of a historical macroperiodization, tracing the transformation of the postrevolutionary pact.

Chapter 3 covers the period from 1910 to 1940. It starts at the onset of the breakdown of the *Porfirato* and ends with the completion of the apparatus constituting state corporatism. A crucial aspect of this strategy was the creation by the state of a corporatively controlled labor movement that nevertheless failed to offer substantial benefits to make this political control palatable to the rank and file, hence the gradually widening gap between the mass of workers and their leadership and the consequent brittleness of this organization. The end of the period witnessed the dissolution of this system, provoked by mass desertion from the official labor organization under the pressures generated by the worldwide depression, and the creation of a new independent labor movement, which threatened to enroll the peasant masses as well. The new organization was soon endorsed and reinforced by the state (as well as separated from peasant organizations) and thereby brought back under control, but at the cost of substantial concessions. Social insurance, though not adopted during this period, is seen as a major focus of bargaining between labor, capital, and the state, along with the revision and federalization of the labor code, which radically transformed relations between labor and capital in Mexico from an antiquated nineteenth-century model to a modern capitalist one.

The second period, analyzed in chapter 4, goes from 1940 to 1970. It is associated by most students of Mexico with "stabilizing development" that spurred steady economic growth in the midst of growing conservatism, inequality, and the repression of change-oriented social movements (among peasants, teachers, doctors, and students, as well as workers). Few studies of the political system give much importance to the momentous struggles that took place *within* organized labor during this period: first, the battles between the Lombardist and Velazquist tendencies inside the Confederación de los Trabajadores de México (CTM— Confederation of Mexican Workers) in the early 1940s; then, the period of internal struggles for union democracy, which culminated in the *charrazo* of 1948 that institutionalized the practice of state-appointed union heads. Ten years later, mass insurgency erupted against *charro* unions, spurred by oil, railroad, and telegraph workers' movements. Following a period of relative labor quiescence (but of strong protest movements among doctors, teachers, and students), the end of this period was marked by the traumatic events at Tlatelolco Plaza in October 1968, when the massacre and imprisonment of hundreds of students called into question the legitimacy of the postrevolutionary regime.

The third period, analyzed in chapter 5, extends from 1970 to 1990. It can be described as the process of increasing pressures from below, accompanied by attempts on the part of state actors to preserve the alliance between the state and the popular classes. This period corresponds to the resurgence of labor struggles for internal democracy and the difficult birth of an independent labor movement. Midway through this period, a reversal of the government's reformist orientation occurred with the economic crisis of 1976. This brief period of fiscal austerity saw the return to a closer alliance of the state with capital (1977–1979)—the *Alliance for Production*—and the twilight of social programs.

The oil bonanza of 1980–1982 briefly rekindled state efforts for social reform in an atmosphere of euphoria, in which the demands of capital, the laboring classes, and the unemployed masses were no longer seen as mutually exclusive. The economic and financial debacle of 1981–1982 triggered by the sudden downturn of international oil prices, left Mexico unable to pay even the service charges on the towering foreign debt incurred during the brief moment of oil-led wealth. This last period witnessed the shrinking of the state under the onslaught of the debt crisis, a corresponding attempt to diminish state involvement in social policies, and efforts to debilitate labor's organizational bases and leadership.

The last section of chapter 5 sums up the changes experienced in the first two years of the Salinas administration. These years witnessed, simultaneously, the first steps in the transformation of the corporatist system linking labor to the state and the introduction of the Program Nacional de Solidaridad (PRONASOL—National Solidarity Program), a new welfare package. This final subperiod was undoubtedly one of intense change in the cast of actors as well as in the institutional means at their disposal for transforming the pact of domination. Chapter 6 reviews the findings of the four periods, focusing on their implications for the hypothesis that has guided the analysis and discussing some of the theoretical problems the study raises.

2

Popular Struggles and
Social Reforms:
An Interactive Approach

Contemporary analyses of the Mexican Revolution[1] all emphasize the active role played by the popular classes[2] in the struggles that toppled the Porfirio Diaz dictatorship in 1910. Equally secure is the hypothesis that popular support has been the key to the consolidation of the Mexican postrevolutionary regime—characterized in most of the literature as a kind of soft authoritarianism and limited welfarism in contrast with the more "exclusionary" forms of authoritarian rule that have been displayed in several Latin American countries during the twentieth century.[3]

Although no student of Mexico would likely disagree today that the presence of the popular sectors of the official party is responsible for the mild character of Mexican authoritarianism, few would be prepared to point to any specific popular actions to account for this phenomenon, beyond the mass mobilizations of the early revolutionary period and the late 1930s. These abruptly stopped in 1939 and have not been duplicated since. Yet, other than agrarian reform, most of the social reforms that have improved the standard of living of the masses—social security, extended public health, mass education, public housing, food subsidies, and so on—postdate the era of popular mobilization, sometimes by several decades. Rather than attribute these gains to struggles from below, most analysts of Mexican politics have turned to the state for explanations, minimizing (or altogether leaving out) popular forces supposedly deactivated since 1940.

Despite the episodic return of popular turmoil (as during the *Henriquismo* movement in 1952,[4] the railroad conflict in 1958 and 1959, and the union insurgencies of the 1970s), pressures from below were long neglected in political analyses of Mexico. As a result, these analyses consistently offered a mixture of structural determinism (presidentialism, official party control, centralism, corporatism) and voluntarism (the president's personality, the values of political elites) to account for virtually every fact of Mexican political life.[5] In this context, the social reforms that have been the hallmark of the Mexican postrevolutionary regime were regarded as the normal product of elite rationality. The occasional popular protest, on the other hand, whether expressed in the mass desertion of corrupt official unions in the early 1930s, the battles for union democracy in the mid 1940s, or the student demonstrations of the late 1960s, have been regarded as an anomaly. As a result, protest has not been centrally incorporated into explanations of the Mexican political system, serving instead as evidence of the capacity of the state for repression, periodically illustrated in the violation of human rights, electoral fraud, and censorship that have invariably followed upon such manifestations.

In the 1980s, civil society forcefully reappeared in analyses of Mexican politics, partly as a result of scholarly interest in the processes of transition from authoritarianism, which was taking place in the rest of Latin America, and partly as a consequence of the reawakening of electoral politics under the impetus of the electoral reform of 1979.[6] It was not clear, however, whether this new interest was triggered by the emergence of a new phenomenon in Mexican politics or simply reflected the influence exercised by debates taking place in other countries of Latin America.[7] Moreover, this new interest in political change tended to overlook the implications of political change for social policy, so that the consequences of the expected liberalization of Mexican politics for the welfare state were not addressed.

The electoral advances made by the conservative political current, from which the majority of studies initially inferred a process of liberalization,[8] indicated strong preferences among the middle and upper sectors of Mexican society for an exclusionary type of democracy (Remmer, 1986), that is, one that would reduce welfare rolls as well as state economic intervention. The opposite could be said about the grass-roots movements that had intensified during the mideighties under the effect of the economic crisis and the 1985 earthquake. They potentially represented new political actors calling for a restoration of precrisis living standards and hence a renewal of the state's redistributive role. Yet their capacity for joint and effective political action was doubtful, hence their relative neglect by analysts of political change, except those who specialize in the analysis of social movements.[9]

Despite the political turbulence of the late 1980s and the heated discussions it elicited among scholars prior to the momentous 1988 election, institutional continuity prevailed. After the administration headed by President Salinas de Gortari took office among clamors of electoral fraud and proclamations of civil disobedience by the losing electoral contenders, public displays of political dissidence gradually subsided. Far from being weak and embattled by debt and discontent, the state stood as the main architect of economic reconstruction and political change, as Mexico experienced a new era of political stability.

In this new context, the resurgence of the welfare state came as somewhat of a surprise, given the fiscally precarious situation in which Mexico still found itself in 1989 and the neoliberal discourse the new government was adopting in economic policy. Yet there was little doubt as to its origin: once more, the state had acted forcefully to resolve a problem. Dissidence would have to regain its erstwhile epiphenomenal quality in the eyes of its analysts, as the manifestation of malaise calling for change but with no capacity to threaten the established order.

The difficulties of contemporary analysts in diagnosing this situation stem in part from the theoretical discontinuities that have plagued scholarship on Mexico. In the 1970s, civil society had been excluded from analyses; in the 1980s, it was reinstated, but in ways that failed to restore its past contributions in the making of Mexico's political system. Finally, the resurgence of presidentialism in 1989 caused societal actors to sink back quietly into oblivion, forcing analysts' attention back on state-promoted change.

This study attempts to steer clear of these sweeping analytical shifts and restore the importance of civil society in the past as well as the present. Starting from the premise that societal actors have always been important in Mexican political life and state stability always dependent upon striking a multiplicity of bargains with various groups (Purcell and Purcell, 1980), it reconstructs the tense symbiosis that has characterized relations between organized labor and the state since the Revolution. This symbiosis has been largely responsible for the reformist style of government that has set Mexico apart from other countries in Latin America. Rather than regard the 1980s alternately as the end of these arrangements or the prelude to a new form of authoritarianism, this study looks upon the "lost decade" as a transition toward a new set of state-society relations, in which the stability of the state and the acquiescence of subordinate classes remains as dependent—if not more so—upon softening the brunt of free-market policies. This means renewed emphasis on welfare, albeit in different form from that previously adopted.

The Mexican political system is presented as shaped and transformed since 1910 by a dynamic process of social tensions between the state and various sectors of organized labor, which have been partially resolved through limited state concessions leading to the slow buildup of a skewed welfare system. The intention is to dispel the belief, still strongly entrenched, that the rules of political domination (whether authoritarian as pictured in the 1970s or protodemocratic as described in the 1980s and 1990s) are bestowed from above, leaving popular classes inactive beyond the initial insurrectionary period. To achieve this reconstruction, I show how selected confrontations between state elites and organized labor have been determinative in the making of Mexico's welfare system. I also attempt to project what the new political configurations emerging in the 1990s portend for the future and what role welfare policies will play in that process.

This chapter begins with an examination of the literature on the Mexican political system, with the object of theoretically grounding the emergence and transformation of the welfare state. In the second part, I propose a conceptual framework to analyze the relation between organized labor and the state, which permits us to view the historical record in a new light.

THE TOP-DOWN VIEW OF SOCIAL REFORM

The view that social reforms in Mexico are preemptively granted by the state with little or no participation by the intended beneficiaries results from the combination of two broad waves of conceptual insights: the authoritarian model that inspired the study of southern cone military regimes in the 1970s; and the debates among smaller circles of Mexicologists. Through this combination, Mexico was incorporated into the general debate over the authoritarian state, but as an exception. To mark its exceptional character, a wide variety of qualifiers to its authoritarianism was offered, all of which attempted to express the more privileged position of Mexico's subordinate classes in relation to their counterparts in military dictatorships.[10] The differences between these qualifiers and the disputes over their applicability are less important for our purpose than the implicit conceptualizations of social reforms they often have in common. Although these arguments have been critically reappraised since their formulation by Guillermo O'Donnell (1973), they still inspire much of the thinking on Mexico's political present and future. Therefore, they serve as a useful starting point.

The Magnanimous State

The view of Mexican politics that takes its point of departure in the seminal works of O'Donnell (1973), Linz (1970), Schmitter (1974), Stepan (1978), and others characterizes Mexico's political regime first and foremost as "authoritarian" and "corporatist".[11] In this view, the building blocks of state power in Mexico are the all-powerful executive branch headed by the president, an extremely weak legislature, in which the dominance of the official party is guaranteed (if need be by electoral fraud), and an all but impotent judiciary. The cornerstone of executive power is its ability to appoint (via the suppression of democracy within the sectors) the heads of the three sectors of the official party—the Confederación de los Trabajadores de México (CTM—Confederation of Mexico's Workers), the Confederación Nacional Campesina (CNC—National Peasant Confederation) and the Confederación Nacional de Organizaciones Populares (CNOP—National Confederation of Popular Orgaizations), representing the worker, peasant and popular sectors, respectively.

Rather than a system of interest representation, as intended in Schmitter's original definition, this system is understood within the Mexican context as a mechanism for the limitation of the articulation of subordinate class interests via state control over sector leaders, who, in turn, must ensure that the rank and file vote for the official party.[12] The emerging image in the 1970s was that of deactivated grass-roots and co-opted popular leadership. In such a view, initiatives for policy came unilaterally from the executive branch. They were faithfully rubber-stamped by a legislature entirely dominated by the official party. The electoral reform of 1979 and its subsequent amendments in the 1980s have somewhat changed this image, by allowing for a sizable representation of opposition groups in Parliament. Yet, differential rules of representation were enacted so as to prevent the possibility of the victory of any opposition party.

The explanation for social reforms generally offered by authors sharing this uncompromising view of Mexico's political regime is the predisposition of each individual president (or his immediate advisers) to understand the delegitimizing potential of mass poverty and to foresee the possibility of enhancing state power (or simply his own popularity) through strengthening his ties with the popular sectors. Each president qua individual (i.e., as socialized, motivated, perceptive, etc.) is capable of understanding the potential for state power enhancement of cooptative reforms. Alternatively, the reformist stance of the Mexican state can also be represented as the solution to the systemic needs of capitalism (Reyna, 1977) or as a mechanism triggered by "periodic self-examinations" of the political system (Cornelius, Gentleman, and Smith, 1989b:12)

Whether seen from a teleological or a voluntaristic perspective, social reforms, in this top-down view, represent incentives, handed down from above, that go hand in hand with the "constraints" characteristic of all authoritarian regimes (Collier and Collier, 1979). Mexico differs from other authoritarian contexts only in that it may have somehow yielded a higher ratio of incentives over constraints. Yet, unless we can produce a compelling rationale for why Mexican presidents are somehow more likely than presidents of other countries to think of reform as a good thing, this overrepresentation of incentives cannot be explained. It also leaves open the mystery of why some Mexican presidents undertake reforms while others do not, which has made the ratio of incentives to constraints extremely variable over time, even within the confines of Mexican history. When the system of presidential succession produced a Miguel Alemán (1946–1952), an Adolfo Ruiz Cortinez (1952–1958), or a Gustavo Diaz Ordaz (1964–1970), few if any reforms came forth; when a Lázaro Cárdenas (1936–1940), an Adolfo López Mateos (1958–1964), a Luis Echeverría Alvarez (1970–1976), or a José López Portillo (1976–1982) occupied the presidency, some reforms were undertaken. So, how do we know (or, for that matter, how do presidents know) when reforms are needed? There is no answer to that question unless one is willing to concede that something "out there" in society is happening that makes the *mandatario supremo* think that reforms should be carried out. Most defenders of this line do agree that something is happening to trigger reformist episodes, but it must never be large enough to be threatening, so that reforms can be interpreted as preventive rather than curative interventions. In this way, far from being seen as diminishing presidential power, concessions to pressures from below are regarded as conducive to strengthening the status quo.[13]

Few scholars have adhered wholeheartedly to this extreme version of Mexican authoritarianism, but many have come very close to it, especially in the early seventies, when the reaction to modernization theory was strongest. The best examples can be found in Daniel Cosio Villegas's *Estilo Personal de Gobernar,* in which the Mexican political system is seen as governed in a "personal" as opposed to an "institutional" way (1972:12); in Lorenzo Meyer (1977), who argues that authoritarianism, of which personalism is a key feature, has been embedded in Mexican political life since long before the Revolution; or in Arnaldo Córdova (1985), who qualifies the regime as presidential paternalism. We also find a strong stance on Mexican presidentialism among American scholars such as Susan Kaufman (1973, 1975), Peter H. Smith (1979), Judith A. Hellman (1983), Thomas Skidmore and Peter H. Smith (1984), Judith A. Teichman (1988) and Wayne Cornelius and Ann L. Craig (1988). Even among Marxists, it is agreed that dominated classes have occupied no significant political space in a process that has generally been labeled a bourgeois revolution, devoid by definition of a significant immediate potential for proletarian struggles.[14] The coercive hold of corporatism over popular groups is integrated into Marxist thinking alternately as an instrument in the hands of a Bonapartist state (Leal, 1975, 1986; Hodges and Gandy, 1979; Semo, 1985) or as an instrument at the disposal of a paternalist state acting at the behest of monopoly capital (Córdova, 1985; Saldivar, 1985; Reyna, 1977). The explanation of "who gets what", therefore, does not need to involve the participation of subordinate groups.

The most obvious failing of the hard-line view on authoritarianism is its tacit assumption that the state rules society through invariably effective organizational means (whether seen as corporatism or presidentialism), so that the only changes that can occur are those decided by state actors. To temper this overly structural view, many analysts appeal to the peculiar circumstances of Mexico's postrevolutionary history, which have generated sui generis mechanisms for bargaining between top and bottom.

The Responsive State

Intermeshed with the argument of sheer coercive and preemptive/co-optative presidential power are three interrelated features that soften the authoritarian character of the regime, setting it apart from others as more inclusionary: the first is a political culture argument; the second is clientelism; the third stresses interelite rivalry.

The political culture argument pictures Mexican politicians as socialized by the give-and-take atmosphere of official party politics, thereby making the state apparatus more "open to pressures and suggestions from the bottom" (Cardoso, 1979:47) than the hard technocrats of bureaucratic-authoritarian regimes. This apprenticeship explains these politicians' capacity for anticipating demands and preempting them. This feature has been said to account for the flexible and pragmatic character of Mexican politics, in which bargaining and conceding are preferred to naked imposition. We are not far from Samuel Huntington's earlier pronouncements that government elites respond to the interests of the masses because "the rise to the top in an institutionalized civic polity broadens a man's horizons" (1968:97).

Clientelism, on the other hand, provides the fluid structural channel through which such bargaining takes place, creating power brokers who are capable of exerting sufficient pressures to obtain limited benefits for their clients—as well as for themselves (Gonzalez Casanova, 1970a:129). Social reforms are a natural outcome of such informal mechanisms. Popular leaders are no longer pictured as bosses (*charros*) unconditionally docile to orders from above, as in the hard-line model, but as union leaders (*dirigencia sindical*), a concept that conveys the notion of at least partial independence from the state through bargaining on behalf of the rank and file. The president himself is viewed as a paternalistic figure who gives and concedes, not just out of cold-blooded rationalism, but also because he has a deep understanding of how people can be motivated rather than coerced, an understanding acquired in the long political career that has presumably preceded his ascent to the presidency. This line of argument has lost ground with the increasing recruitment of higher civil servants and presidents among technocrats since the 1970s (Ai Camp, 1983). Nevertheless, the personal qualities of the *político* (Grindle, 1977a) or "political entrepreneur" (Collier and Collier, 1991) is still very much in the center of theoretical imagery in studies of Mexico.

Lastly, the competition between elites within the "revolutionary family" has been seen as opening up the power structure to popular demands (Collier, 1982; Collier and Collier, 1991). Such processes, as subsequent chapters make clear, may well have taken place during the first formative years of the postrevolutionary regime but have long since been replaced by intraelite party discipline.

The factual validity of these arguments may vary a great deal from one historical moment to another. Their theoretical value lies in their emphasis on the flexibility of institutional mechanisms, as evidenced in the traditional pragmatism of Mexican politicians (Coleman and Davis, 1983; Levy and Szekely, 1985); the capacity of different political actors to bargain with the state (Bennett and Sharpe, 1980, 1985; Story, 1986; Reyna, 1977); the ability of the urban poor to organize themselves to obtain limited benefits (Lomnitz, 1974, 1975; Montaño, 1975; Cornelius, 1975; Eckstein, 1977; Ramirez Saiz, 1990); and even a certain softness of the institutional core leading actors to bargain on a case by case basis, as opposed to a system of fixed bureaucratic mechanisms (Purcell and Purcell, 1980). How much bargaining actually takes place informally, what forms it takes, and how such forms have evolved over time varies from case to case and from one arena to another. Yet all case studies point to the existence of unspoken rule dictating pragmatism and flexibility when dealing with conflict and the avoidance of violence. Yet a culture of conflict avoidance could as easily lead to secret deals and corruption as to reform. Therefore, the question of why some social reforms were undertaken at all is far from resolved by the political cultural or clientelistic version of Mexican inclusionary authoritarianism.

Despite important differences separating these two versions of Mexican politics, they can be considered complementary regarding the mechanisms they identify as central for social reform. They both suffer from an overrational view of the state, which pictures state bureaucracy as a powerful machinery at the service of skilled operatives, accelerating here and braking there but ever watchful of obstacles and careful of avoiding collision. By all accounts, state machinery in Mexico is impressive. Its longevity is even more impressive, especially after the 1988 political upheaval. It is also a fact that most state elites have all the trappings of good administrators, especially those close to the top.[15] Finally, there is no possible doubt that reforms have been carried out: the level of literacy is extremely high (even if the average number of years of formal education is still low); public health coverage is near universal (even if the distribution of these resources is still inequitable); and the majority of the urban population has access to basic food products at controlled prices (even if a high proportion of the rural population suffers chronic undernourishment), despite the open-market global economic strategy.

It is tempting to attribute all these achievements to the goodwill and professional craft of those standing on top of the state machinery, especially when existing case studies indicate the absence of popular demands for specific social policy outputs. Thus, Kaufman (1975) convincingly argues that labor had not been making demands for profit sharing in the years immediately preceding the 1961 decision to make profit sharing mandatory. Likewise, peasants had not requested the crop storage facilities or community food stores offered by CONASUPO during the Echeverría administration (Grindle, 1977a). Neither did they call for the creation of the Mexican Food System (SAM) instituted by the following administration (Redclift, 1981; Spalding, 1985; Luiselli, 1985; Austin and Esteva, 1987). In fact, when the de la Madrid administration (1982–1988) quietly dismantled the SAM and the Salinas administration (1988–) did the same for CONASUPO, no protests were heard. Spalding (1978) and Mesa Lago (1978), on the other hand, show that the issue of social security divided more than united organized labor.

We see an equal absence of demands from the groups that became incorporated into social security in the 1950s and the 1960s (see Spalding, 1978; Wilson, 1981) or from those who were to benefit from the 1973 decision to open selected social security benefits to nonaffiliates. When this program initially failed to be implemented, no one protested. The IMSS-COPLAMAR (Mexican Institute of Social Security–General Coordination of the National Plan for Depressed Zones and Marginal Groups) primary health care program (renamed IMSS-Solidaridad after 1988), instituted in its place seven years later, was as placidly accepted as its earlier absence had gone unnoticed. After a long period of reduction of welfare budgets from 1982 to 1988, a complex package of measures directed at the urban poor was created in 1989 under the name of PRONASOL. In this case as previously, no policy-specific demands had been made, and no protests were voiced at the deterioration of welfare benefits suffered since the beginning of the crisis.

From such evidence, the identification of the state as the sole initiator of social reforms would seem inescapable. What causes state reformers to make their moves can be left sufficiently vague that elite concerns can serve as primary causes and organized forces in society as inactive recipients of state bounty. Until the 1980s, few scholars would have disputed this thesis. Still fewer would have been prepared to accept as plausible the hypothesis that popular struggles have been the detonators of presidential reformist decisions. The paradigmatic changes that have taken place in the 1980s alter this general panorama, however, raising new questions regarding the role of popular forces in political change.

THE LOST DECADE: RECONSIDERING THE MEXICAN STATE

Until the whole edifice of state-led developmentalism came crashing down in August 1981, when Mexico declared a moratorium on its external debt, little dissensus could be discerned among analysts of the Mexican political system regarding the primacy of the state. A decade after the acute crisis that befell the Mexican economy, the belief in the near-inexhaustible power of the state to contain popular aspirations has not entirely subsided. Even at the time when opposition to the Institutional Revolutionary Party (PRI) was strongest and loudest, its profoundly loyalist character was never in doubt (Loaeza, 1987; Cornelius, Gentleman, and Smith, 1989a, Cornelius, 1987). The tacit acceptance of fraud by opposition forces after 1988 and the PRI's genuine electoral success in the legislative election of 1991, following presidential promises of party reform, still place the state at the vanguard of political change.

In the years immediately preceding the 1988 election, the electoral process became the focus of scholarly attention (Molinar Horcasitas, 1987a, 1992; Gomez Tagle, 1988a, 1988b; Luna, Tirado, and Valdés, 1987; Bravo Mena, 1987; Arriola, 1987;

Loaeza, 1987; Carr, 1986). The question asked by most scholars was whether Mexican politics was evolving toward a more competitive electoral process. This reflected the unusually high political mobilization and electoral gains made by the conservative National Action Party (PAN) in the 1980s, coupled with the relative ineffectiveness of labor and leftist parties during the same period. For this conservative opponent to the official party, who advocated privatization and the adoption of free-market policies, the issue of the welfare state was likely to get short shrift. Loaeza notes, for example, that the PAN's 1988 electoral platform made no mention of a party commitment to social justice, commenting that this reflected "the dominant sector's recognition of inequality as a cruel but natural—and therefore inevitable—phenomenon" (1989:361).

The unexpected emergence in 1987 of the National Democratic Front (FDN) as a contender in the 1988 presidential and legislative elections took most analysts by surprise. Leftist opposition forces, which up until then had been dispersed and divided between warring splinter parties (Semo, 1988), localized social movements with little political clout, and small dissident union sectors (mainly teachers and oil workers), had united under the banner of neo-Cardenism under the leadership of Cuauhtemoc Cárdenas, the son of the revered Lázaro Cárdenas, president of Mexico during the 1930s. The movement had its origin in the rejection by the official party leadership of a call for internal democratic reform by a small group of party members. This "democratic tendency," as the group was called, was ousted from the PRI and set about building a separate party. This new contender greatly changed the nature of the political stakes that faced the official party in 1988. Rather than compete with an opponent whose conservative demands implicitly excluded the poor majority of Mexicans, the official party had to contend with a new political actor who revived the revolutionary discourse on social justice, at a time when the PRI's record of protecting the welfare net was less than perfect and discontent at the government's economic policies was high.

The literature on social movements gave little forewarning of this groundswell. Although it documented the rise of social movements in response to the economic crisis (Ramirez Saiz, 1986, 1990; Alonso, 1985, 1986; Calderón, 1986; Foweraker, 1989, 1990; Davis, 1990; Street, 1991; Cook, 1990; Prieto, 1986), it provided little evidence that these movements could turn into a new social base of popular mobilization. In fact, most authors agreed that they lacked the capacity to put the system under any real threat (Carr, 1983, 1986; Needler, 1987; Foweraker, 1989; Street, 1991; Ramirez Saiz, 1989) or to generate new forms of political demands. Rather than be regarded as direct agents of change, social movements were viewed as underground gestators of profound changes in the institutional mechanisms that had heretofore ensured the stability of corporatist arrangements.

This diagnosis left virtually untouched the thesis that the state was the dominant force in the initiation of social reforms. The scholarship on social movements had therefore done little to undermine the top-down view of Mexican politics inherited from previous decades. Given the decline of labor as a force capable of pressuring the state into making concessions (Middlebrook, 1986; Carr, 1983), the clock of the late 1980s seemed to be set back to defining the state as the central agent of change. This time, however, change pointed in the direction of a withdrawal of the state from redistributive responsibility and a reliance on severe wage controls to enhance Mexico's international competitiveness. The popular mobilization achieved by the Cardenist front, clearly oriented toward a renewal of welfare measures, therefore failed to make any imprint on the scholarship on Mexico. Like previous mobilizations, it would likely be seen retrospectively as a process of "letting off steam" (Gonzalez Casanova, 1970), followed by periodic "self-reappraisal" (Cornelius, Gentleman, and Smith, 1989) of the political system.

In many ways, the top-down view might be as true for the 1980s and 1990s as for previous decades, if it is understood as an appreciation of the state's capacity for containing opposition and imposing solutions during conjunctural crises. Any attempt to measure the strength of popular forces by pitting their power against that of the party-state leads to the conclusion that the party-state is the dominant force. Student demonstrators in 1968 were no match for the soldiers who decimated them. The administration that perpetrated the deed was able to maintain political continuity despite the general repudiation of the Tlatelolco massacre among Mexicans. In 1940 and 1988, large-scale electoral frauds appear to have been committed, with no visible consequences for the governments that took power through such means.

The usual explanation for the state's propensity to make concessions to subordinate classes despite its superior coercive power is usually its alleged need for legitimacy. Yet this argument is likely to be circular, unless we are also willing to accept the premise that the state is somehow endangered unless it preserves or recovers its legitimacy. Such a premise implies that relatively powerless groups can be in a position to endanger the state, if they have the capacity to call its legitimacy into question.

Most analysts of social movements either assume a general process of popular demobilization (the authoritarian thesis) or else take the view that dissident groups in Mexico have been too few, too scattered, or too poorly organized to induce changes in the political system. Such assumptions make it impossible even to raise this question inasmuch as they implicitly define the capacity to undermine the stability of the state as a function of the sheer strength of opposition forces, with no repercussions on the rest of the population.

If we start from the opposite assumption, namely that dissidence is dangerous for the state because it sets an example that may ignite general discontent—especially in times of crisis—we must conclude that the continued power of the state depends on the ability of its elites to prevent the spread of dissidence. How can this be achieved on an adequate scale? To convince a large enough proportion of the population that the government is still on their side and, therefore, that the dissenters are mistaken, a government must make true (to some extent) its own legitimating rhetoric. In Mexico, this rhetoric is unequivocally centered on the achievement of social justice by the means spelled out in the Constitution of 1917, that is, by social reform. Social reform therefore, represents a permanent, or "constitutive" agenda (Fowley, 1991) upon which state elites depend in order to maintain social peace.

Under this assumption, a different political reality emerges, wherein the importance of pressures from below lies not in their strength relative to the repressive power of the state but in the possibility (as perceived by state elites) that they might render the system uncontrollable. This possibility arises from the capacity of dissidents to debunk the state ideologically, by showing the vacuousness of government discourse, and therefore to demonstrate the futility of remaining loyal to the system. Loyalty to the regime, in this perspective, is understood not as an internalized "civic culture" or unconditional passivity but as the price paid in exchange for the tacit commitment on the part of the state to improve the living standards of the majority of the population under its leadership. Dissidence opens the possibility of pressuring the state into offering tangible benefits, rather than vague promises. In other words, dissidence creates the conditions for changing the tacit bargain that regulates conditions of inequality in Mexico, hence its potential for altering the system as a whole but also its danger for state stability and regime continuity.

From this perspective, social struggles and public protests are indicative of the pressure points existing in the relation between the state and subordinate classes. Demands from below, if unmet, create a climate of general unrest, which can detonate more forceful demands for change and mobilize other focuses of discontent. Piecemeal social reforms, on the other hand, are organizational weapons in the hands of state managers to prevent such mobilizations and to reestablish a modicum of social peace. The interrelation between struggles and reforms becomes the object of study that can lead to a broader understanding of social peace in capitalist societies in general and the roots of regime stability in Mexico.

THE PACT OF DOMINATION DEFINED

Social reforms, although enacted by the state, have their roots in the conflicts created by the inequalities of Mexico's development. I propose to trace these reforms to short-lived but significant episodes of regime destabilization from below met by a combination of repression and reformism on the part of the state. In this view, subordinate groups, whose individual members submit to legally defined conditions of exploitation everyday, are seen as having a limited capacity to transform these conditions collectively. To analyze these processes, I use a central heuristic tool—the pact of domination—and select from the historical record a number of episodes of social confrontations in which this pact has been renegotiated.

The pact-of-domination construct encapsulates two apparently contradictory elements: the notion of *pact* implies negotiation, conflict resolution, and institutionalization, while that of *domination* connotes inequality, antagonism, and coercion. The juxtaposition of these two terms is meant to express the idea that though people accept subordination and exploitation, they do not do so unconditionally. The notion of *pacted domination* indicates simultaneously the power wielded by the state over dominated classes and the institutional or extrainstitutional means the latter have at their disposal to modify the terms of their subordination.

A pact of domination, as used in this study, is not a clearly identifiable or socially acknowledged entity, as would be the case for the pacted democracies of the southern cone.[16] *Pact* is here understood as an analytical construct that aims at capturing the process whereby deep-seated social antagonisms—particularly, but not exclusively, those originated in class inequalities—are regulated by a legally based institutional order. This concept will be understood as the *institutionally sanctioned and coercively backed set of rules that specifies who gets what at any one time within the confines of a national territory.* It has an important symbolic component insofar as it means simultaneously *who ought to get what* (according to the written rules and official rhetoric) and *who, in fact, gets what.* The degree of discrepancy between the two and the presence of actors capable of calling attention to it are seen as trigger factors for the process of pact renegotiation and transformation.

Pacts result neither from state decisions alone nor exclusively from the actions of subordinate groups but from the interaction between state strategies of control over these groups and the dominateds' modes of resistance (Crisp, 1984, from Munck, 1987:6). To participate in this process of transformation, actors have different sets of objectives and strategic weapons and face different constraints. State elites predominantly pursue limited policy and power goals within the general context of institutional continuity in which capitalist relations of production are taken for granted (O'Donnell, 1977a). Class actors, on the other hand, seek to improve their relative position within this general framework.[17] Both dominant and dominated classes depend upon the state to settle their differences and enforce the solutions adopted. Conversely, the state cannot promote the conditions of institutional stability necessary to its own survival unless a temporary truce in social struggles is obtained. In other words, pacts of domination represent a compromise resulting from prior confrontations between dominated and dominant groups but managed by the state with the legal bureaucratic resources at its disposal.

Not all groups are partners or opponents in a pact, nor do they have an equal voice in its making. Some class factions in Mexico have been altogether excluded (de jure or de facto), either because they are extremely fragmented and unorganized (e.g., the landless rural workers and unorganized labor) or because they have been forcibly eliminated (e.g., the anarchists, the synarchists, and the communists until 1934 and again from 1940 to 1979). The notion of pact negotiation is therefore inseparable from that of membership in a socially active group. Within such groups, however, individuals can change from passive to active (or vice versa) at different moments. Although active participants are usually few, the mass of the inactive who can be mobilized (or demobilized) determines the bargaining power of the active fringe and, therefore, its ability to renegotiate the pact.

The term *pact of domination* is no newcomer in the literature on Latin America. The uses to which it has been put have been so varied, however, that conceptual clarifications are in order. Fernando Cardoso, who coined the term, initially understood it from an instrumentalist perspective on the state. In this context, it was meant to convey the idea that "certain classes dominate others . . . and utilize the state apparatus (coercive as well as ideological) to articulate their domination" (1977a:24). Later, he changed to a structural view, defining the capitalist state itself as a "pact of domination," thereby defining the state as the central mechanism for the reproduction of capitalist relations of production (1979:39). In either case, state domination is understood as an instrument of class exploitation.

In a third essay, Cardoso insists that the dependency approach, as he conceives it, "affirms the existence of domination and struggle" and fundamentally addresses the question of "who are the classes and groups which, in the struggle for control or for the reformulation of the existing order . . . are making a given structure of domination historically viable or are transforming it" (1977b:16). This statement, which makes capitalist continuity dominant yet transformable by class struggles, comes close to my definition of the term.

Apart from Cardoso's work, the term *pact* has frequently been used in the literature on Latin America. For example, O'Donnell defines the state as the "guarantee and organizing agent [of a] pact of domination" (1983:19), yet makes no subsequent use of the concept in his empirical analysis. In the Mexican context, the term is often used, in the expressions *"pacto social"* or *"pacto histórico,"* both of which refer to the postrevolutionary alliance *ex principio* of the state with the popular classes (Cordera and Tello, 1981). In a more recent use of the term, Cornelius, Gentleman, and Smith propose that "the Mexican power structure [can] be viewed as an interlocking series of alliances or pacts" (1989:9). In such examples, however, little attempt is made to exploit the heuristic potential of the term beyond the general notion of consensual arrangements.

The term *pact* is also used to refer to a set of bureaucratic structures and rules regulating relations between the state and specified groups in society, as in the expression *corporatist pact*. In this case, *pact* becomes synonymous with *regime*. Informal but publicly acknowledged covenants between the state and specific sectors of society (e.g., between a civilian government and the military) have also been designated as pacts (O'Donnell and Schmitter, 1986; Karl, 1986), as in the expression *pacted democracy*. In this case, it means that one of the parties to the pact has the power to block the other, should the latter go beyond the agreement. In the case of former military dictatorships, the military agree to stay out of politics only as long as the process of democratization does not go further than they consider appropriate. Lastly, a pact can be a formally designated covenant, as the current Pacto de Estabilización y Crecimiento Económico (PECE—Pact of stabilization and Economic Growth) in Mexico, whereby the major sectors have agreed to freeze prices and wages in order to slow down inflation and promote export-led economic growth.

All the above uses of the term, except Cardoso's, are strongly associated with the notion of a fairly stable rational contract to which all parties to the pact voluntarily adhere. By contrast, in the perspective adopted here, the notion of *pact* refers to macrohistorical processes of structuration and transformation of rules of domination through human agency. Although the actors involved in such processes are assumed to be goal-oriented, their action is not understood as rationally oriented with reference to a known pact. Therefore, a *pact of domination,* as we use the expression, is not something that is present in peoples' minds but a middle-range theoretical construct that goes beyond individual or group rationality. In the context of this study, it will represent the concrete ways in which the conflicts that have periodically arisen between capital and labor have been fought out, negotiated, and eventually incorporated into a set of relatively flexible rules of domination managed by the state. Far from a fixed structure, it is a relatively fluid and contingent process that takes form over time. Its dynamic principle is the historical succession of the struggles of people whose aspirations and means of collective action are constrained by the forces that define their economic interests and political consciousness, on the one hand, and by the pacts that have been established in the past, on the other.

Inasmuch as I am dealing with change over time, I must refer to a multiplicity of pacts, each individual pact a different configuration from that preceding it. Due to the continuity of the political process in Mexico, the changes from one pact to the next are often barely perceptible. The purpose of my analysis is to show these differences and to play them back in fast motion, showing change in the same way as the individual frames of a motion picture displayed in rapid succession simulate movement. This conception requires that we understand the substantive origin of conflicts leading to a given amendment of the pact, how it was settled, the rules and the structures sustaining these arrangements, and their evolution toward new conflicts and renewed agreements.[18]

In sum, while the notion of *pact* has been used alternately to convey the notion of class or state coercion and to imply a relatively consensual political process, my analysis includes both the conflictual and the consensual meanings of the term, whose combination is understood to be the root of dynamic change. Insofar as they serve as instruments to enforce an unequal distribution of economic and political resources, pacts of domination are therefore constantly subject to challenge, no matter how stabilized or coercively enforced they may appear. Their resilience depends on the capacity of subordinate classes to resist exploitation and to transform the political rules of the game; on the ability of excluded groups to forcefully stake their membership claims; on the power of dominant classes to impose policy measures on the state (this is the instrumentalist view, posited here as an empirical possibility rather than a fundamental theoretical principle); or on the relative power of the state vis-à-vis different groups at various junctures.

These internal relations of power, in turn, will be seen to depend to a large extent on the place occupied by a country in the international division of labor and its political and economic ties with other nations, as well as purely conjunctural situations (wars, recessions, etc.). The pact of domination is therefore the very process that relates state to society and different parts of society to each other through historical confrontations, negotiations, stalemates, and compromises that are constrained, yet not determined, by the structural arrangements resulting from past episodes of these confrontations.

THE PACT OF DOMINATION: THE MEXICAN CASE

Inasmuch as they represent simultaneously processes of reproduction and change, pacts of domination are deeply embedded in the past. To take as a starting point the Revolution of 1910 requires, therefore, that we understand the nature of the revolutionary pact at its beginnings and how subsequent events have brought, or failed to bring, certain types of pressures for pact enforcement or redefinition. Contrary to the top-down view, this approach assumes that actors constitute permanent sources of resistance and change (Crozier and Friedberg, 1977), even in the most stringent conditions of domination. Rather than seek to establish the evidence of demand, I look for actions and events that have contributed to the erosion of state control over labor since 1910, despite the formidable machinery of corporatism, and that have subsequently led to welfare reforms.

During the formative period of postrevolutionary Mexico, labor occupied an important strategic position, insofar as its support was a necessary condition for the defense of the regime against counterrevolutionary coups and foreign interventions. As the regime stabilized in the 1920s and official representation of labor interests gradually solidified, the pressure points at which workers could obtain concessions changed. After 1940, these points centered on a system of triangular interpressures between the leadership of regimented labor, dissident elements (within or outside of labor), and the state. Insofar as dissident elements (e.g., independent labor and teachers during several periods, students in 1968) voice grievances that find important echos among rank-and-file workers, they threaten state authority, no matter how organizationally weak they may be. Their strength lies in their potential for spreading social discontent, thereby cutting through the vertical lines built by corporatism.

During periods when dissident activity is on the rise, the bargaining power of official labor leaders to obtain concessions from the state for the benefit of the rank and file as incentives to remain loyal increases. Insofar as these leaders fail to take advantage of such opportunities, however, their power base is undermined, and the edifice of state corporatism is thereby made more fragile.

My task is to analyze historical junctures representing instances of social confrontations likely to lead to the redefinition of the pacts of domination through which the state has regulated relations between labor and capital since 1910. It is understood that confrontations are not necessarily initiated by labor actors or aimed specifically at obtaining the benefits they have eventually received. For example, the bulk of workers fought not to obtain social security but to keep their prewar economic and political gains. Later, they struggled not for the expansion of such benefits or for a share of capital profits but for internal democracy. Public housing, on the other hand, came as an unexpected gift on the heels of the 1968 student uprising. In Mexico, social reforms rarely represent political arenas as such. But they are part of a permanent agenda of social change that constitutes the basis of the legitimacy of postrevolutionary governments. As such, they represent instruments of negotiation drawn by the state as well as by labor elites from the list of permanent demands for social justice.

Often, such reforms have been scoffed at as mere co-optation. In this view, the working class and other subordinate groups are seen as brought to heel with little effort on the part of the state and at little cost to capital. This interpretation, which goes hand in hand with the top-down view of politics in Mexico, is overly simplistic. It confounds state actions aimed at buying off official popular leaders with benefits flowing downward to the rank and file. In the view taken here, co-optation refers to the incentives offered to official leaders to dissuade them from acting as real leaders, in the sense of responding to demands for social justice. Co-optation, therefore, is aimed at suppressing demands. Social reforms, on the other hand, are the price the state must occasionally pay in order to motivate the rank and file to remain within the official organizations. When natural leaders arise out of co-opted structures, or when independent leaders gain an audience outside of these structures, the system of co-optation has failed to yield the expected results. Compliance must therefore be obtained by alternative means. Social reform is one of the means whereby this compliance is renewed throughout postrevolutionary history, but only under the sting of pressures from below that threaten to override state control.

The important point is to determine not whether any given group has been co-opted but what price the state has had to pay, often despite the open resistance of capital (as well as internal resistance within the state), to maintain or reestablish peace. This raises again the problem of incentives versus constraints, which has too often been neglected in the literature on Mexico, despite evidence that selected groups among the dominated classes have gained more concessions in Mexico than in other less stable authoritarian contexts. I argue, therefore, that it is only insofar as real concessions have been obtained for the rank and file that official leaders have been able to provide the incentives necessary to retain the loyalty of their followers.

In summary, the approach I propose emphasizes change and action embedded in Mexican institutional structures, in contrast to the regime approach, which relates policy outputs to a body of fixed rules and structures (Remmer, 1978). The transgression of rules, rather than anomalous or unpredictable, is viewed here as the fundamental mechanism of change. Understood in this fashion, these rules lose the august character they have acquired in the literature that treats regime as the major determinant of state elites' values, policy orientations, and strategies of development. In the present analysis, regime appears as a precipitate from past pacts, which acts as a filtering structural device, inhibiting certain kinds of actions and facilitating others. Despite the normal bias in favor of capitalist interests in the Mexican postrevolutionary regime, the rules it incorporates are not considered impervious to challenges from below. The task of the present research is to uncover change behind the facade of regime continuity and to describe the forces from below that have contributed to such change, despite the appearance of political deactivation.

THE PACT OF DOMINATION: A CONCEPTUAL TOOL

A concept is fruitful to the extent that it allows us to make assumptions about reality that we would not make without it. This, in turn, brings out facts and events that would not otherwise appear significant and helps us draw new implications from the observation of these facts as seen in a new light. Before embarking upon the difficult task of using the notion of pact of domination as a theoretical tool, I might point out from the onset what I think can be gained by adopting it.

From the critique of the literature on Mexico's political system, it should be clear that the very least we can expect from using the notion of pact, as I have defined it, is to avoid falling into the position that defines the state as the only, or at least the invariably victorious, actor. Indeed, the pact-of-domination perspective is diametrically opposed to any approach that would systematically engulf all of society in the state, on the pretext that state actors invariably have the upper hand. In this study, *state* refers to the government (presidency, cabinet, governors, etc.) and to the public bureaucratic apparatus; *society*, to actors outside the state sector. In Mexico, state and society overlap in the official party and the legislature, which are wholly controlled by the president. Labor leaders, however, though imposed on the rank and file by the state, are not invariably part of it; to remain in power, they must also respond to demands from below, as my analysis makes clear.

The notion of a pact of domination also provides a strong antidote to the construction of social order on a normative basis: it presents human beings as accepting their life conditions most of the time, yet without finding them legitimate. This makes them permanently (but not automatically) susceptible to mobilization in efforts to change these conditions. At the same time, it also steers away from the framework of revolution, in favor of piecemeal negotiated change. Social order, in this perspective, is neither harmonious nor built on irreconcilable antagonistic class interests.

Having abandoned proletarian messianism as well as radical pessimism regarding the role of the working class in social change, we can now concentrate on the too-long neglected task of recording what difference—small or large—the actions of organized labor have made to the buildup of the welfare state. Such an examination cannot be divorced from the specificity of inherited political institutions and practices carried over from previous episodes of pact renegotiations, as dictated by my analytical framework.

But neither can they be derived from these institutions a priori, as has so often and unfruitfully been attempted in the past, simply because the process under study is not voluntaristic or deterministic but interactive and open-ended.[19] It is interactive not only in the usual atemporal sociological sense but in the historical sense as well: in this study, the workers fighting for union democracy in 1946 or 1958 remembered what happened in 1928 and 1934, as did state elites. Similarly, state strategies in the 1940s aimed at avoiding the labor mobilizations of the 1930s, while labor leaders attempted to carry through formulas that had proved successful in the preceding decade. Decisions and strategies are therefore built not only on facts and events but on memories of events and their consequences and on anticipations of events and reactions to them born of this collective historical experience. The concept of a pact of domination conveys this temporal and generational dimension. Constructing this concept casts a new light on the primary studies from which this analysis is drawn, transforming and linking up a heterogeneous historiographical collection into a coherent and theoretically significant argument.

3

From Revolution to Institutionalization, 1910–1940

In this first period, the pact of domination forged in the last decades of the nineteenth century was suddenly and violently broken in most of its vital aspects by the series of events that marked what has been called the Mexican Revolution. The latter was unwittingly launched by Francisco I. Madero's call to armed rebellion against Porfirio Diaz on November 20, 1910. This period witnessed a regime change, understood as the radical restructuring of rules of access to and exercise of state power. Simultaneously, there were radical changes in the relations between state and society: first, in the relations of the state with the foreign investors who had taken advantage of Diaz's open-door policy; and second, in the relations among the state, labor, and the bourgeoisie, reflecting the transformation of the pact.

This chapter draws a parallel between these general macro-historical transformations and the new relations that evolved among the state, the industrial and mining bourgeoisie, and labor. The dependent variables of these interactions between state and labor were the protracted debates over social insurance, concessions on work conditions, and bargaining over wage increases. The key theoretical question are: What pacts of domination were defined during the three decades that followed the first manifestations of the Revolution, and in what ways did they differ from those established during the Porfirian period (1876–1910)?

In the broadest sense, strategies and policies were directed at changing the Porfirian power configuration so as to secure the new regime. From the perspective of state elites, the relation between labor and the state can be understood as instrumental to that goal. Yet, as we shall see, if elite goals are fairly constant, the means by which they are attained vary a great deal. From the perspective of labor, on the other hand, the period can be read as a series of strategic moves to obtain institutional (i.e., regime) advances. For some currents within the labor movement, such advances are the stepping-stones toward further political concessions. For the majority, however, they are the means of obtaining tangible benefits. After characterizing in broad terms the Porfirian point of departure, I distinguish three episodes that mark important changes in the transformation of the pact of domination during this period: the constitutionalist decade (1911–1920), the Sonoran period (1920–1932), and the Cárdenas administration (1934–1940).

THE PORFIRIAN PACT OF DOMINATION

The configuration of political and economic power found on the eve of the Revolution was not solely the work of Porfirio Diaz. Capitalist development had begun in earnest in the 1860s, after the dust from the repelled French invasion had settled. It was characterized by systematic efforts on the part of the state to create a national market, chiefly by opening Mexico to foreign investment and undertaking a series of administrative and monetary reforms (Arnaud, 1981:129–57). Foreign capitalists, attracted by copper, silver, and oil, were offered exceptional conditions for the exploitation of mineral resources, in exchange for which they paid only moderate export taxes. For the central government, foreign taxes constituted a stable fiscal basis that could not be tapped by the states, whose governing bodies had consistently shown reluctance to channel local taxes to the central government. Simultaneously, efforts were deployed (mostly unsuccessfully) to suppress internal interstate tariffs (*alcabalas*), which provided the states with independent revenues and slowed down the circulation of merchandise.

Foreign capital investment was also encouraged, via subsidies, to build up the infrastructure in railroads, ports, telegraphs, telephones, and electricity.[1] Limited monetary reforms were undertaken to simplify the monetary system, which, at the time, included several forms of legal tender for different types of transactions (including precolonial cacao seeds). Yet such efforts were undermined by high external demand for Mexican silver (used as the monetary standard in the United States) and by the Porfirian administration's habit of granting multiple concessions to several foreign banks, which fought among themselves for control.

The second half of the nineteenth century also saw the unprecedented growth of haciendas as a consequence of new opportunities in the international market for products such as sugar, hemp, cotton, rubber, coffee, and livestock. Crops that required extensive landholdings impelled landowners to gradually absorb peasant land, mainly by force and fraud. The state generally turned a blind eye on the blatant violations of property law perpetrated by local authorities in favor of *hacendados* (landowners) and allowed local authorities to crush peasant protests, occasionally lending a helping hand with its federal troops, Porfirio Diaz's ruthless *Rurales*.[2] The result of this process was the slow disintegration of Indian communities, whose population became either *peones acasillados* (agricultural workers attached to the hacienda), day laborers, or a landless, floating proletariat, seasonally available for gathering the haciendas' crops.

By 1910, the 834 *hacendados* listed in the census of that year (for a population of over 15 million inhabitants) owned most of the territory.[3] Vast tracks of land also belonged to foreign companies, as, for example, in the state of Sinaloa, where 75 percent of irrigable land belonged to a single U.S. firm (Hamilton, 1982:45). Nevertheless, this process of land concentration was not evenly distributed throughout the country. Whereas haciendas owned 80–90 percent of the land in the north and south, communities of independent small farmers subsisted in central Mexico, as did their ancestral conflict with hacienda encroachments (Womack, 1969; Tutino, 1986). In Morelos, for example, only 23.7 percent of the population lived on haciendas; in Hidalgo, 20.7 percent; in the state of Mexico, 16.8 percent; in Puebla, 20.1 percent; and in Oaxaca, 14.5 percent (Gilly, 1971:29).

Economic activity increased phenomenally during the Porfiriato. Between 1877 and 1911, Mexican exports rose from 40.5 to 288 million pesos, and imports, from 49 to 214 million (Hamilton, 1982:44; see also Coatsworth, 1975; Leal, 1975; and Rosenzweig, 1960). Prerevolutionary Mexico appeared to be a relatively prosperous commodity-export economy almost entirely dependent on the U.S. market (for over 50 percent of its commercial exchanges). Seventy-seven percent of industrial investments were in foreign hands, 9 percent belonged to Mexican capitalists, and 14 percent were state owned (Gilly, 1971:23). Stimulated by this increased economic activity, the population of Mexico registered a steady growth (Brachet-Marquez, 1976). Over 70 percent of the population comprised an impoverished mass of peasants whose internal differentiation followed the lines of organization of hacienda production and regional specialization. The dominant class was composed of relatively integrated sets of landed capitalists, foreign capitalists, and a very small national industrial and commercial bourgeoisie (Hamilton, 1982:51), all closely associated with Porfirio Diaz's government. Between these extremes of wealth and poverty, a small intermediate middle sector of industrial workers, artisans, service workers, and middle-class professionals evolved, principally in urban centers (ibid.:52).

Rather than change the decentralized power structure inherited from earlier administrations, Porfirio Diaz had taken great pains to stabilize it through the creation of an "intricate maze of alliances and armistices" (Womack, 1969:11), which he centrally controlled. As he fell from power under the thrust of Madero's army, these political alliances dissolved and had to be replaced by an alternative structure likely to secure the survival of the new revolutionary leadership.[4] This task was carried out in the context of a generally hostile reaction on the part of foreign governments, particularly the United States. More than the implementation of the democratic or redistributive ideals of the Revolution, the immediate task at hand for revolutionary leaders was the prevention of the possibility of a return to a neo-Porfirian regime and the avoidance of possible foreign military intervention. The alliances alternately formed and dissolved by revolutionary leaders must be seen as means to those ends rather than issues in themselves.

THE CONSTITUTIONALIST DECADE, 1911–1920

Madero tried to reconcile the Porfirian bourgeoisie with the liberal middle sectors that had supported him under the banner of democracy and constitutional legitimacy. His assassination in 1913 and short-lived replacement by the neo-Porfirian dictator

Victoriano Huerta (1913–1914) are proof enough that he failed, alienating his natural allies (the popular masses), arming his enemies (the military), and yet failing to rally the old Porfirian bourgeoisie.[5]

The group that brought Madero to victory was highly heterogeneous, with little possibility of reconciling its internal differences. The split between industrial workers and peasants was total (Knight, 1986). The working class, literate and secularized, had little in common with the highly religious, traditionally oriented peasantry (Knight, 1987a; Carr, 1976).[6] Although representing in 1910 a mere 195 thousand souls as compared to over 11 million peasants and rural workers, the working class was regionally concentrated along the northern border, in the Valley of Mexico, and in ports. It was also receptive to many different currents of ideas, political clubs, and labor organizations. This meant that it was divided internally between the Catholic tradition of mutual aid societies and cooperativism and the anticlerical anarchist-syndicalist tradition.[7] The cultural and experiential gap between workers and the peasantry resulted in totally different expressions of political dissent: for the peasantry, moral outrage at injustice and the reclaiming of ancestral rights; for workers, the liberal Constitution of 1857, which gave them the right to organize and bargain.[8]

The anarchist fringe of the working class, under the leadership of the Magon brothers, had initially borne the brunt of the opposition to Porfirio Diaz in the repression of the great strikes of 1906–1908 in the mining and textile sectors (Ramos-Escandón, 1987; Gamboa Ojeda, 1991). These bloody episodes, followed by superficial concessions in the most industrialized states (Nuevo Leon and Mexico), crippled the capacity of what was left of its vanguard to join in the early phase of armed insurrection. In 1911, this early anarchist-syndicalist movement all but disappeared, its leaders either exiled, dead, jailed, or working in some slave labor camp of Yucatán. At the same time, the Mexican Labor Party (PLM), which had been the stronghold of this movement, veered toward a more liberal position congenial to the urban middle sectors and the progressive provincial bourgeoisie, who endorsed Madero in 1910. Madero, rather than revive the flame of working-class militancy for revolutionary ends, explicitly disassociated himself from the Magon brothers, accusing them of "inflaming the country with a revolution that cannot succeed [and for which there] cannot be a plausible pretext."[9]

On the eve of the Revolution, the working class was relatively politically demobilized and amorphous. Madero's supporters among the working class were both few and devoid of passion. They counted some ex-Magonists, who sought limited reforms and personal advance, and not a few opportunists. Nevertheless, the rank and file expected positive change, as soon became evident in their propensity to strike. This could be considered the result of Madero's generally favorable attitude toward worker organization.[10]

By contrast, the groups that rallied around Emiliano Zapata and Francisco Villa embodied the moral outrage and fervent aspirations for justice of the rural masses (Knight, 1986), specifically the return of land confiscated by the haciendas, the suppression of debt peonage, payments in kind, and the elimination of company stores (*tiendas de raya*). These movements were regionally and locally limited, however. They failed to rally the support of other peasant communities, even as Zapata's victorious army advanced through the territory (Tutino, 1986).

The dominant classes were also divided. They were split between two fractions, one closely associated with the Porfirian state and the other opposed to that regime, for a variety of reasons. In the first category were most of the *hacendados*, foreign investors, and the Catholic Church.[11] The second category, even more heterogeneous, included the Mexican owners of small industries alienated by the policies favoring foreign investors, politicians who had fallen from favor, and professionals, intellectuals, and liberals from many different walks of life, including some *hacendados* themselves, such as Madero and Venustiano Carranza.

Given such divisions, no single group could entirely dominate the insurrectionary movement. Madero's appeal was strongest among disaffected members of the Porfirian upper bourgeoisie and the liberal urban middle sectors. Zapata's Plan of Ayala, calling for wholesale agrarian redistribution, was abhorrent to most constitutionalists, other than a few radicals (Gilly, 1971). Many of Madero's supporters could not tolerate a total suppression of their acquired rights and privileges on land and wealth. Yet, they accepted the expropriation of a few single *hacendados* as punishment for their defense of the Porfirio Diaz regime. Such actions were the exception, however.

The direction of the Revolution was bound to be constantly weakened by such profound internal differences, oscillating between the interests of its various supporters. In particular, the feasibility of the social reforms proposed by Zapatistas, Villistas, and the leftmost wing of the constitutionalist camp were contingent upon Madero's capacity to make these reforms acceptable to at least a substantial coalition of interests, while successfully resisting the armed rebellions of those opposed.[12]

Madero perceived no need to forge alliances based on anything more than democratic principles to consolidate the fledgling Mexican democracy. He had "faith in the people's capacity to govern themselves with serenity and wisdom" (Madero, from Krause, 1987a:68). To exercise coercive power or suppress the expression of divergent interests was against such principles and personally abhorrent to him. As soon as his military victory was consummated by Porfirio Diaz's capitulation (Juarez Agreement, April 1911), Madero permitted a pro-Porfirio interim president—Francisco León de la Barra—to take office while he ran for election again, despite the fact that he had clearly been the winner of the 1910 rigged election. He also disbanded his victorious army while a pro-Porfirio legislature and bureaucracy remained in place. This de facto (if not strictly intentional) adoption of a virtually unchanged Porfirian power structure forced him into a political position that made any change in the Porfirian pact of domination (either from above or in response to demands from below) virtually impossible.

Madero's futile attempts to retain Zapata's support while responding to neo-Porfirian and middle-class liberal pressures to deny agrarian reforms have usually been singled out as the most important facts about his administration, as well as the primary cause of his demise. Though less heroic, the history of his relationship with the working class is equally instructive of the lack of incorporation of this group as a supporter of the still weak constitutionalist coalition.

Madero's arrival produced no ground swell of popular enthusiasm among urban workers. His Plan of San Luis, publicized during his 1910 campaign, made no mention of workers. As a result, his campaign of 1911 had little to say about labor reform. Only weeks after his triumph over Porfirio Diaz, de la Barra broke a strike with Madero's tacit approval, and guns were used against striking miners in Coahuila (Ruiz, 1976:188). Nevertheless, Madero's presidency broke the barriers to a transformation of the relations between capital and labor, which the Porfirian state had erected by suspending the Constitution of 1857. By reinstating constitutional order, Madero's government unwittingly transformed the institutional means by which workers were able to pursue their interests. In effect, the 1857 document specifically advocated the organization of unions and the resolution of industrial conflicts through mutually binding labor-management agreements, both of which had been violently opposed by the Porfirian regime. Madero's government, and after him, Carranza's, respected this resurrected document by (often unsuccessfully) offering the mediation of the state to ensure the orderly resolution of industrial conflict.

This policy did not, as it had in the agrarian sector, trigger the opposition of important power centers whose support the new government needed. Foreign industrial and mining companies, who owned over 70 percent of capital investments in Mexico, generally offered their workers better pay and working conditions than did Mexican-owned companies, most of which were smaller and, therefore, more vulnerable to competition. Madero and his brother (minister of the treasury), on the other hand, believed in the liberal credo that big business, more modern and progressive, ought to be favored over small and middle-sized enterprises (Ruiz, 1976:191). Thus, the thrust of worker demands, which focused on "old-fashioned" Mexican enterprises, especially in the textile industry concentrated in the state of Veracruz, coincided both with the president's bias and with the interests of large foreign-owned enterprises. In the textile industry, for example, wages among male, female, and child workers varied greatly, each category being made to compete against the other.[13]

The situation of the working class on the eve of the Revolution was precarious. Labor was abundant and easily replaceable. Real wages were depressed by the slow but continuous inflation of prices throughout the Porfiriato without compensating pay raises.[14] Simultaneously, working conditions worsened, with workdays of twelve to fourteen hours, six- and often seven-day workweeks, and harsh discipline in the factories, enforced with heavy punishment and fines. Yet the essence of the majority of worker demands (Gran Círculo de Obreros Libres, Casa del Obrero Mundial [COM], Unión de Ferrocarrileros, Unión Minera, Confederación de Artes Gráficas, etc.) was not revolutionary heroics but concrete change. Though the majority of unions adhered to ideologies of broad social change, the demands from below were mostly decent wages, shorter work hours, and six-day workweeks. Above all, workers wanted their right to bargain respected. As Madero took office, strikes multiplied: between January and September of 1912, forty strikes erupted (ibid.:187–188). At one point, nearly 80 percent of the factories in the mining and textile sectors were paralyzed by strike (Ramos-Escandón, 1987).

Madero anticipated this eruption of labor mobilization. Antedating his election was a proposal to the legislature for the creation of a Department of Labor (Departamento del Trabajo) within the Ministry of Development (Ministerio del Fomento), which was enacted barely a month after he took office. The department was instructed to convene workers and industrial employers to a General Convention of Industrial and Textile Workers in April, 1912. The purpose of the meeting was to confront labor and management proposals for wages and working conditions, mainly in the conflict-ridden textile industry. Workers were urged to form the Central Committee of Workers (Comite Central de Obreros) to present their demands; yet this body had no voting power. Objections to the convention came mainly from small Mexican firms, while large and foreign firms, generally in charge of drafting the proposals, had little objection.[15]

The Department of Labor played an important arbitrating role in the disputes aired in this meeting. Yet its efficacy in lessening the exploitation of labor was low: the most important labor demands, such as the ten-hour workday and six-day workweek, the 1.25-peso daily minimum wage, the 10 percent overall raise, the raise of women's wages, and restrictions on child labor, were not met. Either the government was unable to overrule management's adamant opposition—notably, to the pay increase and the plight of women and children—or it could not enforce the agreements reluctantly arrived at. In too many cases, management simply ignored these agreements, sensing the department's weakness.[16] Even the basic constitutional rights of labor to form unions and send labor representatives to the bargaining table failed to be recognized at that first meeting. Nevertheless, it represented a first step toward arbitration and conciliation, a procedure that was soon to become established, serving as an instrument alternately of state support and of control of labor demands.

In this context of blocked liberalization, the issue of social insurance surfaced briefly. In 1908, limited employer liability for work-related accidents had been legislated in the industrial states of Nuevo Leon and Mexico, the two states where the strongest labor mobilizations and repressions had taken place between 1905 and 1906. But these measures were never implemented (Spalding, 1978:87–89). During the rigged presidential campaign of 1910, both the Democratic and the antireelectionist parties endorsed the principle of protection of workers from accidents at work (Garcia Cruz, 1972). In his second campaign in 1911, Madero reiterated his commitment to social insurance (Gonzalez Díaz Lombardo, 1973). Yet after he was elected, this issue disappeared from the agenda. The Department of Labor did not include social insurance as part of its program. The constitutionalist position, therefore, was not to seek worker support (and consequent confrontation with employers) via advanced labor legislation but to reestablish basic labor rights under the Constitution of 1857.

Labor organizations also took the return of a constitutional framework as their reference point. Their immediate concerns were desperately needed wage increases, less flagrant wage inequalities among different factories, regions, and categories of workers, and fractionally more humane working conditions. Earlier demands of the anarchist-syndicalists for eight-hour workdays, equal pay for equal work, and compensation for injuries were still far from this immediate agenda. Those few labor organizations that had such measures on paper (as, for example, the anarchist COM) were regarded with hostility by the Madero administration and had only a modest following among workers. In such circumstances, it was unlikely that the tiny and poorly endowed Department of Labor, criticized by other more powerful state agencies for being too favorable to labor (Ruiz, 1976), would take much initiative.

When Madero's government fell, following his assassination in 1913, no public protest came from labor circles, save a perfunctory speech on May 1, 1913 (Meyer, 1971:7). Contrary to expectations (and contrary to official Mexican history), Victoriano Huerta, the neo-Porfirian usurper, turned out to be relatively more liberal toward workers, whose support he badly needed, than the "apostle of democracy" himself. To start the economy flowing again, he regulated prices and wages and ensured the flow of raw materials, providing military convoys to protect merchandise (Tuñón, 1982). The movement toward new labor-capital relations, timidly started during Madero's administration, was not only not reversed but was in fact perfected: the functions of the Department of Labor were enlarged (e.g., by the creation of a labor exchange that provided employment to many unemployed), and its budget increased; the agreement of 1912 on the textile industry was made law (May 1914), and factories found to be in violation were taxed an additional 8 percent (Tuñón, 1982).

On the whole, workers initially had few reasons to fight Huerta. Unlike Morelos peasants, their means of livelihood and their very lives were not threatened by the dictator. In fact, they offered their collaboration to "defend the country" against the U.S. Marines, who had taken Veracruz in 1914, reflecting the belated U.S. effort to cut off Huerta's arms supply line from Europe[17]. Huerta declined the offer and sent them to fight Zapata's popular army instead (Meyer, 1971:7). Nevertheless, although Huerta was capable of granting concessions to workers, he opposed labor representation in principle. Accordingly, he constantly harassed syndicalist organizations, in particular the COM, thereby forcing their choice of the constitutionalist camp.

Constitutionalist forces regrouped under Venustiano Carranza, the governor of Coahuila. Carranza's initial rejection of social reforms had very nearly lost him the leadership of the campaign against Victoriano Huerta, in which Zapata's southern army and Villa's famous División del Norte were winning militarily and threatening to unite as a single force. It was in order to resolve this deadlock that the Aguascalientes Convention was convened in 1915; the result, however, was the triumph of Zapata and Villa and the consummation of the split within the constitutionalist camp between reformists and liberals. Carranza's subsequent alliance with Alvaro Obregón, the ostensibly propeasant and prolabor caudillo, and his program of social reforms from his temporary military retreat in Veracruz (1914) changed the balance of forces.[18] The Villa-Zapata group, on the other hand, had apparently little appeal for workers (Knight, 1986) and sought no political rapprochement. Villa lacked a program of social reforms, altogether, and Zapata was perceived as exclusively interested in agrarian reform, despite the fact that his proposal at the Convention of Aguascalientes included labor legislation, such as the limitation of work hours, the protection of women and children, the institution of industrial accident insurance, the establishment of cooperatives and mutual aid societies, unionization, and the right to strike (Wolf, 1969:39–40).

The final separation between peasants and workers was sealed with the formal pact, signed in 1915, between Carranza and the anarchist COM. The COM agreed to suspend its syndicalist activities organization and send 3,100 men (the so-called *Red Batallions*) to aid the constitutionalists (Meyer, 1971), which at the time meant fighting the popular army of Pancho Villa. Most historians (Meyer, 1971; Carr, 1976; Cumberland, 1972; Basurto, 1975) present the final outcome of COM's association with Carranza as a heavy setback for the working class and evidence of the government's disinclination to admit this group into the revolutionary coalition. This interpretation is founded on the final breakup between Carranza and the COM in 1916, followed by the forceful liquidation of this organization by government forces. These facts, although undeniable, obscure more fundamental evidence that, during this period, the pact of domination was changing in favor of workers, as could be observed from the content and frequency of labor demands and the organizational capacity that labor demonstrated. The final conflict with the state was precipitated not so much by the illegitimacy of those demands (or the personal antipathy of Carranza toward workers so often invoked) as by the incapacity of the government to satisfy them in the face of staggering inflation triggered by the issuance of fast devaluating paper money; the hostility of the United States; and the capitalists' stubborn resistance to the government's labor reforms.[19]

Carranza's administration opposed labor demands only insofar as they tended to defeat his policy of billing consumers for the cost of the war and the consolidation of his rule via the devaluation of the various paper moneys that were issued during his administration. Five different currencies were issued (in addition to scores of others, issued by various constitutionalist generals, only some of which were eventually recognized by the *Primer Jefe*). These monetary manipulations resulted in rates of inflation as high as 500–600 per cent, especially with respect to basic foodstuffs.[20] Workers, who unlike the rural populations were fully dependent upon the cash economy, turned out to be the only political force with the organizational capacity to oppose this policy. Given the hostile disposition of most foreign governments toward the new regime, this left Carranza little alternative but to fight back.[21]

A cursory examination of the content and intensity of labor demands during these years gives us an idea of the importance of the changes that had taken place since the first negotiations in 1912–1913. The ten-hour workday which represented a victory in comparison with the twelve-and fourteen-hour days customary until 1912, was now considered excessive, the old anarchist demand of eight-hour workdays becoming generalized. Compensation for work-related accidents also appeared in several worker demands in different parts of the country, especially in those states that had instituted more advanced labor legislations (Veracruz, Yucatán, Coahuila, etc.). The Department of Labor repeatedly granted pay increases to public employees and imposed the eight-hour day on commercial firms. Yet, the real problem was that wage increases never kept up with the rate of inflation. It was therefore inevitable that unions would soon start making wage demands: they demanded that the minimum daily wage should be fixed at one gold peso or its equivalent in paper money. This demand was never granted and finally led to the violent conflict between the COM and Carranza, ending in 1916 in the jailing of the COM leaders, followed by the dissolution of the Casa. This conflict was also instrumental in ensuring the success of Obregón's coup against Carranza.

By 1916, the organizational strength of labor had become awesome: in January of that year, eighteen out of the thirty-six COM-affiliated unions formed the Federación de los Sindicatos Obreros del Distrito Federal (FSODF—Federation of Workers' Unions of the Federal District) to represent them through a federal council. Although the FSODF was based on the anarchist principles of noninvolvement in politics, Carranza forestalled the possibility of having to bargain with a powerful rival by dissolving the Red Batallions. In March, the FSODF (led by Luis Morones, head of electricity workers) convened the First National Preliminary Labor Congress in Veracruz. During this meeting, antigovernment feelings were freely aired and the liberation of jailed COM leaders was forcefully demanded. Out of this meeting emerged the first nationwide labor organization—the Confederación del Trabajo de la Región Mexicana (CTRM—Labor Confederation of the Mexican Region).

The CTRM immediately adopted a defiant stance, giving employers until May 22 to start paying a minimum daily wage of one gold peso, and to limit workdays to eight hours. As employers failed to respond before the deadline, a strike was launched, whereupon the government declared that workers who did not report to work on the following day would be automatically dismissed. Simultaneously, the administration pressured employers into making concessions, stipulating that wages would be paid in *infalsificables* instead of the totally devalued *Gobierno Provisional de*

Veracruz bills that workers had been receiving. A month later, the *infalsificables* themselves were badly devalued, and the FSODF reiterated its previous demands again, adding to them an additional 50 percent increase in wages. Only a few progressive employers paid spontaneously. The rest made vague declarations that they would organize in order to study the problem, while de facto disregarding these demands (Ulloa, 1983:304–05). A general strike was called for July 31, which virtually paralyzed the whole economy (water, electricity, transportation, etc.). Seeking Carranza's arbitration, the FSODF's strike committee requested an audience, thereby giving Carranza the opportunity to have them jailed and to close COM's headquarters. Thereafter, the FSODF virtually disappeared.

The clock of social reform seemed to have been turned back. Yet, three months later (on October 23, 1916), the government decreed that wages should be paid in *infalsificables* indexed to gold, with the exchange rate determined every ten days by the Treasury. The following month, 50 percent of wages were to be paid in gold, and the rest in *infalsificables*. Many industrial companies refused to obey, some responding with lockouts, others with mass dismissals. Workers went back on strike but this time in support of the government (Ulloa, 1983:320). A decree in the Federal District stipulated that dismissal without just cause would call for payment of two months' wages, one half in gold and the other in indexed *infalsificables*. In the mining sector, the Department of Labor avoided a massive strike by obtaining the payment of 75 percent of wages in gold. The following year, the country went back to the gold and silver standard.

In the agrarian sector, a similar picture was emerging. Although Zapatistas were fought relentlessly, a new Law of Agrarian Reform was issued, calling for the restitution of all property confiscated in violation of the law of 1856. Governors were given the authority to settle claims. Despite many violations, a limited proportion of this redistribution went to peasants in states fortunate enough to have progressive governors. In other cases, lawful titles were issued in the governors' own names, giving birth to a new class known as the "revolutionary millionaires."

Important labor reforms were also to be incorporated into the Constitution of 1917, even as COM leaders remained in jail. Despite the virtual dictatorial powers that had been conferred on Carranza and constant military threats to the regime, the government's intention to restore civilian constitutional order never wavered. A constitutional assembly was called in mid-1916, with preparatory decrees determining the rules of suffrage. In particular, it excluded all military personnel and all those guilty of having "helped with arms or carried out public functions in governments hostile to the constitutionalist cause," a clause especially drafted to exclude Zapatistas (from Ulloa, 1983:496).

It is generally agreed that the initial draft that Carranza proposed to the representatives assembled in Queretaro differed little from the Constitution of 1857, which he intended merely to amend (Ulloa, 1983; Carr, 1976; Córdova, 1985). In particular, the proposed draft virtually ignored agrarian and labor issues. This text met with the overwhelming opposition of the General Assembly and the committees of revision in charge of drafting proposed changes, which were heavily pro-Obregón. Carranza's project was replaced by proposals more in keeping with the important changes that had taken place in the pact of domination since 1911. The whole of Section 6 of Article 123 was devoted to labor. In addition to the issues most recently fought for and won by labor, this section included items that were barely entering the agenda. The already familiar issues were the stipulations of eight-hour workdays and six-day workweeks; the prohibition of child labor for children under twelve years (with maximum workdays of six hours); the disposition of minimum wages (to be determined by special committees); the payment of wages in legal tender (rather than company currency redeemable in company stores); the right of workers and employers to organize unions or professional associations; the creations of tripartite conciliation and arbitration committees (Juntas de Conciliación y Arbitraje), with equal worker and management representation and to include one government representative to arbitrate industrial conflicts; the right to strike (excepting military establishments); the obligation to pay three months' wages for unjustified dismissal, including dismissal on grounds of unionization (which implicitly incorporated employers' right to violate the Constitution); and the prohibition of lockouts unless authorized by the juntas.

The newly introduced issues included principles of social insurance, incorporated in the provision of compensation for accidents or illness suffered as a result of working conditions; the principles of equal pay for equal work, regardless of the sex or nationality of the worker; the prohibition of dangerous or unhealthy work for women and children under sixteen years; three months' fully paid maternity leave; profit sharing; 100 percent wage increase for overtime; the provision of "comfortable and hygienic housing for workers with moderate rent, in addition to schools, dispensaries and other necessary community services" (Para. 12, Art. 123, Sec. 6).

Many authors regard Article 123 as the embodiment of reformism from above, which subsequent postrevolutionary administrations are alleged to have adopted (Córdova, 1985; Carr, 1976; Basurto, 1975). This position fails to make the connection between the provisions contained in Article 123 and the grievances fought for during the stormy years from 1911 to 1917. The position taken here on the basis of the evidence produced is that in most of its paragraphs, Article 123 was merely giving legal status to the conquests achieved through the struggles that had taken place over the years among workers, the state, and capitalists. The anticipatory character of some provisions (e.g., the prohibition of unhealthy working conditions, social insurance against accidents, or profit sharing) cannot obscure this fundamental fact. In effect, those proposals that were still in advance of their time were to remain dead issues for several more decades, until new confrontations would bring them to the fore.

It is widely recognized that the Constitution of 1917 as a whole laid the foundations for a strong central state whose prerogatives would eventually restrict the capacity of labor to advance beyond the terms that negotiations had reached by 1917. Yet, this distant future could not be predicted in Carranza's time. By the end of Carranza's administration, the Mexican state was far from assured of a stable future. The economic destruction wrought by the Revolution had not been brought under control, due partly to Carranza's efforts to counter pro-Porfirio and pro-Huerta economic interests and partly to his inability to force foreign companies to renegotiate the terms of the concessions granted under Porfirio Diaz (Hamilton, 1982:64–65). Although Carranza recognized the necessity of destroying the Porfirian state, particularly the Porfirian army, he failed to see the necessity of strengthening the popular base of support that he had partially created, which eventually tipped the balance in favor of Obregón. A confirmed federalist, Carranza also failed to take steps to concentrate power at the center. During his administration, government authority existed more on paper than in fact.

The weakness of the state instituted by Carranza and the pivotal role of labor in reasserting its authority were to become evident in 1919, when Carranza stepped down in accordance with the revolutionary rule forbidding reelection. Carranza's attempt to create a puppet regime under Manuel Bonilla, a colorless bureaucrat, assured Obregón of labor and peasant support, even before taking power by force. Only eight hours before Obregón led a successful coup against Carranza, he had signed a secret agreement with the Confederación Regional Obrera Mexicana (CROM—Regional Confederation of Mexican Workers), created in May 1918 through the good offices of Espinosa Mireles, the prolabor governor of Coahuila. In exchange for its support of Obregón, the CROM requested a separate Ministry of Labor headed by someone "identified with the moral and material needs of workers" (from Carr, 1976:113). Labor and agriculture ministers were to be appointed only after consultation with the CROM. The government was to recognize CROM's legal authority to discuss labor problems directly with the labor minister and to agree to provide maximum assistance to ensure the implementation of measures decided by the CROM's central committee or other assemblies. These clauses granted the CROM a virtual monopoly over the representation of the Mexican working class. In 1919, the CROM created the Mexican Labor Party (PLM), which immediately started campaigning for Obregón.

Carranza's presidency ended in increased labor insurgency in favor of Obregón (who escaped from Mexico City disguised as a railroad worker) and general political chaos. On April 22, 1920, Obregón proclaimed his Plan of Agua Prieta, which laid out his program and disclaimed Carranza's authority. A large part of the armed forces followed him. Carranza was militarily defeated and was executed as he attempted to escape to Veracruz. To resolve the crisis of succession, Congress appointed Adolfo de la Huerta (the governor of Sonora) as interim president from May to December 1920. During this interim, Obregón campaigned and won the election.

THE SONORANS, 1920–1932

The ascent to power of the Sonoran dynasty—Alvaro Obregón (1920–1924), Plutarco Elias Calles (1924–1928), Emilio Portes Gil (1928–1930), Pascual Ortiz Rubio (1930–1932), and Abelardo Rodriguez, (1932–1934)—was to signify several important changes: the continued exclusion of landowners and the Catholic Church, the gradual loss of power by the military, the slow marginalization of peasants, and the increasing importance of the new revolutionary bourgeoisie. Simultaneously, the state was to become both stronger and more centralized, as a result of systematic policies of demilitarization, the control of elections, the founding in 1928 of an official party, and the creation of central instruments of economic and monetary policy (e.g., the Bank of Mexico in 1925).

Despite such changes, the state was to remain weak with respect to the foreign bourgeoisie, failing in its various attempts to renegotiate the leonine terms obtained from Porfirio Diaz. As a result, relations with the United States were to remain tense, despite Obregón's initial assurance to Woodrow Wilson that U.S. economic interests would be safeguarded[22]. Obregón's capitulation in the conflict with the United States over ownership of the subsoil, marked by the Bucarelli Agreement signed in 1924, was an agreement to the nonimplementation of Article 27 of the Constitution, which had declared the sovereignty of the state over the subsoil. This concession ensured U.S. collaboration and strengthened the government's capacity to repel the coup attempted by de la Huerta in 1924, leaving the more conservative Calles as Obregón's successor.

Obregón's administration is usually presented as having inaugurated the patrimonial style of limited preemptive reforms from above, considered characteristic of Mexico. If we look upon the events that opposed labor and capital during his administration (1920–1924) from the perspective of a changing pact of domination, however, a different picture emerges.

It is more than probable that Obregón intended to control labor demands through his secret agreement with the CROM (whose very existence did not become known until 1930); if this was the case, events did not turn out exactly as planned. First, the president fell far short of fulfilling his part of the bargain: no separate Ministry of Labor was created (the bill, which lacked strong presidential support, was defeated in Congress); the CROM was not consulted on major cabinet appointments (least of all agriculture); and neither was the CROM officially defined as the sole representative of labor, which would have been blatantly anticonstitutional. CROM leaders had to be content with secondary appointments in government, limiting their capacity to exercise control over the working class. The CROM was shunned by both the right and by the left wing of the labor movement—The first, out of mutualist and cooperativist conviction, the last, out of a preference for direct confrontation with capital and no collaboration with government.

Despite the incompleteness of research into the precise content of labor demands during Obregón's administration, this period can be read as an effort on the part of labor organizations outside of the CROM to assert their bargaining capacity and make effective several of the paragraphs contained in Article 123 of the Constitution, especially the eight-hour workday. Insurance against illness and accidents also began to appear in the *pliegos petitorios* of the time.[23] The CROM attempted to slow down this movement but was unable to play an effective role. Rather than deflate rank-and-file demands, its failure to support them increased the power of the more militant organizations, particularly the General Confederation of Workers (CGT) allied to the recently created Mexican Communist Party (PCM). The state met these clashes with alternating repression and concession. By and large, however, conflicts were resolved in favor of labor more often than in favor of management: of the total of 951 strikes recorded between 1920 and 1924, 30.9 percent were resolved in favor of labor, 17.4 percent in favor of management, and 51.6 percent represented compromises (Basurto, 1975).[24]

Labor's initial intention to make good its constitutionally established claims was demonstrated by the sudden increase in the frequency of strikes, from 173 in 1920 (supposedly an extremely favorable year for labor demands due to de la Huerta's good disposition) to 310 in 1921 (Basurto, 1975:226). According to Basurto, the main cause of strikes in 1921 was the refusal by employers to grant wage increases, despite losses in real wages due to inflation. This year was also characterized by the creation of the Confederation of Railroad Societies (CSF), an independent federation sympathetic to CGT, that was initially opposed by the government. After months of often extremely violent confrontations, the CSF was, reluctantly, officially acknowledged.

In 1922, the majority of strikes (a total of 192) are said to have been triggered by employers' refusal to recognize unions as legitimate bargaining agents. In 1923 and 1924, the number of strikes further declined, to 146 and 125, respectively. Their major cause is said to have been the nonimplementation of the eight-hour workday (Basurto, 1975: 226). These crude data give an approximate idea of the character of labor demands and the role of government in arbitrating them: workers were still fighting, shopfloor after shopfloor, for the implementation of the gains they had made since 1910. Some telling examples give an idea of the intensity of interest among the rank and file in these issues. For example, workers at the Swedish telephone company Ericson struck to obtain higher wages and the implementation of a previous agreement regarding medical insurance that would cover illness (as opposed to only work-related accidents). They also requested equal wages for equal work, and "good treatment" (Basurto, 1975:232–33).[25] The president intervened by forcing the firm to accept a compromise agreement. The first day of illness was not to be paid; the following fifteen days were to be fully paid, followed by an additional fifteen days of half pay. Ericson was also forced to pay 50 percent of the wages for the duration of the strike (Basurto, 1975:232).

On other occasions, government intervention recalled the old Porfirian days: in 1921, a demonstration by textile workers in Queretaro was met by gunshots. The following year, another worker protest, at the Idelfonso textile mill, of the nonimplementation of an agreement on a wage increase, was followed by the abduction and disappearance of its leader. A mounting wave of violent protest and solidarity strikes engineered by the CGT followed this event, further widening the gap between the CGT and the CROM (the first being commonly referred to as the Reds, and the latter, rather aptly, as the Yellows).

Obregón is said to have been increasingly intolerant of labor demands in the last year of his term. This is typically reported as an unexplained change of heart. If we focus upon labor's potential for creating social disruption instead of Obregón's alleged personality change, however, we can reinterpret these changes in terms of the changing power game between state and labor in these years. Throughout Obregón's administration, the government's active intervention in labor disputes had disarmed many employers and demobilized a large proportion of the rank and file, as the decline in strike activity indicates. Despite the government's marked preference for CROM-affiliated unions, we can as yet discern no systematic pattern of government repression of independent unions via the conciliation and arbitration mechanism. The terms of the pact of domination had been improved for all sectors of organized labor, to the extent that the government imposed respect for the Constitution upon reluctant capitalists.

In 1923 and 1924, what remained of labor agitation took a different turn, associated with de la Huerta's growing ambition to succeed Obregón. On de la Huerta's side were the CGT and the railroad federation; on Obregón's side, the CROM. This internal split is illustrated in the CGT-affiliated tramway workers' conflict of 1923. An earlier strike in 1921 had been settled in favor of the union, with the intervention of the governor of the Federal District. Two years later, management declared its intention to dismiss 10 percent of its staff. Given that many workers had over fifteen years of service, the CGT demanded a compensation of one month's wages per year of employment, in addition to the statuatory three months' severance pay. In exchange, workers offered to abandon their claims on profit sharing, which they should have been receiving according to the Constitution. Other demands were full pay and the reimbursement of medical costs in case of illness and full pay in case of strike. Following management's refusal to agree to these demands, a strike was declared.

Rather than face the CGT head-on, the administration allowed the CROM to infiltrate the independent union and take over its direction, lending a helping hand with the forcible expulsion by the police of protesting CGT leaders. The new leadership immediately requested an affiliation with the CROM and was instantly recognized by the government as the lawful representative of the tramway workers. Predictably, the new union was willing to settle for much less than what the CGT had requested. Yet it demanded far more than management had been prepared to offer: the statuatory three months' severance pay, the respect for seniority in the selection of workers laid off, and payment for time lost during the strike. The CGT tried to obstruct this settlement with violent street fights, but its militants were dispersed by mounted police. Prisons were emptied to provide scabs to replace striking workers. Other CGT-affiliated unions came to the rescue, provoking more street fights and the intervention of the army, which shot protesting CGT members. At this point, de la Huerta, then minister of the treasury, intervened in favor of the CGT, forcing the company to hire back dismissed workers. Other companies that had retaliated against demonstrations of solidarity with the CGT were forced to take back dismissed workers as well. Many of those who had been jailed were released, also as a result of de la Huerta's intervention.

The issues of social insurance and profit sharing also illustrate the change in the administration's disposition toward labor demands. In his 1921 annual presidential address, Obregón declared that insurance against illness and old age was urgently needed

(Basurto, 1975:225; Spalding, 1978:91). He proposed that a reserve fund be created: employers would pay 10 percent of all wages into the fund and would be absolved of their constitutional obligation to pay profit sharing (which until that time had not been mentioned). This fund would pay workers' indemnity for occupational risks, old age, and certain kinds of survivor pensions (Spalding, 1978:91). A bill to that effect was eventually presented to Congress but never reached the agenda, owing, allegedly, to lack of presidential support (Clark, 1932). One may wonder why Obregón selected this issue at all, given that social insurance was not salient among formal labor demands. Very likely, however, it was a popular issue among the rank and file and therefore provided the government with an opportunity to soften the police actions against the leadership of selected militant unions with an uncontroversial measure that would benefit the rank and file directly, without the need for union leadership support. In his second campaign, in 1927, Obregón made a similar proposal, but this initiative was cut short by his assassination.

By 1923, it became clear that Obregón had chosen Calles, the CROM's favorite candidate, as his successor, rather than the more prolabor de la Huerta. De la Huerta tried unsuccessfully to use the support he had acquired among the more militant working class to engineer a coup against Obregón. Why he failed where Obregón had succeeded four years earlier is an interesting question. First, Obregón's administration had been significantly more favorable to labor as a whole than Carranza's had been. Second, the CROM was not omnipotent, as it would later become, although it controlled a substantial proportion of unions. Last but not least, the United States had become more accepting of Obregón, after the Bucarelli Agreement left untouched all issues of foreign ownership of the subsoil. The government could now count on a steady flow of weapons to fight internal coups. Labor support to repel these coups had, therefore, become far less indispensable to the survival of the regime.

From 1924 to 1934, a period known as the *Maximato* (from Calles' nickname, the *Máximo Jefe*), the power of the state was further increased through the continuation of policies of centralization, demilitarization, and control of popular movements. Analyses of the history of the labor movement during this decade usually emphasize the loss of power of the Mexican working class, resulting from the CROM's ascent to the position of sole government-supported representative of labor interests. Yet, it does not follow, as these studies usually imply, that the state stopped intervening on behalf of labor in conflicts with capital. The changes that took place in the pact of domination during the Calles administration were often carried out in opposition to the industrial bourgeoisie, who, nevertheless, was eventually to benefit from them.

During the Madero, Carranza, and Obregón administrations, the first mechanisms of state intervention in labor-capital relations had been created. But they remained very fragile, as evidenced by the constant violations of agreements perpetrated by industrial firms, which, in turn, triggered endless rounds of labor protests and further state interventions. State boards of conciliation and arbitration were weak institutions with little power to implement their decisions. As for the Department of Labor, we have seen that its power was also limited. All too often then, the president himself had to intervene, supporting a strike here, crushing one there, and endangering his alliances with various elites in the process. Despite these constant state interventions, conditions of industrial production remained chaotic, with adverse effects on the economy, which had still not recovered from the damages wrought by the period of armed struggles.

A major impediment to the control of labor conflicts was federalism. Each state had its own statutes and power structures. As a result, progressive states with advanced labor legislation (e.g., Yucatan, Coahuila, Veracruz) could coexist with states dominated by the neo-Porfirian bourgeoisie (e.g., Nuevo León). The federal executive was dependent upon state governors for carrying out its policies but had no guarantee that they would be implemented. The latter could independently set the rules of the game in labor-capital relations, backed by local industrial firms. State governors were tempted to yield to business pressures in their own states, make their own deals with foreign firms, and look the other way when even the most solid paragraphs of Article 123 (e.g., the right to unionize) were openly violated, thereby provoking industrial conflict. It was imperative for central authorities to create mechanisms to offset these centrifugal forces without alienating the bourgeoisie, while at the same time keeping the support of the working class.

Calles did not immediately address the problems of federalism, however. To strengthen the hand of the state in labor-capital conflicts, he first perfected the alliance with the CROM handed down to him by Obregón. A new arrangement was signed, giving the CROM significantly more power than it had enjoyed under Obregón and transforming this organization into a virtual state agency for the regulation of labor and capital conflicts. The CROM was defined as the only legitimate spokesman for labor interests. The government agreed to pay the CROM's operating costs (above and beyond obligatory dues), to mediate any conflicts with particular state agencies, and to help in conflicts with any other organizations likely to "vitiate" the pact (sic). The CROM, in return, was to give advance notice of all initiatives undertaken by affiliate unions against private firms and to support all government actions. The CROM was to authorize all strikes. To seal this arrangement, Luis Morones, the head of the CROM, and his closest associates were given lucrative government posts: the Ministry of Industry, Commerce, and Labor to Morones, and half a dozen middle-level posts to his immediate subordinates (in particular, the control of printing, which could be used to suppress antigovernment publications).

Simultaneously, labor-management relations were being defined and codified, leaving little to the imagination of union officials or individual firms: procedures for lay-offs, obligatory severance pay, indemnifications for accidents, seniority rules, minimum daily wages by region, and so forth were precisely defined. Following established U.S. custom, collective bargaining was introduced (as opposed to the previous factory-by-factory arrangements). Enforcement of these new rules was ensured by the constant presence in workplaces of inspectors from the Ministry of Industry, Commerce, and Labor.

Understandably, the independent bargaining power many shop-level unions had enjoyed during the previous administration was drastically curtailed. Yet, the real losers in these new arrangements were not the rank and file but the leadership of independent unions, most of which were of anarchist-syndicalist orientation. After 1924, all CGT strikes were pronounced illegal and forcibly broken by government intervention. CROM-affiliated unions, on the other hand, had little say in the drafting or negotiation of collective contracts, which was left entirely to Morones and the president. Nevertheless, thanks to the CROM's superior bargaining capacity (a capacity backed by the coercive power of the state), CROM affiliates benefited more from improved wages and working conditions than did independent unions (Basurto, 1975:248; Clark, 1932:110).

The regulation and bureaucratization of labor relations also significantly curtailed the power of individual employers, cutting short their capacity to override signed agreements or to rely on the complacency of local authorities. This, in itself, was bound to lower the propensity to strike of the working class, given that violations of basic constitutional rights and signed agreements over wage increases had previously constituted the bulk of industrial conflicts (e.g., refusal to recognize unions as bargaining agents, dismissal of workers forming or joining unions, wage disparities, etc.). Employers now faced a single organization and a set of bureaucratic rules backed by the state. Their capacity to coerce the working class or bend the rules had been drastically reduced. At the same time, the institutional capacity of worker organizations to change the terms of the pact of domination had also been reduced.

These policies helped strengthen the hand of the state and contributed to the development of capitalism: strikes (that is, legally acknowledged strikes) virtually disappeared. New foreign firms (e.g., Ford, Palmolive Peet, Dupont), accustomed to modern labor relations, began to take advantage of the unique fiscal conditions and low labor costs Mexico offered. Yet these arrangements did not bear the expected fruit. In 1926 and 1927 a serious economic crisis caused by the drastic lowering of international prices of oil and silver, Mexico's main exports, put these new arrangements to a hard test. The increasing corruption of CROM officials also endangered the capacity for state control of industrial conflict, increasing the possibility of violent confrontations with labor. After 1927, Calles began to decrease his reliance on Morones and to restrict the states' control over labor relations.

Before he could give his full attention to the new Federal Labor Code, however, the president had to resolve the immediate and acute crisis caused by the presidential succession of 1928. Calles' creation of the Partido Nacional Revolucionario (PNR—National Revolutionary Party) is often pictured in retrospect as a calculated rational move to strengthen the state. In truth, the official party was created in traumatic circumstances in which decisions looked more like last-minute inspirations than calculated strategies. In 1927, the no-reelection rule dictated that Calles should find a suitable successor. Yet, he was unable to find a candidate who would not unleash strong opposition within the revolutionary clan. Weary of creating a situation that might lead to a new round of violent struggles, Calles resorted to presenting

Obregón for a second term, thereby violating the no-reelection rule. Obregón's candidacy was accepted by a majority of the clique of revolutionary generals who formed the core of government support, and he was duly elected.[26] Yet a few weeks before taking office, he was assassinated under mysterious circumstances in which the CROM was strongly suspected. The crisis of succession was wide open again.

It was under these circumstances that Calles created the official party, in a desperate effort to control the increasing internal dissensions that threatened to dissolve the regime. As Hellman remarks, "few people observing the motley conglomeration of semi-independent parties, movements, interest groups and political cliques that was the PNR in 1929 could have believed that it would develop into a unified and enormously powerful political organization" (1983:33). At the time, the PNR was conceived as a mechanism to form consensus among elites, in order to ensure the peaceful handing over of power from one administration to the next. Specifically, Calles used it as an instrument to name presidential candidates who would continue to respond to his command. Agrarian and working-class interests were absent from the PNR: the PLM and the PCM had been excluded, and radical peasant groups (e.g., the National Peasant League and the National Agrarist Party) expected so little from it that they had initially abstained from joining (although they were later forced to do so).

Inside the party, "consensus" was fashioned via the systematic expulsion of all individuals who were not unconditionally loyal to Calles or expressed the slightest doubt regarding the wisdom of presidential decisions. This strategy was followed scrupulously by all presidents of the party (who were appointed by Calles), including Lázaro Cárdenas, who occupied this post in 1930. As a result, the PNR fulfilled its function of solving subsequent crises by making the selection of presidential candidates, until 1934, an unquestioned prerogative of the Máximo Jefe, hence the term Maximato to refer to this period.[27]

In 1927, shortly before the political crisis triggered by Obregón's assassination, Calles took the first step toward bringing labor affairs under federal jurisdiction, creating the Federal Board of Conciliation and Arbitration with the power to authorize and arbitrate all strikes. This made the prohibition of anarchist-syndicalist strikes more "legitimate," while simultaneously taking some power away from the fast-decaying CROM. Shortly thereafter, Calles entrusted President Ortiz Rubio (1930–1932) with the elaboration of a Federal Labor Code.

Private firms were initially opposed to the new labor code. But Calles's support of capital, coupled with the growing distance between the regime and subordinate classes (as evidenced by the CROM's control over labor demands and the halting of agrarian reform) allayed the fears of the industrial bourgeoisie. As a result, Calles succeeded where a more radical president might have failed: the Federal Labor Code was adopted in 1930.

Nevertheless, employers felt threatened by the move toward further federal control and protection of labor. The state's initiative to propose social insurance legislation in 1928 was the catalyst that decided them to organize the Confederación Patronal de la República Mexicana (COPARMEX—Mexican Employers' Confederation) to defend their interests, as much against the state as against labor itself (Spalding, 1978:98). Yet, the Labor Code was no more than a codification of rules that had become legitimate under the impetus of nearly two decades of rapid changes in the relations between capital and labor.

No research has been carried out to date regarding the linkage between labor demands for social insurance and the formation of a full-fledged Social Security Party, credited with having helped reelect Obregón in 1927. Although the union leadership (least of all the CROM) had failed to make any demands in this respect, it is clear that social insurance represented an important issue for the rank and file, who would be motivated to vote for Obregón despite the CROM's open opposition to the candidate. After Obregón's assassination, Calles was under some pressure to take an initiative regarding that issue. In 1925, he had proposed a limited social insurance scheme (covering work-related illness and accidents), to be jointly financed and administered by employers, workers, and the state (Spalding, 1978:93). Yet the depression of 1926–1927 had not provided a favorable context in which to make additional demands on industrial firms. Calles made no attempt to override their opposition, but he did institute limited schemes for civil servants and the army in 1925, with no prompting from either group. Both decisions increased the direct dependence upon the state of two potential sources of internal opposition: the corps of civil servants and the lower ranks of the armed forces. School teachers, who had initially been excluded from the social insurance plan, were included three years later, following prolonged strikes (Mesa Lago, 1978).

The second proposal for social insurance during the Maximato came in 1928, as part of the draft project of the Federal Labor Code. As the federalization of arbitration and conciliation, this could be understood as a preemptive move, aimed at simultaneously weakening the CROM's power and attracting the rank and file of independent unions. Rather than continue to privilege CROM affiliates with benefits while starving out other labor organizations, the new strategy was now to offer an inducement likely to unite the whole working class under direct state control. For the first time, this second proposal went beyond the customary coverage against work-related accidents and illness, presumably under the growing influence of the International Labor Organization (ILO) founded in 1925.[28] However, the government lacked the necessary fuel of worker conflict to confront employer opposition. After an initial airing of the issue in a convention of industrialists and labor representatives, the proposal was quietly dropped in 1928, in the face of adamant business opposition. This time, again, economic conditions were unfavorable: the country was barely recovering from the 1926–1927 slump. A more modest proposition was still included in the draft project of the labor code, which "unleashed a storm of employer opposition and checked the impetus for state action in support of worker rights" (Spalding, 1978:97).

In the early thirties, Mexico began to feel the effects of the Depression. The Máximo Jefe was beginning to lose his capacity to control open demonstrations of opposition to the government or the strengthening of interests potentially dangerous to the clique in power. It is difficult to evaluate the weight of challenges from below in this process. Hamilton (1982:115) states that the historical record is ambiguous enough to lead to diametrically opposed conclusions, according to whether the observer wants to interpret the incoming change as a revolution "from below" or as one "from above": peasant, worker, and consumer revolts during the late 1920s and early 1930s are seen alternately as profound social disruptions or as mere ripples on the surface. The latter imply that, due to their organizational weakness, popular forces were not capable of posing a serious threat to government; the former that Cardenism, the movement centered on the figure of Lázaro Cárdenas, rode on a new wave of class struggles triggered by the Great Depression.

All agree, however, that state control over the popular classes were becoming more uncertain. The clearest evidence was the mass desertion by workers from the corrupt CROM and many other scattered worker federations and the concomitant rebirth of militant labor represented by the creation in 1933 of the Confederación General de Obreros y Campesinos Mexicanos (CGOCM—General Confederation of Mexican Workers and Peasants) by Vicente Lombardo Toledano, a disaffected member of the CROM. It is also clear that the working class suffered the consequences of the economic depression in the United States (Cárdenas, 1987:36) and, therefore, no longer had strong reasons to support the CROM.

After 1930, the balance of power within the official party was also changing. Calles's failure to enact the political and social reforms favored by many of those who had initially supported him was thinning the ranks of his supporters (Brandenburg, 1964:71–76; Basurto, 1975; Cornelius, 1973:437). Despite the virtual police methods employed to maintain internal cohesion (such as the customary expulsion of dissident members from the PNR), a left party wing—the "Reds"—had slowly asserted itself over the "Whites" (Garrido, 1985). Soon these reformers rallied behind Lázaro Cárdenas, an avowed proponent of land reform and labor legislation (Hamilton, 1982:117). In the early thirties, the PNR was almost evenly divided between Callistas and Cardenistas. To redress the balance of power in his favor, in 1931 Calles tried, unsuccessfully, to co-opt the National Peasant League. He succeeded only in bringing into the state a group that was capable of voicing the grievances of the peasantry (Hamilton, 1982:100).

In a belated effort to rally labor's faltering support for Calles, a new social security proposal was presented to Congress in 1932. This initiative was cut short by Calles's abrupt removal of Ortiz Rubio and his replacement with Rodriguez, his third and last puppet president (1932–1934). Rodriguez convened the First Mexican Congress of Industrial Rights, in which representatives of capital and labor further discussed the issue of social insurance, while Lázaro Cárdenas was being nominated as the next presidential candidate. During this congress, an important proposal was presented by two social security experts—Fritz Bach and Adolfo Zamora—around which all subsequent discussions of social insurance were to revolve. It encompassed a wide range of benefits regarding occupational risks, retirement, survivor pensions, illness, maternity, and employment services. It contemplated the gradual coverage (as decided by the president) of all workers and their families, white collar and industrial, as well as rural (Spalding, 1978:99–100).

In response to this initiative, private firms took the new Federal Labor Code, which many had initially opposed, as the basis for refusing the principle of social insurance. They argued that their constitutional responsibility did not go beyond workman's compensation as provided by that law (Spalding, 1978:100). Workers and the state both advocated a centralized program with wide-ranging benefits. In the haggling over who would pay how much for what, the employers' constitutional obligation to provide profit sharing abruptly emerged as an apple of discord: employers argued that their contribution to social insurance should correspond to profit sharing (i.e., that they should be absolved of profit-sharing requirements if they accepted social insurance), while workers argued that it was their own contribution that should come out of profit sharing. In both cases, social insurance would have been a highly unstable institution, depending for its survival on the level of profits. Another interesting feature of that debate was that, for the first time, labor sided with capital in its opposition to a dominant position of the state in the proposed Social Security Institute. This proposal, however, was to have no immediate effects during the Cárdenas administration, despite the importance of labor support of Cárdenas, especially at two key junctures of his eventful administration (1936 and 1938 respectively). Why the administration no longer pushed for social insurance was a function of the abrupt change in the role that labor was to play in the stability of the new government.

CARDENISM, 1934–1940

In 1933, under pressure from radical agrarian organizations and Cardenistas, Calles persuaded President Rodriguez to resign, and the party to nominate Lázaro Cárdenas as the new party presidential candidate. Cardenas had the support of many different groups: the worker and peasant masses, who saw in him a new opportunity for social and economic reforms (Garrido, 1985); the military, who had been marginalized under Calles; and Callistas themselves, who mistakenly thought that he would remain responsive to the *Máximo Jefe*'s directives. His willingness to fill half of his cabinet with proven Callistas gave enough evidence of his good intentions.

From the Callista elites' strategic point of view, the nomination of Cárdenas was a calculated risk. Given the even split between Cardenistas and Callistas inside the PNR in 1933, keeping the peace was no longer a simple matter of making multiple and precarious interpersonal deals, a skill in which Calles (not unlike Porfirio Diaz) excelled. This time, the explosive potential represented by the combination of simmering popular discontent and the political aspirations of young Cardenista⟩ had to be weighed against the seemingly minor risk of losing some political ground. Subsequent events were to demonstrate that Calles had simply miscalculated.

The absence of state-administered social reforms benefiting labor during the administration of the most prolabor president in Mexican history can appear paradoxical. The key to this riddle is simple, however. It is given in speech after speech by the presidential candidate and, later, president: workers must organize and "claim their rights" (Anguiano, 1986:49) by exerting pressures on employers to make economic concessions.[29] The campaign was only the first part of a grand master plan. The second part was the organization of the popular masses and their incorporation into a new official party, "purified" (*depurado*), democratized, and rebaptized the Partido Revolucionario Mexicano (PRM—Mexican Revolutionary Party). The support of peasants, workers and the military, rather than interpersonal coalitions among caudillos of the Revolution, became the basis of presidential power: peasants were incorporated into the Confederación Nacional Campesina (CNC—National Peasant Confederation), while workers entered the Confederación de Trabajadores de México (CTM—Confederation of Mexican Workers) under the leadership of Lombardo Toledano.

Calles was quick to respond. On June 12, 1934, barely a few months after Cárdenas took office, he publicly condemned the escalation of strikes that had been duly authorized by the Federal Board of Conciliation and Arbitration, blaming party radicals, chastising government and calling strikers "traitors to the national interest." The document concluded that "exactly the same thing had happened to Ortiz Rubio's government," clearly implying that Cárdenas would be removed from office unless he mended his ways.

Instead of precipitating the president's resignation, as most seasoned political observers would have predicted, this move led to the stunning victory of Cardenism, backed by all sectors of the organized working class. The following day, a terse presidential statement reiterated the government's intention to "fulfill the program of the Revolution and carry out the dictates of the six-year plan without regard to the alarm expressed by the capitalist class" (Hamilton, 1982:125). The text also strongly suggests the illegality of Calles's intervention. Simultaneously, Callistas were removed from key positions in the cabinet, the party, and the military.

Faced with overwhelming odds against his political recovery, Calles abruptly left the country. The following year, however, he was back, renewing his attacks. This time, the accusations were no longer veiled: he publicly accused Cárdenas of "carrying the country to communism" (Cornelius, 1973:452). This precipitated the final purge of Callista elements from the Cárdenas government and the party, accompanied by massive labor demonstrations in support of Cárdenas. On April 12, 1936, Calles and his closest entourage (including Morones) were taken to the airport and asked to leave the country. The expulsion was made a public act.

Scholars are divided on their evaluation of these strategies. Some (Anguiano, 1986; Córdova, 1985) regard it as an immense hoax played on workers and peasants; others (Cornelius, 1973; Hamilton, 1982) manifest their admiration for a master strategist who circumvented the maneuvers of his enemies and restructured Mexican society. All agree, however, that the president's success was not a mere reflection of his formidable personality. As Cornelius states, he "held a strategic position in the coalition game. As a president of the republic, he exercised unparalleled power over the distribution of authority positions throughout the government-official party apparatus; it was within his legal prerogative to redesign the winning coalition almost at will" (1973:448). The president, in other words, had become the presidency, and the fluid coalitions of the Revolution had crystallized into a solidly entrenched regime.

Yet, this view fails to see the degree to which the power of the presidency rested upon the maintenance of a fluid balance between power centers—foreign and domestic capitalists, party influentials, labor, and peasants—a task that was particularly difficult to achieve in the early 1930s. Each of these actors could potentially destabilize the state. In this respect, the newly independent working class was a force to reckon with. Two years before Cárdenas took office, the CGOCM had been created, in open defiance of the system of a co-opted and corrupted labor organization, upon which the state had relied for more than a decade to control rank-and-file demands. In 1934, this new organization threatened to represent the peasantry as well, which would have created a coalition of awesome proportion and potentially disruptive power.

Should any attempt have been made to revive the Maximato at this juncture (as intended by Calles), Mexico would have faced an explosive situation potentially leading to a crisis of governability. Hence the possibility that a conservative coup d'Etat would put an end to the postrevolutionary regime. What happened instead was the confluence of a reformist presidency—whose selection was the result of strong pressures both from below and from within the official party—and a strong working-class organization that became the government's unconditional ally. This confluence, far from being the mere reflection of presidential control over labor (as some scholars argue), must be understood in the context of the threat to government stability. In exchange for unconditional labor support, the government of Lázaro Cárdenas was willing to let the working class change the terms of the pact of domination. "Class struggles,"—to quote the very words constantly used by the administration—had been legalized.

The Cárdenas administration's agenda aimed not only to redistribute the pie but to increase its size as well. It achieved both ends with varying degrees of success. More land was redistributed (50 percent more than by all of Cárdenas's predecessors put together), and *ejidos* (communal farms) were renewed through a new credit system (Banco Ejidal) to help small farmers.[30] Vast irrigation dams were built in the northern states where commercial agriculture started developing under the impetus of the Green Revolution. Roads and harbors were built, industrialists were granted extensive tariff and other fiscal concessions to facilitate import-substitution industrialization, trade was stimulated, and so forth. Despite widespread conflicts with the owners of industry and numerous expropriations, the gross national product grew by over 30 percent between 1934 and 1940 (Hamilton, 1982:184).

At the same time, government expenditures also expanded as the administration strove to respond to the demands of the masses in education, health, and basic services. The fiscal pressure exerted by the state on private enterprise had been kept low, in order to stimulate investment. Like its predecessors, the Cár-

denas government still depended on oil revenues to finance public expenditures. Yet, these had become insufficient to cover the
vast reform programs undertaken. Cárdenas soon found himself
in the awkward position of having to request loans from the private sector for programs the latter disapproved of (Hamilton,
1982:193). Unable to obtain these private funds, he increasingly
resorted to deficit financing.

Paradoxically, the legislative fight for social insurance stopped
during the Cárdenas years. How can this fact be explained? One
argument to explain this omission is the undeniable priority Cárdenas granted to agrarian problems, particularly his attempt to
rebuild and provide institutional support for the *ejidos*, the indig-
enous communal farms that were, for a variety of reasons, threatened with extinction. In this context, his administration made
significant strides toward providing health care: over a hundred
rural health centers were created following the spontaneous organization by a few selected peasant communities (particularly
in Michoacán, his native state) of cooperative health services. A
Department of Social Medicine was created to coordinate these
efforts. As in the social security schemes proposed earlier for
labor, these rural health programs had a tripartite structure composed of the Department of Health, peasant groups, and the
Banco Ejidal.[31]

Another reason for Cárdenas's restraint in social insurance
was that neither employers nor workers had been interested
in the kind of formula the state had previously offered. Employers still expected the state to contain industrial conflict and,
therefore, felt no pressure to make any new concessions. Union
leaders, on the other hand, preferred to exercise their newly recovered bargaining freedom by demanding social insurance directly from management. The government's insistence on social
insurance would have been tantamount to curtailing this freedom. Lastly, social insurance could also have endangered the
fragile working-class coalition that backed Cárdenas, given the
internal division between the left (anarchist-syndicalists and communists), who advocated demanding social insurance benefits
through collective contracts, and the center (ex-CROM), who
would have accepted state-controlled benefits.

While the legislative fight for social insurance stopped
throughout the Cárdenas administration, the issue never ceased
to be alive. It became closely associated with the historic events
that led to the nationalization of the oil industry in 1938. Until

1934, labor militancy in the petroleum industry had been contained as much through management repression of its organizations as through government control of strikes. Oil companies (whose taxes accounted for 60 percent of federal revenues) were, therefore, little prepared to accept the government's avowed policy of integrating labor organizations and encouraging their demands. This sudden policy reversal terminated the established gentleman's agreement whereby foreign companies discouraged labor militancy (e.g., by firing labor leaders) while the state looked the other way.

In spite of overwhelming obstacies, some unions had nevertheless sprung up, but they were mostly small shop-level "company" unions, isolated from each other and easily manipulated. Their integration into the Sindicato de Trabajadores del Petróleo de la República Mexicana (STPRM–Petroleum Workers' Union of Mexico), undertaken by the Cárdenas administration in 1937—a necessary step to ensure that the working class would side with the government against the Calles coalition—changed this situation profoundly. Once integrated, the STPRM immediately demanded a revision of the collective contract to include higher wages and several additional benefits, among them social insurance. As oil companies refused, the union took the issue to the Federal Board of Conciliation and Arbitration, which, contrary to the established custom of the previous administration, ruled in favor of labor. After the oil companies still denied the legality of the proposed collective contract, the issue was brought before the Mexican Supreme Court, which upheld the decision of the board (March 12, 1938). Thereafter, the Federal Board of Conciliation and Arbitration declared the existing contract to be void and the attitude of oil companies "rebellion" (Hamilton, 1982:229). On March 18, the STPRM ordered the suspension of work.

The Cárdenas administration was caught between two equally risky choices: if it bowed to the foreign companies, it was bound to lose labor support and be replaced by a neo-Callist government through a violent coup. If it nationalized the petroleum industry, its popularity would improve, but federal revenues would drastically decrease, at least initially. Nationalization was also bound to unleash countless retaliations, including the possibility of foreign military intervention. Cárdenas nevertheless chose the latter. On the evening of March 18, 1938, he announced publicly the expropriation of all foreign oil companies. Massive demonstrations of popular support of the decision were unleashed: for the first time, foreigners had been put in their place, and the state had stood by workers. The expropriation was widely supported by the national bourgeoisie and even by the Catholic Church, whose parishes organized public fund collections to pay for indemnification. In the uproar that followed this decision, accompanied by U.S. threats of intervention and general economic boycott of Mexican products (forcing Mexico, for example, to sell oil to Germany), all initiatives for new social reforms (including social insurance) vanished.

From a strictly cost-and-benefits point of view, the Mexican bourgeoisie profited far more from the Cárdenas administration than from the Calles administration. The state had taken over activities, such as oil, that would need extensive investments to stay profitable or, like the railroads, that could not be profitable in the long run. Moreover, these expropriations affected only foreign capital. The state was also financing the infrastructure with foreign debt and deficit financing, instead of with taxes from corporate profits. Private banking, industrial production, and commercial agriculture greatly benefited from Cardenism, as evidenced by the 25 percent increase in industrial production between 1934 and 1938 (Mosk, 1950:59; Cárdenas, 1987). The expanded market, indirectly provided by the policies of income redistribution, made possible the absorption of this growth into the internal market.

By all objective rational indicators, therefore, the national bourgeoisie as a class should have supported Cardenism, realizing that the damages to the economy resulting from social reforms were minimal in comparison with the benefits obtained for capitalist development. Nevertheless, while the beneficial long-term consequences of Cardenism were not yet clear (or at least not clearly perceptible to Mexican businessmen), the atmosphere of social unrest and hostility against capitalists generated in the process of radical change did little to assuage the fears of individual businessmen or to console those who actually lost money in the bargain. They reacted with their most powerful weapon of dissuasion: capital flight. This, in turn, precipitated an economic crisis that forced a devaluation and finally constrained the government to adopt a more conservative posture, as well as to seek a less radical successor.

The expropriation of oil companies momentarily strengthened the faltering popular alliance and rallied the most progressive sectors of the national bourgeoisie. But it also further antagonized the more conservative sectors of capital and contributed to strengthening their resolve to undermine this alliance. Increasing internal opposition to Cardenism was manifested in massive investment cutbacks, capital flight, credit and trade blockage, and even a military revolt (that was quickly repelled). It also led to the creation of the right-wing Partido de Acción Nacional (PAN—National Action Party) and the mobilization of fascist groups (Sinarquistas and Gold Shirts) (Hamilton, 1982:277). The most imperative task for the administration was to slow down capital flight and prevent U.S. intervention. During the last year of Cárdenas's term, the government started mediating, and occasionally forcefully stopping, labor demonstrations. Workers were to go back to the fold of the official party and let their demands be monitored and controlled by the CTM.

As in the previous administrations, the only employees who gained access to social insurance during the Cárdenas administration—workers from the nationalized railroad, electricity, and petroleum industries—had not fought for it or otherwise manifested their opposition to the status quo. Oil workers, in particular, were endowed with a social insurance scheme that, to this day, is the envy of all other labor organizations. In addition, the middle and lower ranks of the military who had served the regime faithfully (particularly when called upon to provide protection against the Calles intervention) were rewarded with more extensive benefits. These actions created precedents that contributed to further activating the issue. But they also had the effect of fragmenting the working class into different categories of beneficiaries, which would eventually create obstacles against the creation of a unified system of coverage.

CONCLUSION

Our analysis shows that labor's power over the regime throughout this period can be described as alternately defensive and offensive. From 1910 to 1924, labor's defensive potential for the Revolution was a major piece in the new coalition's claim to legitimacy within the popular alliance, hence labor was a valued ideological as well as military ally; from 1924 to 1934, although labor's defensive potential for the state came to an end and its offensive capability was diminished by corporatism, the state was obligated to compete with independent labor for the loyalty of the rank and file; finally, from 1934 to 1940, as labor once again became a crucial defender of government survival, it was further induced to support the state by the renewal of its lost institutional power.

Defensive Power (1910–1924)

Madero's administration (1911–1913) represented a failed attempt to form a coalition centered on the Porfirian bourgeoisie and the middle sectors. Attempts by the armed peasants of Morelos to enter this alliance and transform the conditions of their subordination were rejected, leading them into insurrection. The working class also felt excluded. Nevertheless, the return of constitutional legitimacy allowed isolated and scattered working-class organizations to begin mobilizing in order to lighten the exploitative character of the relations between labor and capital established during Porfirio Diaz's dictatorship.

Labor's weak bargaining position during Madero's short-lived administration was changed by the onset of armed struggles from 1913 to 1917. Labor and peasant support became a powerful political asset in the rivalry that developed between Obregón and Carranza from 1917 on. This particular situation, far from reflecting typical interelite processes of rivalry, as one analyst suggests (Collier, 1982), was an isolated instance that never successfully repeated itself.[32] Therefore, we must look elsewhere for an explanation of the constant liberalization of labor-management relations and the concomitant improvement in labor's economic situation during this early period.

During this first period, the fledgling revolutionary state was extremely vulnerable to any kind of internal dissension. To discourage coups and armed rebellions (which could rely on external help), the support of the popular masses, which had accompanied the military campaign to reconquer the national territory from 1913 to 1917, had to be maintained and consolidated at all cost. In this sense, it was not the military power of the Red Battalions, of Zapata's army of peasants, or of Villa's División del Norte that enhanced the power of the constitutionalist camp (although this element cannot be undervalued) but the public demonstration, through their involvement in the campaign against Huerta, of where the regime stood with respect to the "people." After 1917, this alliance was in danger of disintegrating: Zapata and Villa, the two folk heroes of the heroic stage of the Revolution, had been eliminated, and the leaders of the Casa del Obrero Mundial were in jail. All the more reason to exalt peasants and workers. Obregón's insistence on imposing Article 123 of the 1917 Constitution on a reluctant Carranza, therefore, was not inspired merely by presidential ambition; it made good political common sense. How else could the leaders of the new regime prove their credibility? Precisely by consolidating the popular alliance in one single document of enormous symbolic significance and potential for institutional change.

To reap the fruits of this legitimacy, the fledgling Revolution needed to do more than manipulate symbols (as an already established regime might do); it needed also to demonstrate respect for the very institutions it had put in place. Labor's recovered rights to organize, bargain, and strike were only one small element in this larger construction. The problem, however, was that granting these new rights to labor also threatened social peace by pitting labor against management, hence the inconsistent government response to individual strikes and demonstrations. Until the 1930s, the consequences of state intervention for changes in the pact of domination remained unclear. On the one hand, workers were in a position to exert pressure directly on their employers; but employers systematically ignited social unrest by firing recalcitrant workers, refusing to bargain, or failing to implement agreements. Labor's increased rights to pursue its interests, therefore, did not automatically lead to improving the pact of domination. It was not until the state intervened (weakly at first, but more effectively later on) that the resistance of management could be overcome and the pact of domination effectively transformed to reflect the greater bargaining power of labor.

Can we say of this short period that the government acted on behalf of labor because labor had the capacity to upset the constitutionalist coalition? As I have argued, workers were not part of the group that elected Madero. Neither did they appear to have the capacity to alter the balance of power by deserting the constitutionalist camp. Rather than interpret labor's defensive power in strictly strategic terms, we should look upon the state's dependence on labor support for regime stability at this early stage in the general sense of workers' participation in the popular alliance and the negative potential their mobilization against the regime could have in the solidity of this alliance.

Offensive Power, 1924–1934

In 1924, labor's defensive capacity for regime stability came to an end with the general strengthening of the revolutionary coalition through state centralization, demilitarization, and U.S. support. Its offensive power had become a serious hindrance, however. First, the power of the more militant among labor organizations had been curbed, by traditional repressive methods at first and, later, by the differential treatment of CROM-affiliated and independent unions. Far from resulting in a worsening pact of domination for the majority of the rank and file, however, government favoring of the less militant CROM had a price tag: CROM-affiliated workers were better paid and their rights better protected than independent unions. Both the CROM and the labor code served as a regulatory instruments to maintain this pact.

Defensive Power, 1934–1940

This second phase was interrupted by a convergence of factors straining these institutional arrangements: the CROM's increasing inability to deliver the goods to the rank and file, with the consequent loss of government control over the labor movement; the internal reverberations of the Great Depression on employment and investment levels exacerbating these problems; and the fortuitous circumstances that placed labor in a privileged position to protect the government against a coup in 1934.

It is immaterial whether president Cárdenas announced measures permitting labor to exert greater pressures on capitalists before or after his government became dependent upon the latter's support to protect his government against an internal coup. For this argument, the relevant fact is that the problems facing the new government could not be resolved unless a strong popular alliance was forged on a new basis, attractive enough to convince the independent CGOCM to become the CTM, that is, to become integrated into the state. Labor's potential for destabilizing the state should it fail to respond to labor's aspirations was twofold: first, it could mobilize the peasantry (as it had begun to do between 1932 and 1934) and foment a populist coup; alternatively, it could remain inactive and let Calles take power without a fight (as it had let Huerta). In either case, the Cárdenas administration was in jeopardy. To convince this new political actor to do neither, something more than the limited kind of government-regulated bargaining this group had publicly rejected was needed: campaign exhortations to labor to unionize and "claim their rights," that is, to transform, with the government's blessing, the pact of domination, was the inducement needed to secure labor's collaboration. Without the enhanced power achieved through independence, however, labor would have been in much the same condition as the peasantry: "organized" by the state and receiving state bounties directly, while remaining a passive object of these transformations.

4

From Alliance to Confrontation, 1940–1970

Most political scientists and sociologists chose to see Cardenism as the cornerstone of triumphant state corporatism and capitalist development resting on a docile labor force. Labor historians, on the other hand, generally present a far more turbulent process of alternating confrontations and negotiations among state, capital, and labor for this period, setting a highly hazardous course for capitalist development in Mexico, and eventually leading to the political and economic crisis of the 1970s.

Perhaps the greatest misunderstanding clouding the interpretation of this period is the waning of the direct political role played by labor organizations in the government process, reflected in turn in the active discouragement (by state and labor leaders alike) of political activism among the rank and life. This view leads many authors to the conclusion that reforms introduced after 1940 are mere top-down co-optative devices imposed upon a silenced labor force.

In this chapter, I show the changes in the pact of domination that accompanied the decline of labor's political activism and the circumstances in which the welfare state was introduced. Three periods are distinguished. The first, from 1940 to 1946, represents an attempt to conciliate government support of labor demands with the pressures exerted by an aggressive coalition of forces demanding a shift to the right in government policies. The second period, from 1946 to 1958, witnessed the state's failed attempt to restrict labor's institutional power to make demands within the corporatist system, which triggered reactions that reinforced labor's independence and threatened state stability. During the years from 1958 to 1968, the alliance between labor and the state was recemented, despite the generally repressive atmosphere, from 1964 on, that permeated the last part of this period culminating in the tragic events of Tlatelolco.

The economic context of the first two periods has been characterized as growth with inflation (Solis, 1970:94), whose main cause is seen as the financing of government expenditures through monetary expansion. As a result, the gains obtained by wage earners from 1934 to 1940 gradually melted away. To correct these inflationary tendencies that were slowing down Mexico's export capacity (which at the time was still growing faster than import substitution), two devaluations were carried out—in 1948 and 1954—further cutting down the purchasing power of the urban lower and middle classes and leading to renewed labor mobilizations in the 1950s.

The third period has usually been characterized by its byword, "stabilizing development." Accumulation took place without inflation, as public spending was financed by internal debt, foreign loans, and a large influx of foreign capital. During this period, wage earners slowly regained the position reached in 1938 (Bortz, 1984). Nevertheless, the gap between the poorest groups (the rural population and the urban marginals) and the rich remained large. This period ended tumultuously, with the tragic events of 1968 and their aftermath.

Throughout the three periods considered, a gradually expanding proportion of the population gained access to basic health services. As a result, life expectancy gradually rose. Yet, fertility remained practically unchanged, bringing up the rate of population growth from 2.05 percent between 1921 and 1950 to 3.1 percent in the 1950s and 3.4 percent between 1960 and 1970. This demographic explosion, added to the massive migration of the rural population to the cities, exacerbated the restrictions imposed by "stabilizing development" on the absorption of new workers. It also weakened the market position of wage earners, who had to compete with rural migrants. In spite of such profound structural and market disadvantages, rural migrants carried out their recurrent efforts to improve their economic position, to which the state responded with a slow buildup of the welfare apparatus.

FROM CARDENISM TO NATIONAL UNITY, 1940–1946

The presidential succession from Cárdenas to Manuel Avila Camacho marked a moment of extreme vulnerability for the postrevolutionary regime. In 1939, the Cárdenas government had to contend with a coalition of conservative opposition to its reformist policies strong enough to take over power (whether by constitutional or unconstitutional means), echoed by strong centrifugal tendencies within the official party itself. The PRM, as fashioned by Cárdenas, had the legal capacity to determine through an open vote the choice of a candidate for the official party. This provision of internal democracy left the presidency little maneuvering room to contain the battles raging among its different factions, particularly within the labor sector—where the CTM was still struggling for hegemony, against the old CROM as well as against independent unions—and between labor and the military. The upshot was to be the most embarrassingly visible (although too often forgotten) electoral fraud since that of 1910, which had launched the Revolution. The compromise government that emerged from this conflictive process had to walk a thin line between responding to labor demands and restoring business confidence. Out of this explosive mixture emerged a major piece of social legislation—the Seguro Social (social insurance)—which opened the era of the welfare state in Mexico at the same time as it consecrated the principle of unequal development.

The brittleness of the regime and its dependence upon the CTM's support can be envisioned by quickly reviewing the situation prevailing on the eve of the nomination of the presidential candidate. The official party was divided between the military, the peasant sector, labor, and an as yet legally undefined "popular sector," each constitutionally empowered to nominate its own candidate. The opposition, on the other hand, showed fewer internal divisions. After an initial internal split between two candidates, it had coalesced around the more moderate of the two— General Andreu Almazán, considered an authentic caudillo, although initially on the side of Victoriano Huerta in the violent coup that had brought down the Madero administration in 1913.[1]

To many Mexicans, Almazán represented the voice of reason and the return to order after the social turmoil of Cardenism. He represented tranquility for capital, the end of religious strife, and moderate reformism for labor. To workers willing to shun the official party, Almazán made golden promises: the creation of production cooperatives, higher wages, the fulfillment of the constitutional promise of public housing, social security, and a moderate scheme of profit sharing. This platform was intended to attract the vote of several unions (especially railroad workers, electricians, and primary school teachers, who stood apart from the CTM). The official party, on the other hand, was split between General Francisco Múgica, representing the extreme left of the party (and Cárdenas' favorite), Sanchez Tapia, a party man with an ill-defined ideological profile, and General Avila Camacho, considered by most factions to be both moderate and manipulable.

In the norm-violating tradition of Mexican politics, a candidate selection process very different from that predicted by statutes of the PRM began building support for Avila Camacho as easy as 1938, despite the protests of other candidates. The first unofficially acknowledged initiative came from a group of governors summoned by former president Portes Gil. In late 1938, the members of this group signed an agreement to block the candidacy of Múgica, considered overly radical, and promote that of Avila Camacho (Contreras, 1985:14). Subsequently, a similar coalition of congressmen called *mayoritarios* (the majority) was formed under the leadership of Miguel Alemán, a member of the pro-Avila Camacho group of governors. According to Contreras (1985), these two blocks represented anti-Cardenist landowners and local cacique interests. Yet his data are too global to support this hypothesis. In addition, why such interests would have chosen Avila Camacho over Almazán is not immediately evident, given the fact that, at this early juncture, Almazán could easily have become PRM's candidate.

After this initial congressional endorsement, Avila Camacho was also selected by the CTM at its annual convention in early 1939. Although some authors opt for a personalist interpretation of this choice, showing that Lombardo Toledano was a personal friend and unwavering political ally of Avila Camacho (especially against the right wing of the military), it seems more plausible that Avila Camacho's candidacy was closer to Lombardo Toledano's aim of forming a left-center coalition under the CTM's hegemony.[2] In addition, Lombardo Toledano was confident that the official candidate would endorse the PRM's Plan Sexenal (Six-Year Plan), in which the CTM was bound to have a large influence. This plan, published by the PRM in 1939, seemed to bear out this hypothesis. It called for more agrarian reform, giving preference to collective *ejidos;* state intervention in economic decisions; and a policy of expropriations whenever "entrepreneurs unjustly den[ied] workers the improvements compatible with their real economic situation" (Partido Revolucionario Mexicano, 1939).

Not all labor organizations were unanimously in favor of the majority candidate, however. The more radical unions (railroad, electricity, textile) endorsed Almazán as a counterstrategy to the CTM's attempts to control the labor movement (Contreras, 1985:81–83). Similarly, in 1939, a group of primary school teachers seceded from the CTM-controlled Sindicato de Trabajadores del Estado de la República Mexicana (STERM— State Workers' Union of the Mexican Republic) and joined the pro-Almazán opposition (Contreras, 1985:92). Other groups had left the STERM, so that by 1940, it was practically defunct, incapable of channeling votes toward the officially designated candidate. Only the peasant sector seemed disinclined to support Almazán or even Múgica, the candidate closest to its interests. Shortly after the CTM's convention, the CNC also endorsed Avila Camacho. When the PRM convention took place, the choice of Avila Camacho was a foregone conclusion. The president, who preferred Múgica, remained in the shadows of this process during the whole period. Even the president of the PRM, considered too close to Cárdenas, deemed it wise to withdraw.

Although it solved the succession crisis, the formation of a pro-Avila Camacho coalition did not resolve internal differences among his supporters. Among the CTM's faithfuls, the main split was between Lombardistas and moderates. The Lombardistas strongly insisted on the Six-year Plan, intending to orient the new administration toward a milder form of Cardenism. The moderates were prepared to adopt a more conciliatory attitude toward capital. Avila Camacho, on the other hand, announced his own program, very different from that proposed by the PRM. It proposed guarantees to private enterprise, private ownership of land (a wording that opened the door to dismantling collective *ejidos*), and important welfare measures, including minimum wages, profit sharing, social security, and public housing. Each of these promises, launched in the middle of a fiscal crisis and capital flight, spelled danger for the official party. In other words, the ideologically safe principle of state-directed welfarism replaced that of class struggles, still included in the Six-year plan, to attract labor's rank and file (including those shunning the CTM) while offering guarantees of social order to the bourgeoisie.

In addition to this compromise program, the majority coalition counted on the personal aura of the candidate to allay the fears of the bourgeoisie and the middle sectors. The concerted effort on the part of the government and the CTM leadership alike to tone down labor unrest throughout 1939 was thought to lead the way to a relegitimization of the regime among disaffected groups without jeopardizing labor's position. Nevertheless, the CTM, and especially Lombardo Toledano, were generally identified with union militancy by the right, while accused of bureaucratism by the left.

The presidential election took place on July 7, 1940. Despite Cárdenas's reiterated promises that the electoral process would be "clean," state and municipal authorities had little intention of letting Almazanistas carry the day (Medina, 1978:117–20). They systematically blocked or canceled opposition votes by force, including shooting opponents when necessary. Almazanistas answered in kind. The result was a large number of deaths, mostly in large urban centers where the position of the official party was most at risk. There were strong rumors that the proponents of Almazán were expecting fraud and would take over the government by force in case of electoral defeat. Despite Cárdenas's attempts to make good his promise, on the day of election, the vote was determined by whoever got control of each polling booth, either by denying entrance to the opposition or by burning votes. Only the Federal District remained relatively "clean," with the resultant defeat of the official party. An analyst of this period soberly sums up the situation: "Any recommendation turned out superfluous simply because there was no way of establishing order in the electoral process; the official side had resolved to prevent any legal manifestation of the opposition, and the latter had decided to follow the same course" (Medina, 1978:120).

All appearances of foul play notwithstanding, by August 15 the electoral college had established the legality of the election: the final and unappealable verdict was 2,476,641 votes for Avila Camacho against 15,101 for Almazán, and 9,840 for Sanchez Tapia, who had waged no electoral campaign to speak of. Shortly thereafter, Almazán left the country in the hope of obtaining U.S. support (or at least its neutrality). Simultaneously, Cárdenas carried out a vast reshuffling of army commands. The U.S. government, which had been duly consulted on Avila Camacho's candidacy, demonstrated its collaboration with the new government by denying Almazán even an entry visa. Avila Camacho's *sexenio* had begun.

Under such inauspicious circumstances, the presidential program of *unidad nacional* (national unity), aimed at reconciling the right and the left, appeared less a clever strategy than an absolute necessity. Peace had to be restored and the economy set to work under the new stringent conditions imposed by the war upon a fledgling industrial apparatus and a timid capitalist class accustomed to exporting capital at the slightest provocation and highly dependent upon U.S. imports for production. The very first step taken in the direction of ideological and programmatic unity was the exclusion of the military from the party in January 1941, barely a month after the president took office.[3] This decision removed simultaneously the possibility of a military coup engineered by partisans of Almazán among the military and the presence in the official party of constant opposition to the CTM. The latter, still under the leadership of Lombardo Toledano, remained the staunchest ally of the president and his program, preaching the unity of labor and capital against fascism and imperialism while recommending a postponement of class struggles to a later stage of development.[4] The second step—probably less the result of a presidential initiative than of mutual agreement—was to let Lombardo Toledano step down from the CTM so as to project a less militant image of the labor organization. Fidel Velazquez replaced him but for the moment stayed close to Lombardo Toledano's line.

The convergence between the CTM's new program of class collaboration and the presidential program of national unity culminated in the Pacto Obrero (Workers' Pact), signed the following year. Many labor historians (such as Basurto, 1984) denounce this pact as a sellout by the CTM's new leadership and proof that labor had already lost power. Evidence for that interpretation is seen in the fact that labor, in order to aid in the war effort, agreed to temporarily renounce its right to call strikes. This reading, however, is both biased by hindsight and incomplete. In fact, the Pacto, as initially launched, can be considered a labor victory. It was to be the CTM's reward for backing Avila Camacho, rather than a candidate closer to labor's interests. It proposed not merely to stop strikes (the only point usually mentioned by its critics) but to lay the institutional foundation of labor power in the conduct of capitalist development: through the legal principle of *tripartidismo* (tripartite decision making), it defined the legality of co–decision making among labor, capital, and the state in shop-level as well as major national policies. A Consejo Obrero (Worker's Council) was to be created, which would sit with representatives of capital and the state on a National Tripartite Commission endowed with wide powers. Simultaneously, shop-level committees were to be formed on the same model. These were to examine appropriate levels of profits and wages. The architect of the pact was Lombardo Toledano; its most adamant opponents were business leaders (Durand, 1986:67).

For the actors involved, the Pacto Obrero had all the appearances of a major labor victory. If implemented, it was capable reviving economic growth and financial stability, provided that each side was willing to negotiate and respect the bargain. Labor's aim was to preserve the 97 percent gain in real wages obtained since 1934 (see Bortz, 1984). Capital sought to restore pre-1937 profit levels without industrial strife, but in 1942, the economy was no longer riding an upward wave. Despite the obvious advantages of no longer having to compete with U.S. products, the economy suffered from the lack of internal integration and external dependence on capital goods and various other imported inputs. As a result, rather than bringing an industrial boom, as in most Third World countries, wartime production declined slightly with respect to the 1930s (Contreras, 1985; Rivero, 1990:37). Also, exporting scarce foodstuff to the allies or conducting internal black market operations became a better business than strengthening productive capacity or expanding the internal market.

The Mexican bourgeoisie, which had steadily resisted the progressive social reforms contained in the Constitution (particularly social security, proposed as early as 1928), had not yet evolved to the point of believing that industrial conflict should be regulated, rather than merely suppressed. Many were still dreaming of the good old days when labor contracts could be violated and employees thrown out for no reason other than their desire to organize. Expectations of a return to this previous pact of domination were encouraged by the fact that the new administration originated in a center coalition. The new cabinet, in accordance with the idea of national unity, was a political collage of all ideological colors, including the old-guard supporters of

Calles, with only Cárdenas (this time as secretary of defense) representing the left.

A straightforward implementation of the Pacto depended on the government's willingness to exert considerable pressure upon the bourgeoisie. But this was precisely what the program of national unity—an absolute and immediate political necessity at the time—was meant to avoid. Any confrontation with the bourgeoisie was bound to bring back the anti-Cardenist feelings that had very nearly toppled the regime in 1940. It soon became clear that the bourgeoisie did not consider the Pacto binding, except for the no-strike clause. Government authorities just stood by while violent clashes between workers and management took place, intervening only in the gravest cases of violation of basic constitutional rights. To further exclude the possibility of a head-on collision between labor and business, the creation of the Tripartite Commission was abandoned, leaving the Consejo Obrero with no real function to fulfill other than to provide some semblance of unity within the labor movement and a forum for worker grievances. Individual enterprises, on the other hand, refused to create internal tripartite commissions capable of overseeing their profits and determining wages. In short, Mexico was not to be the birthplace of comanagement between capital and labor.

The failure of the Pacto Obrero was to alter profoundly the strategies of the actors involved. It was to intensify the division within the organized labor movement and trigger attempts by several splinter groups to shake off its dependence upon the state. In response to the CTM's silence on the nonimplementation of the pact, individual unions began to launch independent strike actions. Barely three months after the pact had been signed, the number of strikes went from 19 in 1942 to 562 in 1943 and to 721 in 1944 (Rivero, 1990:39). The CTM was under threat, both internally and externally. Internally, its waning militancy caused the exit of electricians in 1941, railroad workers in 1942, and oil workers in 1946. It also led to the creation from 1941 on of splinter groups like the Confederación de Obreros y Campesinos Mexicanos (COCM—Confederation of Workers and Peasants of Mexico), and the Bloque Nacional de Defensa Proletaria (National Bloc of Proletarian Defense) (Loyo, 1990:87). On the national scene, the CTM's inviolability was also seriously threatened. Its militants were systematically persecuted in several states, particularly Nuevo Leon, Jalisco, Guerrero, and Veracruz

(Basurto, 1984). In Veracruz, the CTM was even forced to dissolve its local organization so as to avoid further assassinations (Basurto, 1984:29–35).[5]

This situation began to accentuate the internal split within CTM between radicals associated with Lombardo Toledano and the moderates associated with Fidel Velazquez, the new secretary. In July 1944, Lombardo Toledano decided to sound out various representatives of the Mexican left on the possibility of founding a new party independent of the PRM (Medina, 1979:116; Durand, 1986). In September 1944, after a series of seminars in which the heads of various leftist groups expressed their views, a first step was taken in that direction with the creation of the Liga Socialista Mexicana (Socialist Mexican League). The CTM was to be the basis of its membership, but it was also to include the middle sectors and the progressive bourgeoisie.

Following this strategy, the CTM signed in April 1945 a Pacto Obrero Industrial (Worker Industrial Pact) with various employer groups, particularly the Cámara Nacional de Industrias de Transformación (CANACINTRA—National Chamber of Transformation Industries), with few implications for labor-management relations save that of independence from the government. This move made it possible for all CTM members to vote for the new party independently of the PRM. The idea of a left-center coalition had become a distinct possibility. The organized working class had changed from an ally of the regime to its rival, exerting pressures capable of transforming it. The situation was not dissimilar to that created by the CROM's dissolution in 1932, yet the international context was very different: World War II was over, and the Cold War, was dawning. The political and economic independence of Mexico were therefore no longer assured.

Following the failure of the Pacto Obrero, Avila Camacho's government changed its strategy toward the organized working class. As workers became increasingly disaffected from CTM with the steady decline of real wages, the political situation became potentially explosive.[6] In response, the president adopted a double strategy of containing labor through a new labor code while vigorously pushing a languishing social security bill. The first, accepted by the CTM but opposed by other unions (Loyo, 1990:90), made the right to strike contingent upon a complex process of advance notice and state arbitration. The second offered organized labor a comprehensive system of health and accident insurance and retirement pensions.

In September 1942, a revised draft of the social security bill was widely praised at the First Inter-American Conference on Social Security in Santiago, Chile. Following a whirlwind of conferences and consultations with labor and business circles, a bill was sent to Congress in December 1942 and approved in January 1943. By this time, the principle of social insurance was no longer associated with a progressive vanguard, as several Latin American countries had already adopted it. In fact, Mexico was behind in this respect. To make social insurance palatable to the majority of employers, it was pointed out that inadequate workers' benefits and noncompliance with collective contracts had been the cause of numerous work stoppages and strikes (Spalding, 1978:149). The resolution of these conflicts through a tripartite commission on social security was presented as the most appropriate solution and the condition for increasing the productivity of the labor force (García Tellez, 1942). The burden on employers was made to look insignificant: according to calculations endorsed by the International Labor Organization (ILO), it would increase production costs by only 1.14 percent, the increases to be introduced gradually. Workers were to contribute 3 percent of their considerably reduced wages, which was bound to cause resistance, especially from unions that had deserted the CTM and were in dire need of causes to promote themselves.

Several independent groups manifested their opposition to the bill.[7] Soon, street demonstrations and work stoppages broke out. Implementation was pushed through, despite resistance. Initially, only workers in the Federal District were to benefit and, even then, only those from large enterprises (thereby excluding the majority of small firms, domestic workers, and rural workers). In 1944, the newly created IMSS had little concrete to offer workers: it subcontracted various private medical establishments, giving services to a mere 103,046 persons (Zertuche Muños et al., 1980). Nevertheless, the law provided for the gradual incorporation of the whole working force. It also represented a new political gain for the CTM, in the guise of the reincarnation of the principle of tripartite decision making.

Almost simultaneously, a vast and luxurious housing complex was built in Mexico City, providing the CTM leaders with ample opportunity for rewarding loyalty and compliance in the key years of 1945 and 1946, when the presidential succession became the central political issue. Through this project, funds originally intended for the construction of health facilities and for pension funds (and paid in part by all salaried workers throughout the country) were made to benefit only a handful, leaving social security more symbol than reality. Nevertheless, its ideological force alone may have determined its efficacy, for in 1945 and 1946, there was also a drastic reduction in the number of strikes, from 721 in 1944 to 107 in 1945 and 24 in 1946 (Rivero 1990:39). As for the minority opponents of social security among labor, they were quickly repressed and their leaders arrested for mutiny, insults to the president, and the illegal bearing of firearms (Pozas Horcasitas, 1990:130). Employer representatives and private insurance companies made vain attempts to amend the law through the legislative process.

Welfare was also to be expanded to the middle sectors during the Avila Camacho period. The PRM was transformed by the official inclusion of a white-collar sector, which had previously been present only de facto. In 1943, the CNOP was created. It included all government employees, among others the newly created Sindicato Nacional de los Trabajadores de la Educacion (SNTE—National Union of Education Workers Union), replacing the defunct STERM, which had failed to rally teachers to government policies. With the CNOP's support, government stability was no longer exclusively dependent upon the CTM. On the other hand, the only easily controllable portion of this "popular" sector was that corresponding to government employees.

Avila Camacho's government also devoted considerable energy to restructuring business interests: they were to be divided into several organizations designated as the official spokesmen for their constituents in negotiations with the government: Confederación de Cámaras Industriales (CONCAMIN—Confederation of Industrial Chambers) for large enterprises, Cámara Nacional de Industrias de Transformación (CANACINTRA—National Chamber of Transformation Industries) for medium and small enterprises, and Confederación de Cámaras de Comercio (CONCANACO—Confederation of National Chambers of Commerce) for trade. This new structure was aimed at diminishing the risk of the crystallization of a common business political front against government policies. These innovations have been interpreted as evidence of authoritarian corporatist government control over business comparable to its control over labor (Kaufman, 1975).

Yet, Mexican capitalists were not barred from membership in the Confederación Patronal de la República Mexicana (CO-PARMEX—National Employers Confederation of the Mexican Republic), which had proven its independence from the state since the 1920s; neither could they be forced to invest in Mexico. The idea of corporatist control over capital is, therefore, an artifact of model builders more than a reality.

The last successful play by the presidency to consolidate the existing regime was to make Lombardo Toledano withdraw the CTM's proposal to form a new party and endorse Miguel Alemán as the official party candidate. How this feat was accomplished remains a mystery. As usual, historians unashamedly invoke the personalist principle: Avila Camacho "convinced" Lombardo Toledano to withdraw his proposal of a new party (Medina, 1979). Why Lombardo Toledano had to accept the offer, rather than carry on with his own plan, is left unsaid. Most probably, internal divisions within the Liga Socialista Mexicana and the beginning of the split between Lombardo Toledano and Fidel Velazquez within the CTM had weakened Lombardo Toledano's hand, making the victory of the new party in 1946 highly improbable. Also, the conservative alternative to Miguel Alemán—Ezequiel Padilla, an old-time Callista—was certain to be less sympathetic to labor interests than Miguel Alemán. Alemán still projected a moderate figure, so much so that the U.S. embassy in Mexico initially branded him as a radical and opposed his candidacy.[8] To seal the repatched alliance around Alemán, the PRM was formally dissolved on January 18, 1946, and replaced by the Partido Revolucionario Institucional (PRI—Institutional Revolutionary Party). Now, as before, it was understood, although not legally stipulated, that affiliated organizations were to deliver the vote of the totality of their membership to the official party. But the PRI's sectors, unlike the PRM's, were not entitled to independently endorse presidential candidates.

Most authors conclude that the Avila Camacho period saw the subordination of labor to the state (if they hadn't reached that conclusion already regarding the Cárdenas administration), opening the way for the systematic repression of labor demands in the following administration. In this context, social reforms are seen as mere co-optative devices—if they are mentioned at all.[9] My review of this period leads to different conclusions. If by co-optation is meant the incorporation of the CTM into the political and bureaucratic apparatus, then nothing new occurred in the 1940–1946 period: the CTM continued to control a number of seats in Congress and some minor appointments in the civil service. Its administrative costs were being covered by the state, and its leaders responded directly to the president (whether out of personal conviction or through corruption).

If we look beyond this formal structure, several new elements indicate that political co-optation, narrowly conceived as buying off leaders, can destabilize, rather than reinforce, a regime's stability. The Avila Camacho campaign showed that political agreements with the leadership of the labor movement do not ensure electoral results. The price of correcting this mistake was an immense and highly risky electoral fraud. The same trick could not be pulled twice in a row without major violence and consequent danger to the regime.

This period also saw the failure of attempts to achieve a formal labor-capital pact acceptable to both parties and mediated by the state. Instead of responding to labor's increased purchasing power by increased production, the bourgeoisie produced less at higher prices, thereby lowering the participation of wages in domestic consumption. For its part, the government continued the tradition of financing development by monetary expansion, that is, by inflation. Far from being the result of "dependency," this narrow road to capitalism was chosen at a historical juncture of great independence from the world market, high internal savings (refugee capital), and therefore, great opportunities to accelerate the rate of accumulation. We find instead a slightly lower production in comparison with the Cardenist years (in most part due to the contradiction of internal demand), production almost entirely oriented toward exports to the allies, which could be only temporarily profitable. The end of the war was bound to spell recession and renewed pressures upon labor to earn less, as well as the opening of frontiers to foreign capital as the only way out of the impasse.

The incapacity of Mexican capital to adopt the long view in labor-management relations prompted the state to compensate for loss of wages by instituting social reforms, in this case, social security and the beginnings of public housing. These reforms occurred at a critical moment, when both the rank and file and the leadership (Lombardo Toledano) of organized labor threatened to abandon the official party, thereby destabilizing the regime.

We may also conclude that the Avila Camacho administration saw the construction of institutional barriers to direct political action for labor organizations; first, through the transformation of the PRM into the PRI; second, by the appointment of Fidel Velazquez to head the CTM; and third, by the creation of the CNOP. The result was a more coercive structure, which would eventually have to resort to fraud and corruption to maintain itself. What had changed in 1945 was the nature of the concessions made by the state in order to secure the link between organized labor and the support of the official party: the working class was no longer authorized to "fight for its rights"; it had to accept what the state deemed necessary. At the same time, however, what the state deemed necessary was in no small measure determined by the events of the 1940s. These events demonstrated the lack of ideological appeal of the new CTM among the rank and file and the need to tie it to the regime with tangible benefits. The destabilizing capacity of the working class had shifted again from a defensive to an offensive position.

TIGHTENING THE SCREWS, 1946–1958

Despite its strong discourse on industrialization and development, the administration that took office in 1946 did not leave Mexico measurably more prosperous than its predecessor had. Above all, it consolidated unequal development by consecrating the principle of low wages and low taxes as the key requirements of economic development. Analysts of the economic situation of this period (Vernon, 1963; King, 1970) are dazzled by the raw figures on GNP growth.[10] Yet, they also note the extreme difficulties faced by the state in building up an enduring economic base.

In 1946, the demand generated by allied forces dried up, and most of the capital that had taken refuge in Mexico during the war was taken out of the country (Vernon, 1963:99). Yet, the commercial and manufacturing bourgeoisie, whose ranks had been swollen by war exports, was in no mood for austerity. Eager to acquire the import luxury goods that now fitted its station, it precipitated foreign currency hemorrhage and balance of payments difficulties. A new offer to foreign investors was needed to lure capital back into Mexico. Prospective investors were offered an extremely attractive package: reduced credit restraints, a protected market (except for capital goods and other industrial inputs); leonine transfer of technology contracts; and increased state participation in infrastructure expenditures (especially irrigation in the north for the new export-oriented agricultural bourgeoisie). Last but not least, the peso was devalued by over 60 percent in order to ease Mexico's balance of payments problems. Simultaneously, wage earners saw their purchasing power dwindle. By 1950, the capital that had fled between 1945 and 1948 was back, taking its cut from the devaluation and participating in a new industrial boom spurred by the Korean War.

The systematic loss of political and economic power endured by the organized working class during this period is often taken as a natural outcome of these macroeconomic processes. Yet, in 1946, if the labor movement was divided by the enduring split between Velazquezistas and Lombardistas and by the numerous defections from the CTM, it was by no means weak. As Medina observes: "The Avila Camacho administration's policy of unification [of labor] had not only reduced interunion friction, but also created a new awareness of the need to strengthen the ties between unions and reorganize them on a national scale" (1979:151).

The fate of Mexico's labor was far from sealed in 1946. During the Avila Camacho years, the official left had kept considerable political clout, yet without triggering massive opposition from the right, as in the previous administration. The new labor legislation, although it restricted the right to strike, also further reduced the power of capitalists to violate collective contracts. Through these gradual changes in the pact of domination, smoothed over by early welfare legislation, workers and capitalists learned to live together, despite the loss of purchasing power for the former and the greater restrictions imposed by the state on the latter.

To the uninformed, Alemán represented the candidate of continuity, chosen to perfect the policy of national unity. Unlike the 1940 situation, the opposition candidate, Padilla, was no great peril to the ruling regime. He suffered from an anticlerical past (Medina, 1979:50), which was certain to weaken the conservative vote. Alemán's electoral victory, therefore, seemed reasonably assured. In this situation, the official party, bolstered by the unconditional votes of the CNC and the newly created CNOP, had no apparent need to make great concessions to labor.

During the first two years of Alemán's administration, Mexico's aspirations of becoming a social democracy were to be frustrated by a combination of government initiatives and self-destructive decisions by the labor elite, which lost the left wing of organized labor the minority position within the government it had retained in 1940–1946. While many writers take a fatalistic view of this outcome, making preexisting corporatist structures responsible for alternately weeding out from the official party *Lombardismo* and other dissident movements and blaming Velazquez for all that happened, historical facts tell a different story. Labor leadership maneuvered itself into a position of weakness, from where it was near impossible to exert pressures on the government; hence the uncompromising posture of the Alemán administration. These actions, in turn, paved the way for the creation of a powerful, repressive machinery to ensure labor's party discipline and subservience to the regime. From then on, change from below would come either from dissident labor or other subordinate groups (e.g., teachers, peasants) and at very high costs.

The year 1946 was to be a major turning point for labor in Mexico, as well as for the Mexican economy. The 1940s had seen the CTM's gradual weakening and its growing disrepute among the larger unions (such as electricians and railroad and petroleum workers). In 1946, relations had reached their nadir. This should have increased the possibility of forming the broad center-left coalition envisioned by Lombardo Toledano. But in 1946, such a move had two clear implications: first, the repudiation of the Velazquez wing of the CTM, that is, the de facto destruction of the CTM; and second, the possibility of an open divorce between the new coalition and the ruling regime. Although several factions from the socialist camp pushed for such a solution, Lombardo Toledano chose to give his full support to Alemán's candidacy. He was still confident that he could make a deal with Velazquez in order to make the CTM the political basis of his Popular Party (PP). In essence, he thought that he could repeat in 1946–1948 what he had successfully achieved in 1934, namely, the unification of the left and the center. But both the world and major national actors had changed since the war, and the formula no longer fit the circumstances. The presence of the PCM in the Lombardista camp was a cause of internal fragmentation and external embarrassment. In the end, it became a major obstacle to Lombardo Toledano's plan for the Mexican center-left coalition.[11]

It is customary to take the *charrazo* (literally, the cowboy coup) of 1948 as the kickoff for this period of labor repression. Yet in fact, the first blow was dealt to oil workers barely eighteen days after the new president took office. On December 8, 1946, a demand for wage increase by the Petroleum Workers' Union (STPRM), the independent oil union, was rejected. The strike was declared illegal, whereupon the army took control of Petró-leos Mexicanos (PEMEX). Simultaneously, a legal offensive was mounted against the striking union: the work contracts of strike leaders were nullified, and the Board of Arbitration and Concil-iation was instructed by the president to reexamine the collective contract considered too advantageous to labor. Playing on Lom-bardo Toledano's desire to create an independent party without antagonizing the president, Alemán even obtained his public condemnation of the strike. At a new convention of the STPRM, a more pliant leadership was elected. Only then were wage con-cessions granted.

In March of the following year, Lombardo Toledano's power base was further undermined through his own doing. When the CTM's secretariat came up for reelection, instead of giving his support to Gomez Zepeda, the STFRM's independent candidate (but also independent from Lombardo Toledano), he made a se-cret deal with Fidel Velazquez whereby his supporters would vote for Fernando Amilpa, Velazquez's designated heir, in exchange for a promise that the CTM would form part of the Popular Party. Instead, Amilpa, following his election as the new secre-tary, publicly repudiated the very principle of an independent party, and ordered all CTM-affiliated workers to vote for the PRI under threat of expulsion and consequent loss of their jobs.

Although such declarations were in clear violation of the legal statutes of the PRI, they were in full agreement with the spirit of the new party. The Alemán administration stood by, letting the Velazquez group do its work. The defeated candidate, on the other hand, left the CTM with his cohort of supporters to form an alternative union federation, the Central Unica de Trabaja-dores (CUT—Workers' Single Central). Shortly thereafter, Lom-bardo Toledano and his closest associates were suspended from the CTM, on the pretext that his recent appointment as head of the Confederación de Trabajadores de América Latina (CTAL—Workers Confederation of Latin America), a left-oriented worker federation, was incompatible with membership in the CTM. An-other big chunk had been taken out of the future membership of the Popular Party. Worse yet, the very idea of the Popular Party was being publicly branded by the CTM's new secretary as part of the conspiracy of international communism (Basurto, 1984:131).

By 1948, it was clear that the Mexican economy could not face the postwar situation. In July 1948, its doors were opened wide to foreign investors with a devaluation of 61.6 percent, which brought the national currency from 4.85 pesos to 8.01 pesos to the U.S. dollar. This measure unleashed a series of labor protests, which had the potential for destabilizing the regime, because they brought down the CTM and also scared away foreign capital. The STFRM, which had already organized several demonstrations in 1947 protesting the high cost of living (Middlebrook, 1981:83), now organized a joint demonstration with CANACINTRA businessmen against the devaluation (Basurto, 1984:218). The Coalition of Worker and Peasant Associations also organized several demonstrations throughout the country (Middlebrook, 1981:83). Also, in response to the loss of purchasing power accelerated by the devaluation, teachers, oil workers, and railroad workers filed strike petitions.

In early January, the STFRM engineered a pact of solidarity between railroad, metal, and oil worker unions. This coalition claimed a membership of 185 thousand members (more than the CTM could count).[12] The pact called for mutual economic solidarity and coordinated general strikes, among other things (Middlebrook, 1981:80). By February, the coalition was joined by Gomez Zepeda's CUT, electrical workers, and several other unions. As a group, they had the capacity to challenge the CTM, marginalize Lombardo Toledano, and oppose the government's economic policies. Immediately following the devaluation, this threat became a reality. The coalition demanded a hundred-peso wage increase. By contrast, the CTM declared that strikes of affiliated unions would be considered legal only if the profits of the individual firms concerned were "excessive" (Middlebrook, 1981:83).

The government faced the choice of either negotiating with this opposition, thereby risking the destruction of the tottering CTM (and hence endangering the PRI), or repressing it. As it turned out, its actions were to be geared more toward breaking up the coalition than repressing the rank and file's economic demands, most of which were granted despite public threats to the contrary. Internal conflict within the STFRM provided the opportunity to divide and rule. In September 1948, conflict broke out between Diaz de Leon, the newly elected secretary (nicknamed El Charro because he dressed as a Mexican cowboy), and Gomez Zepeda, the STFRM's former secretary and now in the process of creating the CUT. Diaz de Leon charged that Gomez Zepeda had embezzled 200 thousand pesos. Instead of following the union's normal investigation procedures, he brought this accusation directly to the attorney general and suspended Gomez Zepeda and his closest associates from the union.[13]

In response to this violation of union norms, Diaz de Leon's own secretariat disowned him and elected a new secretary. El Charro then stormed the union offices with gunmen and expelled the newly elected bureau. The government merely stood by, implicitly legitimating Diaz de Leon's maneuver. Alemán immediately demanded a revision of the collective contract by the Board of Arbitration and Conciliation, threatening to reduce both personnel and wages, as he had in the case of oil workers. Nevertheless, Diaz de Leon prevailed upon Alemán to make no personnel or wage cuts, thereby ingratiating himself to the rank and file. The *charrazo* (literally, the *charro* coup) had been invented and would thereafter be used as a formula to suppress union democracy. This event is important, not only because it represents a political invention that would be repeated in other unions, but especially because it was perpetrated against a union that was both prominent in labor politics and economically crucial. The STFRM and its allies had a long history of opposition activities, including a protest march against antistrike rulings, a call for more economic protectionism, a demand for a wage raise, and a public endorsement of the leftist CTAL (in opposition to Amilpa's open flirtations with the American Federation of Labor) (Middlebrook, 1981:80–81). Its control was, therefore, strategically crucial for the government.

While these events were taking place, Lombardo Toledano's Liga Socialista Mexicana was still debating how to create the new independent party. Apart from Amilpa's CTM and Gomez Zepeda's CUT, an additional opponent of this project turned out to be the Mexican Communist Party, whose very presence in the Liga was a major impediment to broadening its partisan base. Communist leaders considered their first task to be the consolidation of their own party. They also found it difficult to comanage a new party with leftist leaders who had previously been expelled from their ranks.[14] The Asociación Socialista Unificada (Unified Socialist Association), headed by an ex-PCM member, was also opposed to the idea of the new party. Despite these obstacles, Lombardo Toledano insisted that the aim of the PP was not to define the fine points of Marxism but to fight the PRI. In public, however, he claimed that the PP was devoid of electoral ambitions and was merely critical of the PRI.

Against all odds, the PP was founded in June 20, 1948, backed by the Alianza de Obreros y Campesinos de México (Workers and Peasants Alliance), a new independent union federation created in March of the same year.[15] Despite the CTM's repudiation of the new party (and a fortiori the new federation), these developments were potentially dangerous for the new bloc which backed the Alemán administration. First, the new organization threatened to incorporate peasant elements, which traditionally supported the official party with little resistance. Second, it proclaimed itself pacifist, thereby repudiating the Cold War in which Mexico had been involved by the United States. Finally, this movement agglomerated all the forces that stood for union democracy and the independence of labor from the state, including teachers, whose support of the CNOP was weakened by the persistence of a dissident group.

To protect itself, the administration launched a preventive *charrazo*, before this movement had time to gather any momentum. As a result, the UGOCM emerged as a weak organization, publicly branded as communist. The Labor Department refused to acknowledge its legality, thereby denying it the right to bargain for its affiliates. The congressional election of 1949 witnessed the resounding defeat of the PP, doubtless aided though not determined by fraud (Durand, 1990:187–88). The CUT, on the other hand, had also been virtually destroyed by a *charrazo*. In sum, no opponent of the CTM was left standing.

As the Ruiz Cortinez administration prepared to take the reins of government, the state's control over the organized working class seemed perfect. Authors inclined toward the top-down view are quick to point out that the new president was endowed with a "strong state, headed by an executive without fissures" (Reyna and Trejo Delabre, 1981:20). From such a position, the possibilities of any real challenge to the institutional order can be discounted (1981:34), especially when viewed from hindsight. Such a priori judgments notwithstanding, the Ruiz Cortinez years were to see several challenges to the authoritarian and notoriously corrupt political structures built by the previous administration, leading to a substantial transformation in the pact of domination. The events that developed in the 1950s proved that the regime was indeed vulnerable, as even authors associated with the top-down view admit after the fact (Pellicer de Brody and Reyna, 1978:10).

As the Alemán administration drew to its end, the Korean War boom was over. Foreign debt had considerably increased, and the gross corruption of higher civil servants had all but emptied the state's coffers (see appendix 3). It was time to bring back orderliness, monetary orthodoxy and moral probity in government (Vernon, 1963:108). By 1953, the country's economic growth had practically come to a standstill (see appendix 3). Predictably, capital began to flow out again (Vernon, 1963:109; King, 1970:35). The recession hit hard an already considerably impoverished urban proletariat. Throughout 1953, the government was besieged with strike *emplazamientos* (announcements), particularly from railroad and telephone workers, supposedly tamed by *charro* leaders (Reyna and Trejo Delabre, 1981:53).[16] CANACINTRA, on the other hand, which represented small and medium enterprises producing mostly wage goods, continued to side with organized labor, asserting in its second congress of 1953 the need for greater integration in industrial production and social welfare measures for the laboring masses (Reyna and Delabre, 1981:44).

In the face of the slow strangulation of the Mexican economy, the new administration opted for creating new incentives for volatile capital to flow back in: it devalued the peso in April 1954, from 8.50 pesos to 12.50 pesos to the U.S. dollar, and instituted a wage and price freeze. The system of labor representation engineered by the previous administration immediately bore fruit: all "official" labor organizations unanimously applauded the measure. This included not only the CTM but also the Confederación Revolucionaria de Obreros y Campesinos (CROC—Revolutionary Confederation of Workers and Peasants), a new federation that now formally encompassed all the stillborn independent unions except Lombardo Toledano's UGOCM.[17] To compensate for price increases the government decided to monopolize the distribution of maize and beans by creating the Compañía de Exportaciones e Importaciones Mexicana SA (CEIMSA—Import-Export Mexican Company), despite strong opposition from the official chamber of commerce (CONCANACO).[18]

No system, no matter how coercive, is without fissures. As the purchasing power of wage earners further declined, pressures from the rank and file began to resurface via the official union leadership, the very force supposed to suppress them. By then, real wages had declined to 83 percent of their 1936 level, while the price index had quadrupled during the same time interval (Flores de la Peña, 1971:15–31). The following year, it dropped another 13.6 percent. Barely three weeks after the devaluation, telephone workers announced their intention to go on strike, and probably many more unions made similar moves informally. It was time for the government to go back on its initial wage-and-price freeze policy. Yet, it did so only timidly at first: on May 14, Ruiz Cortinez conceded that a 10 percent wage increase was in order but that implementation by employers should be voluntary.

The CTM and the CROC again expressed their unmitigated approval of this proposed and publicly summoned business firms to comply with the presidential recommendation. Simultaneously, several unions asked for wage hikes: the CROM, so docile in the past, was now asking for a 44.5 percent raise (Pellicer de Brody and Reyna, 1978:93). The independent UGOCM, on the other hand, demanded a wage increase proportionate to price hikes. But since no law or presidential decree had been issued, employers shuffled their feet, merely scheduling meetings to discuss the appropriateness of the presidential recommendation. By June, even the more officialist unions had assumed a militant attitude: unless a general wage increase of 24 percent was granted by July 12, a general strike would be called. In response, the government took up the initiative again, instructing Lopez Mateos, the minister of labor, to settle quietly the thousands of cases before the Federal Board of Arbitration and Conciliation. The board conceded raises between 15 percent and 24 percent, despite the manifest ill will of employers.

At this juncture, some of the most top-down-oriented analysts of this period admit that "the majority of the organized working class . . . ha[d] gained some autonomy" (Pellicer de Brody and Reyna, 1978:98), disregarding an earlier assertion regarding the corporatist hold over the organized working class (Reyna, 1974, 1977). But they hasten to add that "the control of the labor movement never escaped the hands of its leaders. . . . The union structures, while they showed discrepancies [presumably with respect to government policies], were an effective barrier for the containment of labor demands" (Pellicer de Brody and Reyna, 1978:99–102). My interpretation of the same facts differs: as the exploitation of labor came close to the limits of what was considered acceptable, rather than endanger their position of leadership by blindly following orders, most official union leaders opted for transmitting rank-and-file demands.

This interpretation is sustained by Solis, who states that "the response of unions to the devaluation shook the entire structure of the party. In order to calm down workers, a wage increase was granted as it became evident that economic growth with price instability was not going to be accepted" (1977:1). This conciliatory government response quickly reestablished stability. The 1954 expansion of the social security system to include new categories of labor followed the same pattern, although, as Spalding shows, it was, at first, more symbolic than real (1978:200). To argue a posteriori that no real risk of regime destabilization existed in 1954 because the rank and file did not actually explode (but merely threatened to do so) flies in the face of available evidence. The eradication of internal democracy in Mexican unions served to delay demands. Yet the events of 1954 show that it could not suppress them altogether.

The case of the STFRM illustrates the limitations of unmitigated labor repression as a general recipe for political stability. In the general process of wage raises that followed the 1954 devaluation, railroad workers (who were government employees) were left behind. They merely received the minimum 10 percent raise initially agreed upon, but which had been more than doubled in many sectors of the economy. In real terms, this raise amounted to a negative increase of −0.3 percent for the 1952–1957 period (Pellicer de Brody and Reyna, 1978:166).

Other demands—such as pensions with full wages, a 30 percent raise for diesel machine operators, and the five-day workweek—were left unheeded (Topete, 1961). As a result, a dissident group began to form in opposition to the all too compliant official union. Its initial strategy was to stage slowdowns in the vital industrial centers of the north, to which the official union and management responded with repression: expulsion from the union (which meant the automatic loss of one's job) and the jailing of suspected leaders. The pension of a retired worker whose activities were declared "contrary to the interests of the firm" was canceled (Pellicer de Brody and Reyna, 1978:160). These and other repressive measures temporarily restored order. A year later, as the collective contract was being renegotiated, the *charro* union agreed to freeze wages for the 1955–1957 period. This submission to government pressures triggered widespread protests among the rank and file, which were met by extreme repression: gunmen hired by the union quieted the agitators (some, for good). These events, rather than bring peace, however, were the midwife of the independent movement headed by Demetrio Vallejo, whose actions were to threaten the whole edifice of corporatism constructed since 1946.

For most workers, real wages began to rise again shortly after the showdown that followed the devaluation, so much so that the gap between capital and wages temporarily ceased to grow (Reynolds, 1974). The years 1955–1957 are characterized as a period of relative "labor peace" (Pellicer de Brody and Reyna, 1978). Yet, several skirmishes were to precede the 1958 explosion. In mid-1956, the workers of seventy-two electrical power firms declared that they would go on strike unless they received a 30 percent wage increase. The minister of labor bargained down to 17 percent and increased fringe benefits (mostly health and pension) from 4 percent to 10 percent of wages. Electricity workers were also the first to be conceded the forty-hour workweek (ibid.:118). Despite these concessions, a new wave of demands for wage increases was launched by electricity workers in 1957. This time, the demands were spearheaded by the CTM itself, whose leadership was weary of appearing less eager than independent unions to defend its members' interests. The conflict was again quickly smoothed over, with a moderate wage increase of 18 percent, in addition to a 12 percent raise in overtime pay. Finally in 1957, Lopez Mateos, who had become labor's favorite presidential candidate, avoided by a hairline a strike of the whole textile industry, by successfully pressuring employers into conceding a raise (ibid.:118). Simultaneously, the CTM requested a large increase in the minimum wage, obtaining 9 percent.

During this period also, the first serious union dissidence among teachers since the creation of the SNTE came to a head. In July 1956, the SNTE's leadership, which had initially demanded a 30 percent wage increase, accepted a mere 14 percent. Most teachers complied, except those in the capital city. The conflict continued to simmer throughout 1957 and resurfaced again at the beginning of 1958 (the year of the presidential succession), immobilizing most primary schools in Mexico City. After an impressive showdown between dissidents and government forces (the latter including police and antiriot troops), the state took a conciliatory stance, granting the wages lost during the strike as well as the wage raise requested.

Simultaneously, telegraph and oil workers began to mobilize to shake off their respective *charros*. In the spring of 1958, a demand by telegraph workers for a wage raise, also originated in a dissident movement against the corrupt official union, was met by immediate concessions (Alonso, 1972:104). Electricity workers followed suit and received a raise of 15 percent. The conflict with oil workers, on the other hand, was not so easily smoothed over. Pressured by their leaders to accept the renewal without changes in their collective contract, a sizeable minority of dissidents declared that they would no longer legally recognize the union should such a renewal come into effect. Despite this warning, the contract was renewed, but for one year only, which represented a compromise in relation to previous proposals. The dissident movement tacitly accepted the settlement. To show their appreciation, the management of PEMEX paid public homage to the "patriotic spirit" of its workers (Alonso, 1972:105).

In sum, we see in 1956–1958 a continuation of the pattern of conciliation shown in 1954, with the government either acting as intermediary to pressure employers into granting raises or making concessions to its own employees, as in the case of teachers. To some analysts, this pattern was interpreted as giving strength and legitimacy to dissident movements while debilitating the official structure of *charro* unions (Alonso, 1972). From such an evaluation, it should follow that the railroad conflict represented a further inroad into state power and, therefore, a threat to the regime. To others, these concessions were a mere ripple on the surface of state power (Pellicer de Brody and Reyna, 1978). This last diagnosis makes the subsequent conflict with railroad workers exceptional (and therefore unpredictable by definition). A closer look at the details of this episode may help us understand the role it played in the relations between state and labor and the eventual buildup of the welfare state in the early 1960s.

In 1958, railroad workers also remobilized in the face of overwhelming odds, but no more so than teachers or telegraph or oil workers. A new dissident movement was created by the initiative of the STFRM's Section 15 to elect a special commission with representatives from each section. The commission's task was to collaborate with the National Executive Committee in the determination of the degree of wage increase considered economically justifiable. Conflict soon erupted between the democratically elected commission and the STFRM's general secretary, after the commission declared that a raise of 350 pesos was in order. Local secretaries were ordered by the STFRM to demand a raise of only 200 pesos, and the commission was declared disbanded. Instead of disappearing, however, the commission organized a meeting in Mexico City on May 24, where it publicly accused STFRM leaders of failing to meet workers' demands (Alonso, 1972:112). From its midst, a new leader emerged—Demetrio Vallejo, who had previously been a comrade of Valentin Campa and Hernán Laborde in Acción Socialista, which formed part of Lombardo Toledano's ill-fated Partido Popular.

What made the railroad workers' conflict different from the others from the start was its symbiosis with other dissidents. Mass protest marches were organized in Mexico City in which workers, students, and teachers began to cofraternize (Pellicer de Brody and Reyna, 1978:151). The years of labor peace therefore ended in an atmosphere of generalized mobilization that threatened to rupture the corporatist principle of separation between sectors and vertical negotiation of conflicts. The railroad workers' conflict was also different in that the principle of union representation, rather than the demand for higher wages, was at stake. In May 1958, Section 13 of the union, headed by Vallejo, launched a program substituting existing union representatives for others elected freely. The Plan del Sureste (Southeastern Plan), as it was named, called for the rejection of the 200-peso raise accepted by the official union. It also rejected the two-month delay accorded to individual firms to implement the raise, demanding instead an immediately payable 350-peso raise. Second, this document called for the removal of all local executive committees. Finally, it summoned the National Executive Committee to recognize the new local leadership and to accept the 350-peso raise. Failure to do so would lead to work stoppages (explicitly considered illegal in the labor law of 1943), starting with one hour the first day, two hours the second, and so on. In other words, what had taken place was a counter-*charrazo* against the official structure.

Objectively, there seemed little chance that this initiative would be followed by other sections of the union. Yet it spread like bushfire. Work stoppages began, as announced, on June 26 (Alonso, 1972:115). The STFRM's National Secretariat refused to bargain with the rebels. Nevertheless, by July, the government had made a conciliatory move by offering a 215-peso raise, instead of the original 200 pesos asked by the secretariat (against the 185-peso raise initially offered by the firm). At this point, the industrial and commercial chambers were still tolerant of the movement. They expected the differences to be quickly settled. Yet despite the insurgents' immediate acceptance of the presidential offer, the conflict continued. It now centered on the problem of union representativity. By August, business interests were no longer so tolerant; they demanded the "repression of illegal work stoppages" (ibid.:122). On August 3, secret police, uniformed police, and the feared Policía Judicial erupted into the offices of several dissident sections and arrested 200 workers. Vallejo managed to avoid arrest. It was charged that a secret pact of solidarity between various dissident sections of teachers, oil, telegraph, and electricity workers had been discovered, its explicit purpose being to coordinate labor struggles in the future. As it turned out, the police were right: this "pact" did exist, although it was barely in its initial phase of negotiation. Its potential for destroying the official union structure was undeniable.

Meanwhile, Vallejo announced that work stoppages would be called off as soon as general free union elections were organized. In addition, he demanded the release of those arrested, the idemnification of the families of workers killed by police, and a stop to government reprisals. In support of these demands, telegraph workers, dissident teachers, and oil workers also declared work stoppages, while electricity workers published a manifesto in support of Vallejo's demands.

At first, the government appeared to give in. It announced that, provided work started again, new elections would be ordered, with secret ballots and under the supervision of both dissident and official union representatives. The government also put a stop to police reprisals. In the election that followed, Vallejo obtained 59,759 votes against 9 votes for his opponent (Alonso, 1972:129). But even this resounding victory did not bring back social peace. Other groups began to agitate. In Mexico City, students seized buses in protest against a price increase in public transportation, demanding the municipalization of public transport and the independent unionization of bus drivers (Hofstadter, 1974:58). Oil workers were also continuously agitating: they had removed their official representatives, replacing them with elected leaders who were not recognized by the Department of Labor. Instead of small fires that could be put out one by one, as in the early 1950s, the outgoing government was now faced with a generalized conflagration.

The importance of the railroad workers' action is not in the fact, as some authors argue, of their challenge—considered individually—of the official structure. Neither does the eventual defeat of this movement justify an assertion that they "did not alter the basic guidelines of the system" (Pellicer de Brody and Reyna, 1978:9–10). Their historical importance lies in the potential they represented, at one particular historical juncture, for drastically altering the institutional means by which workers could transform the pact of domination. This explains the repressive reaction of the state in contrast to other similar conflicts, which were settled amicably. The railroad workers' conflict had profound resonance among other groups, particularly electricity workers, dissident schoolteachers, and oil workers. The oil workers, whose wage demands had been met, had been expected to remain quiet. Yet they joined in the demonstrations when work stoppages reached the six-hour limit; they were soon followed by students. The business sector and the "railroad deputies" responded by protesting even louder against the rebels.[19] Vallejo was accused of using communist tactics to gain the submission of unwilling union members (Alonso, 1972:133).

The repression of dissident teachers took place in September. Despite this fact, the dissident movement among oil workers gained ground in new internal elections. In this atmosphere of generalized labor agitation, Fidel Velazquez himself began to sound militant, demanding a 25 percent wage hike, in defiance of business opposition. Vallejo graciously sent Velazquez a message of solidarity with the CTM's heroic struggles for the working class. All evidence indicates that the labor movement was escaping the hands of the state, driving even the most reactionary CTM leadership to a desperate stand for relegitimation. Even Pellicer de Brody and Reyna admit that "during the second semester of 1958 and the first of 1959, Mexico was very close to political instability. It had been demonstrated that labor, with only a relative and somewhat autonomous organization was capable of beating the system" (1978:196).[20]

A GOVERNMENT OF THE EXTREME LEFT, WITHIN THE CONSTITUTION, 1958–1964

On December 1, 1958, Adolfo Lopez Mateos took office as president of Mexico for the next six years. From the previous administration, he was known for his tolerance of labor demands and his ability as a negotiator, leading a scholar to assert that "he consistently tried to identify with the workers" (Kaufman, 1975:65). Such psychological reductionism notwithstanding, the new president had announced major social reforms during his campaign. In the initial phase of his mandate, he even went so far as to assert that his government, "within the constitution, [was] of extreme left.[21] Yet, his progressive program faced many obstacles: an enlarged and powerful bourgeoisie created by the economic policies of the previous administrations, highly volatile and accustomed to having its way; an important sector of the organized working class, remobilized and threatening to form a larger movement opposed to the principle of an official party controlled through nondemocratic elections; a fast-growing population in need of new sources of employment; an economic recession, originated in the United States, that blocked Mexico's exports; and the end of the "easy" consumer goods stage of import substitution.

As if this were not enough, the Cuban Revolution reawakened the anticommunist craze in the United States and in Mexico's business sector, and any progressive measures to relieve the plight of the work force were seen as a communist plot. It also reawakened Mexican students and intellectuals. No less than Lázaro Cárdenas, the Joan of Arc of Mexican politics, was at the head of the movement—the only man, according to Cosio Villegas (1965), "capable of breaking the PRI in at least two pieces." Out of all this, most improbably, was born one of the most prosperous, as well as socially progressive, periods of Mexico's postrevolutionary history, later known (and much maligned by leftist intellectuals) as its period of "stabilizing development." During this period, the inflation-devaluation cycle was broken, at the expense of a vertiginously growing foreign debt. Economic growth temporarily ceased to be a zero-sum game between capital and labor.

During the first months of the new *sexenio*, the government seemed caught between the now irreversible railroad workers' conflict over union representation, a bourgeoisie made fearful by the general tone of the new government (and made nervous by the Cuban Revolution), and the possibility of a rebirth of the Mexican left. The new administration opted for repressing the dissident railroad workers' movement and red-baiting its leader while revitalizing the official unions through wage increases and social reforms. It also actively supported the Cuban Revolution, while repressing public demonstrations of such support at home.[22] In the economic field, rather than await the recovery of the U.S. economy, the government took the country out of its recession by increasing public expenditures for industrialization as well as for social welfare. As Pellicer de Brody argues, this new style of government "can be explained by the desire to cope simultaneously with the opposition of some business groups to the government's economic policies, and to the pro-Cuban groups under the leadership of Cárdenas. In view of the contradictory pressures exerted by these groups, Lopez Mateos decide[d] to emphasize the progressive image of his administration, a maneuver intended to improve his bargaining position with private enterprise while preventing the pro-Cuban sectors from capitalizing on the initial enthusiasm generated by the Cuban revolution" (1974:23).

The novelty of the administration's approach to the intervention of the state in the economy lay in the shift of public expenditure financing from inflation-producing monetary expansion to internal and external debt. In effect, a series of mechanisms designed to encourage internal savings (already begun on a smaller scale in the previous administration) were established, in particular the system of *encaje legal* (legal cash), which stipulated that private banks must deposit close to 50 percent of their assets in the central bank, to be used for development purposes (and rewarded with high interest earnings). In addition, a number of government bonds were offered at attractive interest rates, capturing not just speculative capital, as in the past, but also less volatile medium and small domestic savings.

There are several interpretations as to why the railroad workers' movement was finally crushed during the first months of 1959. Most of these hang on situational factors that steer away from the more fundamental issue of the threat of union democratization (or any democratization at all) to a regime based on machine government. Among these, we find the penetration of railroad union leadership by Trotskyist communists with more inclination to engage in confrontation politics than to obtain workable settlements. Also cited are Lombardo Toledano's lack of support for the dissident movement and the absence of coordination and discipline in the organization headed by Vallejo.[23] In addition, Mexican railroads, despite their having been nationalized for decades, still retained the old regional divisions corresponding to their original private ownership and lacked collective bargaining. This contributed to the danger of uncoordinated spontaneous actions. As soon as one division obtained a workable settlement, another started strike procedures. The result was chaos in the transportation system, which at the time depended almost exclusively on the railroads, and consequent pressures by business to end the conflict.

My reading of the events that led to Vallejo's jailing and the return of a more docile union focuses more closely on the role model the triumphant free union presented to other unions and to the reawakening left, spurred on by the nationalist revolution in Cuba. Among situational factors, it is also important to note that Vallejo's attempt to alter labor's institutional position within the regime went further than seemed politically feasible at the time. Vallejo overstepped the boundaries within which exploitation could be negotiated by tacitly defining the union he headed as administering the railroads in collaboration with management and by using this usurped (in the eyes of state elites) position to make wage and welfare demands that went well beyond the fiscal capacity of the state, given the well-known reluctance of the bourgeoisie to pay more taxes.[24]

Vallejo first proposed a reorganization of the railroads to put an end to the preferential treatment granted to foreign enterprises. The artificial lowering of the price of railroad transportation was largely responsible for the firm's deficit and its consequent inability to pay its workers decent wages. Vallejo argued that if the government wished to subsidize business firms, it should do so out of the federal budget. Second, he called for both shrinking and shortening the hierarchy, which would have removed 868 well-paid patronage jobs. Third, he demanded higher welfare benefits: a broadening of the very limited social insurance plan to include health services for workers' families; the construction of housing to be rented to workers; and the creation of a savings fund, representing 10 percent of fringe benefits. Finally, he insisted (allegedly under the influence of his communist advisers) on increasing by another 36 pesos the 215-peso increase that had already been granted (Alonso, 1972:139–44). To top it all, Vallejo sent the president an unsolicited report on the oil industry, expressing his disagreement with the possibility of its partial reprivatization (Pellicer de Brody and Reyna, 1978:202).

Although the Lopez Mateos administration was willing to bargain on wages and welfare measures, it was not prepared to share power with a midget representing less than 10 percent of organized labor, much less to run the risk of other unions following suit. Moreover, to make concessions to an openly communist union was not good for the president's rating among capitalists, whose propensity to export capital was on the increase in 1959. Despite Lombardo Toledano's efforts to mediate the conflict, Vallejo remained unwilling to take back any of his demands. Meanwhile, he was publicly branded by the CTM, the commercial and industrial chambers, groups of congressmen, and the umbrella trade union organization Bloque de Unidad Obrera (BUO—Worker Unity Bloc), which formally linked the CTM with the other labor federations.

Despite the government's declaration that the strike announced by Vallejo (in case his demands were not met) was illegal, all work on the railroads stopped on March 28, 1959. Following the work stoppage, Vallejo was arrested, on grounds of "social dissolution."[25] Simultaneously, as many as nine thousand workers were fired. Some leaders among dissident teachers and oil workers were also arrested. By April 3, remaining workers went back to work, and the union was purged of all pro-Vallejo elements.

Most analyses of the railroad movement end in this debacle, either lamenting it or holding it up as a trophy of state power. The point of my analysis is to show the link between what might be called the crisis of *charrismo* in the late 1950s, marked by increased pressures from the rank and file in the labor movement, and the social reforms of the 1960s. The railroad union rebellion is only the strongest manifestation of this crisis. Its repression shows its incapacity to defeat the system singlehandedly and replace it with another but not its inability to prompt reforms.

Before I focus on the reformist initiatives of the Lopez Mateos administration, it is important to recall that pressures from below did not end with the crushing of the movement led by Vallejo. Under the leadership of General Lázaro Cárdenas, the Movimiento de Liberación Nacional (MLN—National Liberation Movement), a new grass-roots movement pushing for redistributive reforms, was born. Although this movement exhausted itself barely a few years after its birth, its presence in the early 1960s, which contributed to the student revolt of 1968, was considered by many as a singular landmark in Mexican politics.

Reformist movements spearheaded by intellectuals and Cardenists were no novelty in Mexico. *Henriquismo* had briefly flourished in the late 1940s and 1950s, before it was slapped down by the Ruiz Cortinez administration. But the movement started by the Cuban Revolution was different from *Henriquismo* for two reasons: first, it brought together a heterogeneous group of students, intellectuals, peasants, and labor; and second, it could not so easily be repressed, given the immense prestige of Cárdenas, its leader. The support for Fidel Castro in Mexico was the internal echo of the desire shared by many for a more just society. The MLN in which this support originated had neither the tactics nor the objectives of the movement that had brought down Batista's rule in Cuba (Pellicer de Brody, 1974:106). It was fundamentally a reformist and nationalist group, with little inclination to follow Che Guevara's path. It called, more modestly, for a rebirth of Cardenist policies: national control of natural resources, which were being bought wholesale by transnational corporations;[26] a more equal income distribution; more diversified exports; and the continuation of the agrarian reform. The defense of the Cuban Revolution was merely a foreign policy position, which never amounted to more than alternately cheering Cuba and booing the United States but nevertheless served as a rallying point for all participants, regardless of differences among them in their opinions on domestic policies.

Initially, the MLN included all leftist critics of the regime. But it soon became apparent that its initial impetus was the desire of established organizations, particularly Lombardo Toledano's Popular Party (which had changed its name to the Popular Socialist Party [PPS]) and the Communist Party, to capture this new constituency. Both parties failed, however, and consequently abandoned the MLN, leaving it divided and disorganized. In June 1962 (less than a year after the creation of the MLN), Lombardo Toledano announced the withdrawal of the PPS, due to "profound differences" separating the movements. Henceforth, all PPS militants were forbidden to participate in the MLN, under the flimsy pretext that electoral law prohibited double militancy. The fact that the MLN was not registered as a political party made this explanation patently spurious. Lombardo Toledano's hostility was in fact motivated by the MLN's refusal to stay within the narrow channels available to opposition parties in Mexico.

The Communist Party also wanted to increase its thinned ranks with new MLN blood in order to regain a foothold in the electoral system, which it lost in the Cold War. In April 1963, it created the Frente Electoral del Pueblo (FEP—People's Electoral Front), urging MLN members to register as members. Few MLN militants responded to this call. Nevertheless, the FEP was able to compete in the 1964 election as a legally registered party but, predictably, failed to gain any political foothold, even the minimum provided by the law, which reserved a limited number of window-dressing seats in Congress for opposition parties. This initiative did succeed in disorganizing the MLN, by creating deep internal divisions. In the end, Cárdenas eased out of the movement. Thereafter, key intellectual figures also withdrew, returning to the university (Pellicer de Brody, 1974:114). Once again, an independent movement had been split and marginalized, more by its own doing than by state repression.

The leftist reformist political climate declined in the second half of Lopez Mateos's administration. Therefore, it cannot be claimed that the social reforms that appeared after 1961 were instituted under immediate pressures. They must be understood as responses to the long-range pressures that surfaced throughout the Alemán and Ruiz Cortinez administrations and up until 1960, of which the president had firsthand knowledge. In addition, many reforms took a long time to elaborate, from announcement to adoption and implementation. The profit-sharing proposal, for example, which increased wages by 5 to 15 percent, had been in preparation since the beginning of 1960. On the other hand, the international climate was more favorable to social reforms after the missile crisis passed and the Alliance for Progress was launched. By then, the economy was on the upswing again, so that less business opposition to reform could be expected.

It is difficult to time exactly the different reformist measures adopted during Lopez Mateos's term, because in examining this period, timeless social science takes over, and history withdraws. Instead of being based on events and actions, available information is often reduced to average figures and broad generalizations. Wilkie's study shows a 30 percent increase (from 14.4 percent to 19.2 percent) in the proportion of the federal budget devoted to social expenditures during the Lopez Mateos administration (Wilkie, 1970:130). This was the first administration to top the 18.3 percent of the Cardenist period, despite the serious economic and fiscal difficulties experienced during its first three years. (In contrast, the effects of the depression were over by the time Cárdenas took office in 1934.) At the same time, the size of the federal pie had also grown, so that by 1954, per capita social expenditures had increased by 80 percent (from 26 pesos to 47 pesos) in relation to the Ruiz Cortinez administration (ibid.:36). Contrary to Wilkie's (1970:38) interpretation of his own data, this amount does not represent a sacrifice of social in favor of administrative expenditures, since the latter increased by only 73.4 percent during the same period (from 59.5 pesos to 103.2 pesos per capita).

The Lopez Mateos administration also continued the existing trend of higher social expenditures in relation to administrative expenditures. According to Wilkie's figures, social expenditures represented 41 percent of administrative expenditures during the Cárdenas administration, 38.1 percent during the Alemán administration, 43 percent during the Ruiz Cortinez administration, and 45 percent during the Lopez Mateos administration (1970:36). Nevertheless, these figures are so aggregated as to give only a vague idea of what was going on. For example, the proportion of expenditures considered economic dropped from 52.7 percent to 39 percent from the Ruiz Cortinez to the Lopez Mateos administration (Wilkie, 1970:32). This flies in the face of all qualitative evidence showing that Lopez Mateos launched a new phase of state interventionism in the economy, buying a number of private companies (in particular, steel and electricity) and setting up new fiscal incentives for private firms, according to a new classification of their economic importance. This new role did not fail to worry private enterprise associations (excepting CANACINTRA, which consistently applauded government policies), which showed their hostility to this strategy on more than one occasion (Martinez Nava, 1982).

We know from qualitative evidence that social reforms were planned from the very beginning of the *sexenio* (as opposed to when the economy recovered) and with a great deal of business opposition to contend it. In December 1959, the social security law was amended to include new categories of workers: agricultural wage earners, the members of agricultural *ejido* and credit associations, individual *ejidatarios,* and small farmers (Hofstadter, 1974). Throughout the *sexenio,* more land was distributed to landless peasants, making Lopez Mateos second only to Cárdenas in agrarian reform. The number of urban people protected by the IMSS, on the other hand, nearly doubled between 1959 and 1964—from 2,657,200 to 5,448,700 (Spalding, 1978:202)—while major institutional expansions were taking place (e.g., the Mexico City Medical Center complex and the Oaxtepec vacation center). Social security was also extended to civil servants (including teachers) in December 1959, with the creation of the Instituto de Seguridad y Servicios Sociales para los Trabajadores del Estado (ISSSTE—Institute of Social Security and Services for State Workers), IMSS's homologue for the public sector. During the same period, oil, electricity, and railroad workers received periodic improvements in their separate social insurance plans (Wilson, 1981:121).

Profit sharing occupied an important place among the measures aimed at assuaging labor militancy. It was also planned at the very beginning of the political cycle, even as the railroad workers' and teachers' strikes were still raging (Kaufman, 1975:73). When the amendment to Article 123 of the Constitution making profit sharing mandatory was eventually sent to Congress in 1961 (after a secretly appointed commission had spent months on the legal preparations), business was taken completely by surprise and openly showed its opposition, complaining that it had not been consulted on the matter (Kaufman, 1975:75). In effect, the measure was equivalent to a fiscal reform, except that it was less likely to encounter insuperable opposition or to trigger capital flight, as any profound fiscal reform most certainly would. By the time the exact extent of profit sharing was negotiated with representatives of capital, business was booming again. The measure therefore passed in 1963 without provoking any political conflict. The extent of actual redistribution it achieved was reduced by the known capacity of private enterprises to give misleading figures on profits and by their ability to set aside various kinds of capital reserves. Nevertheless, it represented an important symbolic gain for labor (as well as an additional factor of inequality with other subordinate groups). Kaufman forcefully argues that profit sharing had not been requested by labor in any way approximating the pluralist model (1975:58). At the same time, although she devotes almost no space to the labor struggles of the 1950s, she does concede that the measure was meant "to do something for the labor movement in order to demobilize it" (Kaufman, 1975:69). This comment indicates that labor has been, in some way, "mobilized," which contradicts the image, conveyed at the onset of her study, of a demobilized society dominated by the president.

Lopez Mateos was also the first president to have included low-cost urban housing as something more than a symbol in his administration's policies of social welfare. Previous administrations had taken early steps to provide low-cost credit for private housing—mainly for the middle classes and the higher ranks of the official labor organizations (Arteaga, 1990; Aldrete Haas, 1991)—although only to a limited extent. Though the demographic pressure on Mexico City was still in its initial phase, approximately 2 million workers were in need of housing, and at least twice as many represented the marginal urban poor. In December 1954, the Instituto Nacional de la Vivienda (INV—National Housing Institute) was created to deal with urban slums and squatter settlements. It was too fiscally unstable, and its economic resources too limited, to provide any viable long-term program, however (Aldrete Haas, 1991:70). Public housing actions during the Lopez Mateos administration benefited primarily civil servants: between 1959 and 1967 (that is, including the first three years of the following administration), a total of 4,279 housing units per year were built by the ISSSTE (Aldrete Haas, 1991). In addition, financial assistance for low-cost housing was offered to the middle classes. The IMSS's housing program, on the other hand, was canceled as part of the bargain with private enterprise on the profit-sharing measure. Nevertheless, large housing complexes were built in various sections of Mexico City (e.g., Tlatelolco), providing some housing to labor. A rent freeze was also adopted in the central part of Mexico City.

In sum, the Lopez Mateos administration represents a second postwar reformist moment in response to the labor mobilization of the 1950s. Aggregate economic data gives us a glimpse of the changes that were taking place for wage earners in the 1960s: according to Robert Looney's calculations, while consumer prices increased by 31.4 percent during the whole period of stabilizing development (1960–1970), real wages went up by 91.5 percent. In the previous period (1950–1959), consumer prices had increased by 85.2 percent, while real wages had risen by only 31.7 percent (1982:59).

THE END OF STABILIZING DEVELOPMENT, 1964–1970

When Gustavo Diaz Ordaz took office, Mexico's working class had largely caught up with postwar losses. Unless new initiatives to restrict these gains were taken, there would be no reason for further working-class mobilizations. During the Diaz Ordaz administration, stabilizing development took an almost exclusive interest in fostering the growth of large capital-intensive firms, showing little concern for launching new social reforms other than the redistribution of land to peasants, an apparent effort to slow down the rural guerilla movement that was under way. During this administration, the political climate gradually deteriorated, as the limitations of "stabilizing development"—particularly the inability to grow at a pace consistent with population growth without sacrificing monetary stability—were increasingly felt. Yet political stability was preserved despite the student rebellion of 1968, because the two best organized subordinate groups—labor and teachers—failed to join the students. Why labor remained inactive and, therefore, allowed the regime to remain stable is the question I address in this section.

Were it not for the fact that this period coincided with the era of student protest, which both preceded and echoed that experienced in several countries of the Western world, analysts might have little to say about it, save that it witnessed the exhaustion of the model of "stabilizing development." This was manifested in the gradual diminution of the proportion of the population protected by the welfare system, under the combined effect of rural-urban and interregional differentials in population growth and the comparative slowness of the incorporation of the labor force into the sectors protected by social legislation. Despite this trend, Mexico appears to have experienced no major challenge to its status quo during these years. An article published by Claude Bataillon only a few weeks before the shooting of student demonstrators in Tlatelolco states that "stability in Mexico does not seem at risk: economic progress follows its course; no social group challenges national unity and political parties continue to play a game that has lasted for several decades (1968:5).

Diaz Ordaz continued to diffuse the rhetoric of stabilizing development, which had proven successful for his predecessor. Yet several changes were taking place. First, the capacity of the state to contain inflation and keep economic growth ticking at the correct pace through extensive external borrowing was pushed to new limits. As a result, external debt, which had increased by 150 percent during the preceding administration, rose by another 100 percent, reaching $3,762.4 million on December 31, 1970 (Green, 1976:150). This placed Mexico among the most important borrowers worldwide. The composition of this debt also changed. As the perception of the Cuban menace to U.S. security became less acute (with the stabilization of the Cuban political system, the death of Che Guevara, and the repression of guerilla movements in most Latin American countries), the contribution of the Alliance for Progress and other international institutions (e.g., the International Bank for Reconstruction and Development) to social expenditures in Mexico declined sharply: from $89 million in 1962–1964 to $25.1 million in 1964–1970. Most of the moneys were borrowed to provide water and drainage improvements, leaving only a tiny percentage for education and nothing for the expansion of existing welfare programs such as health and housing.[27] The rest of the towering debt was in loans for capital intensive projects, leaving the medium-sized and small enterprises on the margins of the economic system.[28]

During the Diaz Ordaz administration, both the sources and nature of demands for institutional change shifted. The major spokesmen for those demands were students, not, as in the past, labor or teachers. Democratic change, rather than economic improvement, was the order of the day. The 1964 attempt by the PRI president, Carlos Madrazo, to democratize the party by submitting its process of candidate selection to democratic internal elections, failed. Under the pressure of local cadres of the PRI, municipal elections were held with the usual *dedazo* (finger-pointing) system, after which the reformer was summarily dismissed by the president (Skidmore and Smith, 1984; Bataillon, 1968). In the same year, the arbitrary decision to reduce the salaries of already-underpaid resident doctors at ISSSTE by denying them their end of year *aguinaldo* triggered a wave of protests and a strike (Stevens, 1974).[29] The protests were met with uncompromising repression: ring leaders were jailed, and striking doctors were forbidden to practice their profession.[30] This strike prefigured the government's style of handling social conflict: from the beginning, government spokesmen refused even to listen to demands. As a result, protest was magnified to the point that, in the end, only police repression could stop it. Nevertheless, following this show of force, new facilities for resident doctors were built.[31] Thereafter, the end-of-year bonus was no longer withheld.

The existing welfare structure established by previous administrations continued to expand during the 1964–1970 interval, as it was fiscally tied to industrial growth. The social security system administered by the IMSS continued to expand, through obligatory contributions from employers, employees, and the state, from 6,228,700 affiliates in 1964 to 9,496,400 in 1970 (Spalding, 1978:202).

A brief description of the student uprising of 1966–1968 illustrates the important difference between this case and the doctors' strike. Whereas the doctors had been a politically isolated group speaking only for themselves and representing little danger to government stability, student demands were clearly of greater political significance. In the spring of 1966, a student strike at the National Autonomous University of Mexico (UNAM) was triggered by the academic reform launched by its Rector, Dr. Ignacio Chavez, a renowned cardiologist. The new regulations stipulated that entrance to all UNAM schools was subject to an entrance examination. Therefore, successful completion of high school was no longer a guarantee of entering a university. Likewise, faculty members had to provide proof of their proficiency through a "defense" examination for each course offered (Molina Pineiro, 1988).[32]

The leaders of the strike (which started in the law school) were joined by various faculties and high school students. After fruitless attempts to negotiate, the rector expelled several ring leaders, an action questioned by strike organizers. Following several weeks of disturbances, during which the police did not intervene, student demonstrators took the Rector's office by force. The latter resigned under duress and was replaced by Justo Barro Sierra, who immediately reestablished the automatic admittance from high school to university (Bataillon, 1968; Molina Pineiro, 1988). A major crisis had been avoided, but a bad precedent had been set for handling subsequent student demonstrations. In effect, the university had shown its inability to control the student body, thereby endangering the principle of university autonomy. Provincial universities were not so lucky: in October 1966, the army stormed into the University of Michoacán. The following year, more student protests took place in Tabasco, Morelos, and Puebla, all of which were also met with violence (Bataillon, 1968).

The year 1968 began with a protest march by Guanajuato students from the state's capital to Morelia (the capital of Michoacán), demanding the freedom of the students jailed in 1966. The army forcefully disbanded the march. The student movement in the capital also began in early 1968, with fights between rival high schools in which the police intervened violently, arresting and injuring scores of students.[33] This display of government strength was followed by weeks of more violence, during which the secret police and *granaderos* (grenadiers), the special riot police, moved against any student gathering in protest of police brutality or in commemoration of the Cuban revolution. In one case, a bazooka was used to forcibly enter a school building (Hellman, 1983:173). These acts, in turn, mobilized UNAM and Polytechnic Institute student populations, who engaged in pitch battles against the police and the *granaderos*.

On July 30, all UNAM high schools were closed indefinitely, despite the Rector's protest. More than ten thousand students, faculty, and parents demonstrated inside the UNAM against this decision. Hundreds were arrested. The spiral of violence continued until the fateful day of October 2, when another student mass rally organized in Tlatelolco was cordoned off, and soldiers attacked the crowd following a flare signal from police helicopters (Mabry, 1982; Hernández, 1971). Hundreds were killed, thousands taken prisoner.[34]

The dimensions of the violence that culminated on October 2, 1968, has prompted most analysts of this period to consider this event as a significant landmark in Mexico's recent political history. It has been called upon to explain, among other things, the reformist zeal of the subsequent administration (headed by the person hierarchically responsible for the deed), understood as an effort to reestablish a modicum of legitimacy for the regime. What is vital to my thesis is not the sheer size of the repression but the extent to which the 1968 student revolt can be considered to have momentarily endangered the regime's stability and, therefore, to have exerted pressures toward implementing new reforms. As a group, students were not vital to the regime, given that they did not constitute a working part of the political machinery sustaining the official party. But their rebellion could be dangerous in two ways: first, they could "contaminate" the middle sectors undergirding the CNOP (to which their parents belonged); second, they could mobilize those elements among labor and peasants who had remained on the margins of the benefits distributed by "stabilizing development." By calling attention not only to inequality and social injustice but also to the institutional features that sustained them—the official party and presidential absolutism—students could stir malcontents into questioning the regime's institutional structure, something that had not happened since the railroad workers' strike.

On the surface, labor as a whole remained uninvolved in the conflict. The CTM's official position was that "the discontent of some disoriented students ha[d] been exploited by subversive agents of the left and right in order to sow discontent and create an atmosphere of chaos in the country" (Hellman, 1983:177–78). But the CTM could not be counted on to control all labor organizations. In 1966, a new umbrella organization—the Congreso del Trabajo (CT—Congress of Labor) was created to replace the ineffective BUO.[35] In an attempt to avoid the reactivation of the more volatile elements among labor, the president launched a major piece of labor legislation in the spring of 1968: it stipulated that firms with more than a hundred employees would have to provide housing for their employees within three years of the adoption of the law and, meanwhile, provide rent money as a fringe benefit (Aldrete Haas, 1991). This represented a significant gesture, one that triggered immediate opposition from COPARMEX, the main business association (Aldrete Haas, 1991). But given the delay of three years granted to comply with the new policy, there was ample time for the firms involved to negotiate with the following administration. In addition, more than 80 percent of the nation's enterprises fell below the one-hundred-employee limit, which split the potential opposition from business at the same time as it left out the majority of workers.

At the height of the student strikes, the CTM requested and obtained a wage raise for its affiliates. Yet, despite the fact that a semblance of labor unity had been achieved, this measure was too limited to ensure overall control of the labor sector. Fortunately for the government, however, the industrial wage situation was not critical in 1968. Between 1964 and 1970, the index of urban workers' real wages in the Federal District rose from 74.2 percent to 96.9 percent of the 1938 level (Bortz, 1984). The threat of labor support for students was, therefore, neither clear nor immediate.

Despite these preventive reforms, the student movement was beginning to mobilize several politically strategic groups: a sprinkling of labor (mostly railroad, electricity, and oil workers), peasants, urban marginals, and white-collar workers. Student political brigades, the best-organized portion of the student movement, actively sought out contacts with labor and peasant organizations (Hellman, 1984:178). The vast crowds that participated in the mass demonstrations of August and September included workers, taxi drivers, street peddlers, shopkeepers, and peasants. In other words, the opposition to the regime threatened once more to break out of the narrow vertical channels provided by state corporatism.

What was new was the middle-class and urban-marginal element, which previously had been absent from challenges to the regime. Its presence betokened the CNOP's inability to agglomerate and neutralize the lower rungs of this heterogeneous group. The Tlatelolco massacre is said to have begun when marches of peasants and workers joined the student gathering (Cockroft, 1983:241). Nevertheless, labor's role in this action should not be overrated. It was the agglomeration of discontent from several sectors, not the individual presence of any one element, that spelled danger for the regime. In addition, the new demands for political liberalization, if they came to be shared by a substantial portion of the population, would be difficult to meet. Yet this is precisely what the following administration would try to do.

By the time the dust from this major conflagration had settled, the government had changed hands. Throughout the presidential campaign, the candidate of the official party stressed the necessity for an *apertura política* (political opening), an implicit recognition that, until then, such an opening had been conspicuously absent. The repressive tactics of the Diaz Ordaz administration prompted the new government to accept the necessity for political reform.

In other words, while the pact of domination was not substantially altered after 1964, the institutional rules on the basis of which future demands for changes in the pact could be made had changed. The limited housing reform, on the other hand, rather than representing a response to an immediate threat, was a preventive measure that would benefit only a small proportion of the rank and file and at a very low cost. This contrasted with past episodes, which had seen the gradual erosion of industrial wages. The combination of price stability and a wage rise, which characterized stabilizing development throughout the 1960s, also prevented labor mobilizations from erupting at the crucial moment when they would have coincided with the student uprising.[36] The policy of carrying on with monetary stability, despite the fiscal crisis it was bound to provoke, was therefore politically wise, if economically foolish.

CONCLUSION

In this chapter I have followed different episodes of the transformation of the pact of domination from the Cardenist period to 1970, focusing on the actions and reactions of state and labor actors as conditioned by general economic factors, the ideological climate of the time, the reactions of the capitalist sector, and the institutional constraints imposed by state corporatism as it evolved from the previous period. While it is clear that the strategy of state actors throughout this period was to limit the institutional capacity of organized labor to act independently, it is equally clear that these strategies were not successful, inasmuch as social struggles have periodically bypassed narrow institutional channels.

By threatening the CTM's hegemony within the official party—and thereby that of the official party itself—dissident forces temporarily acquired the capacity to destabilize the regime. Episodes of political fragility occurred (1) in the 1940 presidential succession, during which various labor groups joined the conservative coalition in a desperate effort to regain some independence (from the regime as well as from the CTM); (2) in 1944–1946, when the possibility of a schism within the CTM threatened to split the labor vote and thereby weaken the official party; (3) in 1948, when the loss of purchasing power brought about the first postwar devaluation reactivated and united labor against this policy; (4) in 1954, when the second postwar devaluation triggered widespread labor protest, causing even the CTM to take a defiant posture; (5) in 1958–1959, when the *charro* system of labor control instituted in 1948 was challenged in the three most powerful non-CTM unions; and (6) in 1968, when student protest threatened to activate subordinate groups, even though labor was not strongly represented among these.

The political response of state elites at each of these historic junctures varied, as we have seen, from conciliation to outright repression. The Avila Camacho administration (1940–1946) attempted to reunite politically divided labor by offering welfare measures: social security and public housing, which were only weakly implemented, and profit sharing, which was shelved. It also attempted to renew the class alliance between capital and labor through a formal pact of collaboration yet made no effort to force compliance on the part of capital. By the end of Avila Camacho's term, the failure or feeble implementation of most of these measures threatened once more to weaken labor support of the regime, leading to the creation of the CNOP, intended to make labor support less indispensable to the state. The Miguel Alemán administration (1946–1952) destroyed union democracy and removed the last remnants of political choice by party members with the transformation of the PRM into the PRI. While these measures temporarily crushed the political power of dissident labor, most of the rank and file economic demands that formed the basis of this power were granted.

Labor's economic demands acquired new strength in the Ruiz Cortinez administration (1952–1958) with the 1954 devaluation and again were partially satisfied, this time in a conciliatory style, except in the case of railroad workers, whose leadership aimed at reestablishing union democracy (and even labor-capital co-administration), thereby threatening to loosen the link between organized labor and the official party. The Lopez Mateos administration (1958–1964) destroyed the movement headed by Demetrio Vallejo but intensified welfare measures in social security, public housing, and profit sharing. Lastly, the Diaz Ordaz administration (1964–1970), although by far the most repressive of the four examined, took important steps to expand the welfare system available to labor by making the provision of public housing by employers mandatory for the first time.

However modest the role of organized labor in the political crisis of 1968 and its violent resolution may have been, it was clear that, in 1970, workers were no longer the only or the main source of social pressures able to potentially threaten the ruling regime. To labor's demands were now added those of the growing number of lower-level white-collar workers (not all of whom were protected by social security), urban semimarginals (street peddlers, small shopkeepers, taxi drivers, etc.), intellectuals, teachers, students, and a sprinkling of peasant groups, some of which had opted for guerilla warfare. The political system could not withstand the concerted assault of all of these disaffected groups simultaneously. Had the discontent voiced by students in 1968 been allowed to continue much longer, the organization of all these forces into some kind of social democratic front would have become a real possibility. The next administration was under pressure to offer progressive social change if it was to reestablish itself by means other than open state terrorism. In the following period, the importance of organized labor must be understood not in terms of its ability to shake the system singlehandedly (as in the past) but as a potential ally of malcontents in other sectors. The threat of labor activation continued to exist, although it now required a much larger effort of coordination than previously to become a reality. The corporatist mandate to negotiate with each sector separately was, therefore, more than ever a requirement of the survival of the regime.

5

From Riches to Rags, 1970–1990

As the decade of the 1960s drew to an end, a number of structural problems ignored, or simply postponed, by the preceding administrations came to the forefront, precisely at a time when social and political reforms were long overdue. The contradictory pressures generated by the economic and political problems faced in the 1970s led Mexico to a fiscal crisis from which it has yet to recover.

This chapter contrasts four presidential periods: that of Luis Echeverría Alvarez (1970–1976), which saw the revival of populism in government discourse, of labor militancy, and of government attempts to enlarge the welfare system, despite strong fiscal constraints. The second, under José Lopez Portillo (1976–1982), witnessed the first signs of a crisis of debt-led economic growth, followed by a brief period of oil wealth, the consequences of which plunged the country into deep economic depression in the third and fourth periods, under Miguel de la Madrid Hurtado (1982–1988) and Carlos Salinas de Gortari (1988–1994), respectively. These subdivisions, more than merely chronological, correspond to different sets of historical opportunities for changes in the pact of domination. The first saw the temporary release of the political constraints that had prevented the spread of independent labor organizations since the 1940s, together with the rebirth of labor militancy. The second marked a pause in this process, yet without strong reversals. The third opened up a new era of austerity for Mexico as a whole, eroded the previous pacts, and shifted the locus of popular discontent. Finally, the fourth saw the rebirth, in different guise, of state reformism in response to the popular discontent of the previous period.

The various ailments that forced themselves onto the agenda in 1970 were by no means new. Mexico's twentieth-century experience has demonstrated (1) that the unplanned and unintegrated model of import substitution (usually consisting of importing capital and intermediate goods in order to produce final goods) tends to generate a high volume of imports that cannot easily be offset by exports; (2) that the subsidization or substitution of private capital by the state can be sustained only at the cost of mounting external debt; (3) that the policy of maintenance of currency parity between the peso and the U.S. dollar causes serious price distortions, inhibits exports, and dollarizes the economy; and (4) that the extremely high rate of demographic growth offsets to a large extent the benefits of high economic growth (reducing per capita growth).

It was also clear that agriculture, which had sustained the effort of industrialization since the 1940s by providing foreign exchange and cheap food to the urban population while keeping the majority of the rural population in abject poverty, had become exhausted through government neglect.[1] Since 1968, agricultural production no longer sufficed to feed the growing population, as families making a living from subsistence farming grew increasingly unable to survive on the land, let alone produce a surplus. Impoverished peasants had been pouring into the three main cities since the 1950s, forming around them large *cinturones de miseria* (poverty belts), some of which had become cities of their own (such as Ciudad Nezahualcoyotl and Ixtapalapa around Mexico City). This population constituted a large and politically unorganized, but potentially mobilizable, "informal sector" of the economy, which would be incorporated at the end of the period into loosely coordinated organizations for the defense of consumer rights (to land, food, water, etc.), in contrast with conventional worker organizations.

What made the 1970s and the 1980s different from the 1960s was the overwhelming size of all these neglected problems. They further stretched out, and finally broke, the fiscal capacity of the state not only to provide basic food and public services to the population (while at the same time subsidizing and undertaxing private capital) but also to service the mushrooming debt generated by this strategy of economic growth. The most crippling restriction on the process of development was the past inability of the administrators of the Mexican miracle to establish a secure fiscal basis of state revenues. Invariably yielding to the implicit or explicit threat of capital flight, neither the Lopez Mateos nor the Diaz Ordaz administrations had been able to do more than marginally improve the ability of the state to extract surplus value from business. As a result, state revenues from taxes yielded a mere 8.2 percent of the federal government's income in the 1969–1972 period (Fitzgerald, 1978:32). This situation was aggravated by the built-in propensity of unplanned and unintegrated policies of import substitution to generate more imports than exports, which brought the balance of payments deficit from $375.7 million in 1965 to $905.8 million in 1970 (from $35.6 million in 1955), reaching 3 percent of GDP (Looney, 1978:20).

Lastly, the myopic sight of state elites on the danger of high demographic growth, despite the existence of a worldwide debate and its discussion in Mexican academic circles, severely limited the already minimal capacity for redistribution imposed by a regressive tax system, as well as the creation of enough jobs in the dynamic sectors of the economy to absorb excess manpower.[2] Victor Urquidi sums up this general situation of increased needs and diminished capacity to meet them in the following terms:

> The important structural problems were not sufficiently dealt with during the "golden decades" 1950–1970. Among them, outstandingly, the lack of enough resource allocation in favor of the petroleum industry; the dangerous combination of unplanned import substitution and high tariff and non-tariff protection with an increasingly (especially after the midsixties) overvalued currency; the neglect of higher education and industrial research; the very limited efforts to improve traditional agriculture; the official refusal to consider a population policy to facilitate a rapid decline in the birth rate; the ineffectual policies to prevent excessive concentration of people and industry in the central metropolitan area. Some of these issues started to come to the fore at the end of the sixties, when the political system began also to be questioned by a more educated electorate. (1988b:7)

In short, "stabilizing development" ultimately became "unstable" (Reynolds, 1977). It yielded a highly vulnerable economy and a polity that was seriously questioned in the 1968 student movement. The Echeverría years witnessed contradictory government efforts to reestablish a modicum of moral authority by offering *apertura política* (literally, political opening), while at the same time limiting the destabilizing effects born of this policy, especially among labor. The latter, in turn, took advantage of the new political conjuncture by renewing its pressures on government to increase real wages and social expenditures, thereby fanning inflation and provoking more wage demands (Barkin and Esteva, 1982).

POPULISM WITHOUT THE PEOPLE, 1970–1976

By all accounts, the political credibility of the new government headed by President Luis Echeverría Alvarez appeared severely limited. Only two-thirds of those eligible turned out to vote; of these, 20 percent voted for the opposition, and 25 percent turned in blank ballots. In effect, the president was elected by about 37 percent of the electorate (Spalding, 1981:146)—ironically, at a time when the reputation for the near omnipotence of the presidency among academics had replaced the "pluralist" paradigm of Mexican politics diffused by social scientists during the 1960s.[3]

The first year of the Echeverría administration was marred by a recession in the United States (Whitehead, 1980), to which Mexico responded with monetary orthodoxy: the suspension of external credits, the reduction of the balance of payments deficit, and budgetary austerity. The following year, throwing monetary wisdom to the winds, the government embarked upon an ambitious program of fiscal, structural, and social reforms, aimed at achieving the structural transformations deemed necessary to redress the imbalances generated by stabilizing development. In essence, the administration intended to maintain the high rate of economic growth sustained during the 1960s, while at the same time attempting to correct the inequalities generated in the past, hence the slogan, "shared development," which replaced "stabilizing development." This program was launched at an inauspicious moment within an international context of "stagflation." While some analysts characterize the administration's policy as economically foolhardy (Solis, 1977a), others argue that it simply postponed the crisis that otherwise would have started in 1974, when private enterprise practically stopped investing, in Mexico as well as in the United States (Pellicer de Brody, 1977).

The government was committed to creating more jobs through the expansion of the parastatal sector, which was also expected to bring additional public revenue.[4] Small farmers were to be offered credit, discounts on key inputs, insurance against crop failure, small irrigation projects, and basic social services (Hellman, 1983:192). To increase production and stimulate exports, import duties were to be reduced, and the production of wage goods encouraged. The legislation on foreign-owned firms was to be tightened, especially with regard to transfer of technology contracts (Nadal Egea, 1977). New factories were to be located in the less-developed regions. Education, social security, and general health services were to be expanded. The linchpin of this economic and social reform package was fiscal reform. After a bitter confrontation with capital, however, it was abruptly dropped in 1972, leaving the whole reform program without a fiscal base other than more debt.

At the core of the political reform was the declared willingness of the executive to enter into an "open dialogue" with various protagonists. In addition to allowing opposition parties minimal representation in Congress, this policy initially led the administration to openly encourage the formation of independent unions and the democratization of official ones, much to the discontent of the latter's official leadership. Setting aside erstwhile official pretenses of legality in union elections, the president himself declared: "How can we speak about democracy in Mexico if the process of election of a union's Executive Committee is undemocratic?" (Molina, 1977:69). In response to this unexpected call, scores of new independent unions sprang up.[5] At the same time, the *charro* structures of old unions began to show signs of wear. For example, old unions brought to heel in the past, like STFRM, the railroad workers' union, created the Movimiento Sindical Ferrocarrilero (MSF—Railroad Workers' Movement) in 1971, in open conflict with the official CTM-affiliated union purged of its independent elements since 1959. Similarly, teachers created the Coordinadora Nacional de los Trabajadores de la Educación (CNTE—National Coordinating Committee of Education Workers) as the democratic alternative to the official SNTE.

As long as this proliferation resulted in the formation of relatively small organizations with no strong ties among them, the government could maintain its democratic posture while still holding the reins. These government-backed (or at least government-tolerated) unions constituted a strategic weapon to offset the power of Fidel Velazquez, the CTM boss, who did not see eye to eye with the president regarding democratization or social reforms. At the same time, the administration could not afford to lose the support of the machine-based unions.

As economic recession was followed by inflation, this fragile equilibrium was threatened. The first spark was set off by an old unresolved conflict within the electricity worker's sector, which opposed the official and the "democratic" tendencies in Mexican sindicalism. This conflict, in turn, was to ignite similar conflicts in other sectors. Following the nationalization of foreign electrical firms in 1960, the industry retained its fragmented prenationalization union structure; labor representation was shared between the Sindicato Nacional de Electricistas, Similares y Conexos de la República Mexicana (SNESCRM—National Electricians' and Related Workers' Union for the Mexican Republic), which was affiliated with the CTM, and the Sindicato de Trabajadores Electricistas (STERM—Electrical Workers' Union), headed by a democratic leadership. The smaller, independent Sindicato Mexicano de Electricistas (SME—Mexican Union of Electricity Workers) which remained at the margins of the conflict, represented workers in the still foreign-owned Cía de Luz y Fuerza del Centro (which was eventually nationalized in 1974). In 1966, and again in 1969, an agreement was signed between the SNESCRM, the STERM, and the Comisión Federal de Electricidad (CFE—Federal Electricity Commission), the government agency in charge of coordinating the sector, according to which the plurality of union representation (and hence also of collective contracts) would be respected despite nationalization. Yet the government, which played a double game of encouraging union democratization while protecting its source of political support in official labor organizations (Molina, 1977:70), favored the SNESCRM's ambition to become the sole representative of labor in this sector. STERM, numerically inferior, understandably resisted all maneuvers in this direction, holding on to the 1969 agreement that guaranteed its survival.

In 1970, the conflict came to a head. STERM publicly accused the CFE of trying to integrate the two unions in a way detrimental to union democracy. This accusation was substantiated in 1972 when, upon a request from the SNESCRM, the Federal Board of Conciliation and Arbitration ruled that the two unions were to be merged and that STERM no longer represented its affiliates (Gomez-Tagle and Miquet, 1976:189–90; Trejo Delabre, 1979:140). In response, STERM declared a strike, organizing a mass protest against the violation of the 1969 agreement (Gomez-Tagle and Miquet, 1976:151). For the first time since the fateful railroad strike or the late 1950s, several unions in other industrial branches, including even moderate ones such as CROM and CROC, participated in protest marches organized in more than forty cities.

Hampered by its policy of *apertura*, the government could not openly reject STERM's demands. A compromise was reached whereby a new integrated union—Sindicato Unico de Trabajadores de la Electricidad de la República Mexicana (SUTERM—Single Electricity Workers' Union of Mexico)—was created, with a 50 percent representation of each rival union in the executive organs (without elections). It was assumed that SNESCRM's numerical superiority would eventually undermine STERM's power base despite these arrangements. But against these expectations, the "democratic tendency," led by Rafael Galván, gained ground after the merger. Gradually, the tone of its demands rose to a level that surpassed anything foreseeable or tolerable within the rather vague policy context of *apertura*, which had been tailored for middle-class aspirations for political participation, not for union militancy.

While this conflict was erupting, other nonlabor sectors started agitating, particularly UNAM personnel and faculty, who formed their own union, followed by employees of most other universities. In 1972 also, the MSF, the new independent railroad union, forcibly occupied the offices of the *charro* leadership and expelled its members. The new representatives were immediately thrown out by the army. As a concession to the insurgents, the government appointed Gomez Zepeda as head of the reinstated union (Molina, 1977:70). The latter, although unconditionally docile toward the government, had at least had a past of democratic action.[6] The following year, a new umbrella organization uniting "democratic" unions—Movimiento de Unión Revolucionaria (MUR—the Revolutionary Union Movement)—was created, integrating university employees and faculty, teachers, telephone, textile, steel, oil, railroad, and brewery workers (Hellman, 1983:245). All these events were faithfully recorded by a radical newspaper, *Excelsior,* which was soon to become the target of government wrath.

In an effort to unite labor support of its program, the administration announced the creation of a housing fund—The Instituto del Fondo Nacional de la Vivienda para los Trabajadores (INFONAVIT—Institute of the National Housing Fund for Workers)—to be comanaged and cofinanced by employers, labor, and the state, following the tripartite principle that had been used to set policy on social security and profit sharing.[7] After the government's stinging defeat over the issue of fiscal reform, the willing participation of employers in this measure represented a partial victory for the government. Private enterprise, on the other hand, cared little about its contribution, which amounted to 5 percent of the payroll. As CONCAMIN spokespersons openly declared, this 5 percent could easily be transferred to the consumer (Aldrete Haas, 1991). In comparison with the provision of 100 percent employer financing, which the previous administration had called for (but not implemented), the new legislation was a bargain for private enterprise. Moreover, the construction industry was bound to benefit from the measure.

This new source of rewards represented a golden opportunity for the CTM to regain some ground, provided that it could control the agency so as to benefit only its affiliates. But instead of delivering INFONAVIT into the CTM's hands (as everyone had expected), the president appointed as head of the new agency Jesús Silva Herzog, an eager and incorruptible technocrat, who immediately proceeded to distribute housing according to need criteria (unerringly determined by an equally incorruptible computer) and to disregard the subtle or not-so-subtle pressures (e.g., sabotage of construction sites) exerted by the CTM. A deep rift was thereby created between the CTM and the presidency, which lasted until the end of the *sexenio*. At the same time, INFONAVIT's program failed to address the needs of the poorest among labor. Contrary to its original program, which called for 40 percent of the credits to be spent on new finished housing, it devoted between 80 and 85 percent of its budget to luxurious and expensive (by labor's standards) housing. This record in new housing was the answer to the unrealistic public declaration by the president that 900 thousand housing units were to be built during his administration. These units, however, were too expensive for the majority of workers, who earned little more than minimum wage (Aldrete Haas, 1991:104).

In fairness, social expenditures during the Echeverría administration were not restricted to labor, so that not all the reforms carried out during that period can be considered as politically targeted responses to pressure. The urban poor also began to be given their share with the creation of their own housing fund— the Instituto Nacional para el Desarrollo de la Comunidad (IN-DECO—National Institute for Community Development)— and the Comisión para la Regularización de la Tenencia de la Tierra (CORETT—Commission for the Regulation of Land Tenure), created to legalize landownership in urban squatter settlements. The middle sectors also obtained a limited housing program, the Fondo para la Vivienda del Instituto de Servicios y Seguridad Social de los Trabajadores del Estado (FOVISSSTE—Housing Fund of the Institute of Social Security and Services for State Workers). Nevertheless, judging by the output, there was little doubt that the lion's share went to labor: in four years, INFONAVIT produced 154,626 housing units, the FOVISSSTE, 14,655, and INDECO, approximately 28,000 (Aldrete Haas, 1991:87).

The middle sectors also benefited in other ways from government reforms. A vast campaign to increase the educational level in the country doubled the number of civil service jobs during the 1970–1976 period. Half of this increase was due to the expansion of basic education (alleged to have reached fifteen million children instead of the previously acknowledged figure of ten million) and to the creation of a broad network of technical schools intended to serve as alternatives to university education. In addition, the forty-hour workweek was granted to public employees in 1972, thereby raising the cost of the bureaucratic payroll.[8] The CONASUPO network of low-cost food stores also cushioned the worst effects of inflation among the lower- and middle-income urban population. Significantly, the network of these stores never reached all rural areas, although the cities were fully serviced.

In 1973, the administration attempted to partially include the rural population and the urban poor into the social security welfare net through the "Social Solidarity" program. Forty percent of the cost of the program was to be financed by the IMSS's pension and disability fund (already called upon to make up for the deficit in health programs) and 60 percent by government deficit spending. This program met with persistent resistance from several actors: the official labor sector, which saw its privileges threatened; social security experts, who questioned its fiscal wisdom; and business people, who opposed the administration's social reforms in general (Spalding, 1981).

Social Solidarity was supposed to extend medical services and pharmaceutical assistance to the uninsured population, especially in rural areas. In fact, its implementation was limited: according to official figures (which were probably inflated), only 1.9 million people gained access to the program. Added to the improvements in the more poorly funded Ministry of Health programs, this reform was supposed to have tripled health coverage in the rural areas. A more conservative estimate of 700 thousand people was offered by nongovernment experts (Spalding, 1981).[9] The only universal health-related services actually offered wherever public health facilities existed (i.e., mainly in urban areas) was family planning, made into law in 1974 (Brachet-Marquez, 1984a, 1984b), and hospital emergency services. Contrary to other social reforms, family planning was momentarily unhampered by fiscal constraints, due to the availability, until 1976, of generous international funds to sustain it.

Despite these reforms, the number of strikes increased steadily from 1972 on, peaking in 1974, when inflation reached its maximum of 25 percent. The price of the basic beans-and-tortilla menu had risen by 50 percent, which by far outstripped the 20 percent emergency wage hike granted in the fall of 1973. A new wave of labor protest was unleashed.[10] SUTERM returned to the headlines in 1975 with the Guadalajara Declaration, reminiscent of the railroad workers movement of the late 1950s. This manifesto, which stressed the principles of independent and democratic unions, demanded a wage increase, a permanent "mobile scale" to adjust wages to inflation, more social security and public housing benefits, the municipalization of public transportation, agrarian collectivization, the planning of agriculture, the nationalization of credit, and the expropriation of imperialist foreign-owned companies.

Clearly, Rafael Galván, SUTERM's leader was treading dangerous grounds. A few months later, an illegally constituted SUTERM congress expelled the democratic leadership (Trejo Delabre, 1979; Hellman, 1983). Thereafter, prominent members of the "democratic tendency" were fired and harassed. Nevertheless, they responded with a national strike, which was stopped by the army. In 1977, they even went so far as to pitch tents right next to the presidential palace but were immediately dispersed by the police. During the same period, the daily newspaper *Excelsior*, whose tone had also risen above the administration's tolerance threshold, was transformed into a docile recipient of government discourse, via the illegal armed storming of its board of directors, who were replaced by representatives chosen by the administration.[11]

In the end, neither INFONAVIT nor the efforts to lower food prices and sustain wages were enough to stem the tide of labor protest unleashed after 1972, when rising inflation began to seriously eat into workers' incomes. The government's strategy of protecting wage earners from inflation in order to use them as a political counterforce against business opposition had therefore not been successful.[12] In effect, from 1974 on, the government faced opposition simultaneously from capitalists, who exported their assets by the carload, and from the official leadership of organized labor, who felt let down by the policy of encouragement of union democracy. Finally, it also faced opposition by independent labor unions themselves, whose major recruiting appeal was to call attention to the deterioration of labor's economic situation and the CTM's inaction in that respect. Even peasants were becoming troublesome, whose opposition was manifested by rural guerrillas and by land invasions in the rich irrigated districts of the north. The CNC, as always, seemed to have had little to do with either prompting these actions or demanding social reforms (Grindle, 1977a). It could only be expected, as always, to deliver the PRI vote for the next presidential election.

The net result of the Echeverría administration's social and economic policies was a deepening of the crisis of state-led developmentalism (*desarrollismo*). Between 1971 and 1975, federal expenditures nearly quadrupled, from 41 billion to 145 billion pesos, and the deficit rose from 4.8 billion to 42 billion pesos. Simultaneously, the balance of payments deficit went from 905.8 billion to 4 billion current pesos, while the current-account deficit continued deteriorating, from 726 million to 3,769 million current pesos (Looney, 1978:65). Exports grew, especially due to the proliferation of assembly plants along the northern border, most of which paid below minimal wages and offered few, if any, social benefits; but imports grew even faster.

In 1976, the 3.5 percent net population growth outstripped the 2 percent GDP increase. The Echeverría administration decided to slow down its mad race to the fiscal abyss. A stabilization program was introduced, including tightening credit and the circulation of money. Despite these measures, the atmosphere of speculation generated by inflation and the agitated political ambience precipitated capital flight.[13] By August 1976, a devaluation seemed inevitable. The parity between the peso and the U.S. dollar changed—from 12.50 to 20.60—for the first time since 1954. Within hours of the devaluation, department stores and shops in Mexico City marked up their goods by 20–40 percent (Looney, 1978:125).

The last five months of the Echeverría administration were extremely agitated. The government, normally weak after the next presidential candidate is *destapado* (unveiled), was unable to impose a price freeze. As a result, price markups soon caught up with the devaluation. The CT, the labor umbrella organization that included most unions, demanded a 65 percent wage raise, to which the administration responded by an offer of 10 percent, established as the ceiling for all wage increases from then on.

Meanwhile, the wildest rumors circulated regarding a military takeover, to prolong Echeverría's rule, or land confiscation. Supermarkets were quickly emptied of food. These rumors, which replaced normal channels of communication (Loaeza, 1977), were exacerbated, in turn, by the president's loud accusations against business, which he held responsible for the climate of insecurity. In response, business accelerated capital flight, triggering the second devaluation in October, bringing the peso to 26.5 to the U.S. dollar (Looney, 1978:127). In November, the administration announced the expropriation of nearly a hundred thousand hectares of irrigated land in the north, earmarked for agrarian redistribution (some of which had already been forcibly occupied by landless peasants, secretly instigated by the government, according to some). Agricultural capitalists were up in arms (large as well as medium landowners). The government loudly protested against this campaign of rumors and accusations, all of them allegedly unfounded.

Despite the opposition encountered in the implementation of its social reforms, we can nevertheless conclude that the Echeverría administration saw the substantial advance (at considerable economic costs) of welfare legislation, with the lion's share given to labor, still the least pliable member of the official party and, therefore, the actor in the best position to destabilize the regime. Nevertheless, labor was no longer alone on the political scene. It was clear that the necessity to mend the government's fences with students, intellectuals, and the middle sectors in general had led President Echeverría to open up the political system to labor militancy.

But the CNOP had also proven troublesome: although created in order to counterbalance divisions within the labor movement, it proved capable of destabilizing the system on its own: teachers, banking employees, and health workers, as well as the less easily controllable service subsectors (e.g., transportation) also had to be reckoned with. The last year of the administration saw the reconciliation between the president and the CTM, most evident in the "unveiling" of the CTM's favorite presidential candidate, José Lopez Portillo, as the official PRI presidential candidate. It was also evident in the public chastising of the head of INFONAVIT in the last presidential annual report (presumably for having done what the president had instructed him to do), which augured a more "flexible" (i.e., corrupt) housing policy for the future.

FROM STABILIZATION TO PETROLIZATION, 1976–1982

The 1976–1982 presidential term must be divided into two distinct periods: the first, from 1977 to 1979, marked by stabilization and fiscal austerity; the second, from 1980 to 1982, which might be subtitled the president's folly, during which the inflation of international oil prices took Mexico on a borrowing binge that brought its economy to a near collapse in August 1982, when debt payments had to be suspended and the dollar reserve was nearly exhausted.

On December 1, 1976, when José Lopez Portillo was sworn in, the country faced a serious political and economic crisis (to which he had generously contributed as minister of the treasury), generating, in turn, a profound crisis of confidence in all sectors of society: among businesspeople, who no longer believed in the currency and feared for their property; among workers and the urban poor, whose standards of living had deteriorated as a result of high inflation; among intellectuals, whose dream of a more democratic Mexico had not been realized.[14] Lopez Portillo's first tasks were to reestablish the government's ties with private enterprise, quiet social protest among labor, the middle sectors (e.g., teachers), and peasants, and repair Mexico's badly damaged international credit situation. The renewal of the presidential cycle created new hope for change, despite this inauspicious beginning.

At his inauguration speech, the new president attempted to mend his fences with virtually everyone: first and foremost with the owners of capital, but also with official labor. Avoiding the sullied populist term of *campesinos,* he addressed the rural population as the "marginalized," whose misfortunes caused him to shed some tears (literally). The administration launched a new motto: the Alliance for Production. The keynotes of his administration were to be productivity, organization, fiscal austerity, and wage restraint, all in the name of saving the national economy. Yet, unaccountably, the ISSSTE, the public sector social security agency, was granted a 263 percent budget increase (Revel-Mouroz, 1980), hardly an austerity measure.

Barely a day after Lopez Portillo was sworn in, the stock exchange was climbing and capitalists were bringing back their dollars, now worth twice their buying price. The new president offered them an olive branch: in addition to the restriction of wage raises to a 10 percent ceiling, the Alliance for Production meant that industry would continue to be subsidized by the state and that some provisions of the agrarian reform would be disregarded (e.g., the illegality of consolidating several plots of land). In exchange, private firms were to produce more efficiently and create more jobs.[15] Unions accepted the 10 percent wage increase and were duly congratulated, in the president's first annual report, for their spirit of sacrifice. The rural poor, on the other hand, were promised a new program destined to improve their capacity to feed the country: the Coordinadora General del Plan Nacional de Zonas Deprimidas y Grupos Marginados (General Coordination of the National Plan for Depressed Zones and Marginalized Groups), better known as COPLAMAR. At this stage, however, this program was little more than a promise.[16]

The new IMF-directed economic policy package, introduced to address the severe debt and fiscal problem, provided for the reduction of inflation, the reestablishment of external balance, and an increase in the rate of economic growth and employment (both of which seemed unlikely expectations in conjunction with credit and wage contraction). Public expenditures were to be reduced via budgetary austerity and greater administrative efficiency, in the hope of bringing the public deficit to 2.5 percent of the GDP, instead of the current 8 percent (Pellicer de Brody, 1977:47). The administration planned to stabilize the economy during the first two years, then resume noninflationary growth. In fact, the first stage was reduced to one year and the second left out altogether. From 1978 on, the administration embarked upon a high-growth program sustained by more debt, conceded by international creditors on the basis of Mexico's newly discovered oil wealth. At the end of this mad race, the government deficit soared to 15 percent of GDP (García Alba and Serra Puche, 1984:30).

The government's strategy to achieve the initial stabilization program while restoring social peace was first to give power back to the official unions, thereby increasing the probability of obtaining temporary restraints on wage demands despite high inflation; second, to redirect away from unions the political struggles that had taken place within the independent labor movement during the 1970s (e.g., the Guadalajara Declaration by SUTERM); and third, to break up the power structure of the most troublesome unions via decentralization. The first two strategies were directed specifically at labor, the third at teachers, a group that was fast becoming a bigger thorn in the side of Mexican corporatism than labor.

To empower official unions, the Lopez Portillo administration started with the tried-and-trusted method of increasing the number of fiefs allotted to the official labor sector: four governorships (of Nayarit, Querétaro, Zacatecas, and Tamaúlipas) and scores of deputy and senate offices were added. Also, a new financial institution—the Banco Obrero—was created, to be administered by the CTM's labor boss. Through this institution, the latter could reward party discipline, as well as improve his own personal financial position and that of his closest associates.

But the most important concession, the plum offered to the CTM in exchange for its renewed support of the government, was INFONAVIT, for whose control Fidel Velazquez had fought throughout the Echeverría period. The day the new president was sworn in, the computer that had been allocating housing according to objective-need criteria since 1972 mysteriously self-destructed. A few weeks later, an internal coup d'état swept away the democratic leadership of INFONAVIT's own union, replacing it with CTM-controlled elements (Aldrete Haas, 1991:127). Simultaneously, the new director declared a policy of "external promotions" to replace that of direct construction. This meant that construction would be carried out by private construction companies owned, more often than not, by labor bosses, and IN-

FONAVIT would be transformed into a financing agency. The CTM had finally obtained control over a powerful instrument likely to ensure discipline within its ranks and the marginalization of independent unions. From then on, it became common practice for workers to belong officially to the CTM and secretly to an independent union (Roxborough, 1984).

The second state strategy to stem the tide of democratization among labor was, paradoxically, the promise of a political reform that would truly give an electoral voice (although not the possibility of winning the election) to the opposition. This reform put independent unions into the hands of leftist opposition parties, who had their own organizational problems to deal with (such as, for example, a rapprochement between the Communist Party and the CTM, to swell the ranks of the PCM). In addition, opposition from the right, as represented by the PAN, was far better organized than that from the left and, therefore, likely to do better in elections than the generally fragmented left. Whatever the potential gains for the leftist opposition of this change in the electoral process, its effect on unions, as the president himself stated, was to siphon off political struggles from the labor movement:

> The limitation of the political participation of some organized groups has gotten to the point of deforming, for example, the union structure. Many groups have been carrying out their legitimate—yet not legitimated—political struggles within the union movement, deforming the latter. On many occasions, the solutions to the workers' problems have been impeded by their association with political opinions that had to express themselves in that context because there was no way out. We believe that institutionally recognizing the participation of all kinds of opinions, even if they don't agree among themselves, provided that we organize it and place it within the institution, will relax these tensions. (*Unomasuno*, Dec. 1, 1977)

With the new institutionalization of opposition, leftist parties, some of which (particularly the Communist Party) had long lost their registration, were able to come out into the open and campaign for more recruits. Contrary to expectations, they managed to form a united front represented by the Partido Socialista Unico de México (PSUM—Single Socialist Party of Mexico). Nevertheless, it was not clear that the electoral aims of this new front were compatible with those of independent unions. Since labor's political action, as we have seen, were usually narrowly focused upon bread-and-butter issues and only occasionally on wider political ones, their association with the PSUM was not likely to guarantee the satisfaction of their demands. According to Bizberg, the program offered by the PSUM had little to do with union interests (1983). Both the PSUM and the MUR showed little concern for issues of internal democracy or concrete worker concerns. This contrasted with the more specifically labor organizations, such as the Movimiento Proletario (Proletarian Movement), which developed in the mine and metal works of SICARTSA, the state-owned steel mill (Bizberg, 1990). Ian Roxborough's study of automobile workers, carried out during this period, confirms this diagnosis: he found Mexican workers to be narrowly concerned about their immediate needs, rather than depoliticized and apathetic (Roxborough, 1984).

A last measure likely to further weaken union democracy was a limit on the number of independent unions. Existing independent unions had not been persecuted, but new ones were prevented from being born by virtue of the government's prerogative not to "recognize" a new applicant to union status. This strategy failed in the case of the Workers' Union of the National University of Mexico (STUNAM), which resulted from the merger of employee and faculty unions. In the face of student, employee, and faculty clamors for amnesty and the release of political prisoners (Alvarez, 1986), the government opted to acknowledge the new union. In general, however, the expansion of independent unionism was over.

Labor conflicts during these years (e.g., in textiles and metallurgy industries and at Volkswagen and Tolteca Cements) are cited by some authors as evidence that even official unions were radicalizing under the impact of stabilization (Hellman, 1983). Yet in most cases, these conflicts were resolved with wage increases that fell below the official ceiling, which was gradually increased. Two exceptions to this rule presented themselves: the doctors' strike in the Ministry of Health and a teachers' strike. These two sectors were the most adversely affected by initial budgetary cuts. Teachers often had to wait for months for their meager pay. In 1981, teachers' wages were considerably increased, which temporarily reestablished order within this deeply embattled sector (Street, 1992; Kovacs, 1989).

Teachers proved more difficult than labor to deal with, however. The palace revolution, instigated by the previous administration, to replace one demanding *charro* with another, supposedly more pliable, had largely failed. The SNTE's new leadership, headed by Jonjitud Barrios, was just as demanding, if not more, since it had to establish its credibility with the rank and file. From the beginning of the 1976 electoral campaign, SNTE demanded (and obtained as fulfillment of a campaign promise) the creation of a new educational vehicle for teachers—the Universidad Pedagógica Nacional (UPN—National Pedagogical University). The UPN was supposed to offer teachers a means to aspire to higher wages (if not a way to obtain them immediately), and the SNTE leaders a basis for reestablishing their hegemony, threatened by the growing dissident democratic movement within its ranks (Kovacs, 1989).[17]

But far from reestablishing government control over the union or corporatist discipline within its ranks, the UPN started a protracted battle between the SNTE's leadership and the Ministry of Education over the definition of what the UPN should achieve. While the SNTE wanted a massive teachers' college that would admit virtually all teachers and thereby establish credentials for higher wages (i.e., in effect, a union-controlled social benefit), the ministry's leadership aimed at a government-controlled academic project designed to upgrade teachers' training, which, by international standards (even those of Third World countries) was extremely poor and, therefore, apt to slow down economic growth. The result was a split project: on the one hand, an open university that took in the majority of teachers, and on the other, a more academically oriented UPN, supposed to create an elite on a technocratic basis.

This concession did not immediately bring teachers more income, however. The SNTE experienced a serious internal crisis, due to the combined effects of inflation and the ministry's policy of decentralization, another technocratic ploy to weaken the troublesome union. The process of change from federal to state education produced chaos, whose immediate consequence was the delay in paying teachers. From this conflictive situation emerged a new democratic teachers' movement in the state of Chiapas whose militants meant to take seriously the government discourse describing decentralization as a move toward democracy (Street, 1992). They demanded more local autonomy (also a piece of government rhetoric to justify the change), specifically the local union's capacity to bargain for increases in wages and social benefits and to demand prompt salary payments (Prieto, 1986). This regional movement soon sprouted into a national one: the first National Forum of Educational Workers and Democratic Organizations assembled in December 1979. On the second day of its meeting, the congress created the Coordinadora Nacional de Trabajadores de la Educacion (CNTE—National Coordinating Committee of Educational Workers): the democratic teachers' movement had emerged out of the very strategies designed to suppress it.

The second half of the Lopez Portillo administration brought few changes in the policies toward labor, except for the gradual and moderate raising of the wage ceiling, thus avoiding open confrontation with unions. Although Mexico openly declared itself affluent in 1980, most of the extra money obtained from oil went back into investments for the modernization of that industry, which had received little official attention except during the Echeverría administration. The state's interest in social reform during 1980–1982 focused on bringing new benefits to the rural population through the subsidization of small farming (chiefly through the Sistema Alimentario Mexicano (SAM—Mexican Food System) aimed at reaching food self-sufficiency. Primary health services to the rural areas, begun on a modest scale in the preceding administration, were also expanded, with the construction of some three thousand rural clinics and scores of rural hospitals throughout the country. These reforms, however, do not fit the hypothesis of response to pressures. The COPLAMAR health system was simply bestowed upon a patient peasantry.[18] In some cases, the process was even reversed, as, for example, when the CONASUPO-COPLAMAR program, which set up a network of peasant small businesses, opened up opportunities for peasants to organize locally (Fox and Gordillo, 1989; Fox, 1993).

The government's conflict avoidance strategy with respect to labor (and the university union) can be seen in its efforts to compensate wage restraints by increases in *prestaciones*, the social benefits tied to wage contracts (chiefly transportation and food allocations). Although wage increases were restrained, these benefits were on the increase, particularly in state-owned and transnational firms (Bizberg, 1984). The ISSSTE, the IMSS, the treasury, and UNAM offered their affiliates anything from potatoes to refrigerators in special stores exempted from the new 15 percent value-added tax imposed on all sales in order to reestablish the government's fiscal solvency. In the comprehensive fiscal reform that was enacted, the government took care to liberate the lowest rungs of the income scale from the obligation to pay taxes (Revel-Mouroz, 1980). The losers in this unequal allocation of social benefits were the employees of small and medium-sized national firms, who had to accept wage ceilings without compensating mechanisms. Also on the losing side were the urban poor, who paid the value-added tax and faced the "liberation" of 140 price-controlled articles, decided under pressure from CONCANACO, the official trade association.

In the case of teachers, conflict could not be avoided. The democratic teachers' movement was spreading like bushfire throughout the national territory, eventually including teachers from more than twenty states. They organized mass meetings, (e.g., the demonstration of twenty thousand teachers from Oaxaca in Mexico City in May 1980) (Street, 1992), which threatened to mobilize teachers in the Federal District. The CNTE, the dissident teacher organization, also organized several national forums that welded together these regional and local grass-roots movements. The state response to this process was administrative harassment, mysterious assassinations, and mass layoffs of demonstrating teachers. This is illustrated in the suspension of the forty thousand teachers who took part in mass marches protesting the assassination of Misrael Nuñez Acosta, a CNTE leader. More marches and protests followed this reprisal, after which the Ministry of Education struck a compromise with the dissidents, conceding them five positions within the SNTE's National Executive Committee and a promise to stop reprisals (ibid.). Peace had been obtained just in time for the presidential campaign of Miguel de la Madrid, whose election needed teacher support even more than labor support, given their numerical superiority.

The urban poor also began to organize toward the end of the Lopez Portillo administration. A number of elements—from the increasing cost of living and inflated property taxes to the threat to housing posed by the vast urban demolition undertaken by Mexico City's regent,[19] Hank Gonzalez, and the administration's creation of PRI-controlled neighborhood councils—paved the way to the creation in May 1980 of the Coordinadora Nacional de los Movimientos Urbanos Populares (CONAMUP—National Coordination of Popular Urban Movements), an independent urban-based grass-roots organization. In May 1982, when inflation and unemployment racked the country, CONAMUP was to mount *paros cívicos* (national days of protest) and establish alliances with various democratic labor and peasant groups (Prieto, 1986:82). Yet the threat of a united front between these movements and labor did not materialize during the Lopez Portillo administration.

If the Lopez Portillo administration cannot be qualified as *obrerista* (prolabor), neither can it be said to have economically punished labor. Therefore, there were no strong reasons why labor protest should have been on the increase, as it had been in the previous administration, when inflation was markedly steeper than wage increases. Throughout the *sexenio,* wage increase ceilings were carefully tailored to reestablish each January the purchasing power gradually lost during the previous year. The imposed increase ceiling (*tope salarial*) went from 10 percent in 1977 to 29 percent in 1981, leaving the purchasing power of wage earners practically unchanged.[20] From this we can conclude that wage earners were not singled out as the sacrificial lambs of stabilization. At the same time, neither can they be said to have benefited from the boom years, except for oil workers, whose union redistributed to the rank and file some of the kickback moneys it obtained from all contracts (Alvarez, 1986:54). For the rest of the mining and manufacturing sector, 1981 was the only year when a gain in real wages (of 8.9 percent) was achieved, just before the big plunge. Finding neither pressures from below nor state responses to their plight, we must, therefore, declare a stalemate for our leading hypothesis, as far as labor was concerned.

The same cannot be said about teachers, whose struggles, although repressed at first, were finally rewarded with some concessions, and whose democratic movement was consolidated within the SNTE, despite government efforts to the contrary. In the strategies to prevent the destabilization of the regime, this organization, which comprised 750 thousand members in 1981 (the largest single union in Latin America), took precedence over labor, which totaled only 605 thousand members among all unions at the time (Alvarez, 1986). Some of the teachers' demands were, therefore, met, while labor ceased to be the main potential source of disturbance on the political stage. Yet, labor's role remained significant: it could become either an aggravating factor in case of teacher insurgence or an additional consolidating factor if it failed to join teacher insurgency. For historical reasons, it still held the best position among dominated classes, with the IMSS,

INFONAVIT, and profit sharing as its protective weapons. Teachers, on the other hand, although they had access to some of these benefits (the ISSSTE and the FOVISSSTE, for health and housing, respectively), were still struggling for basics.

The last months of the Lopez Portillo *sexenio* were also stormy. Although most analysts (and government spokespersons at the time) argue that the sudden decline of international oil prices was the factor responsible for capital flight in 1981, others point to the climate of uncertainty generated by the inconsistencies between stated and actual economic policies (Garcia Alba and Serra Puche, 1984:63). For example, despite the announcement of public expenditure reductions of 4 percent in 1981 and 8 percent in 1982, public money kept flowing. Likewise, the peso was devalued barely twenty-four hours after the president had declared that he would defend it like a dog, and exchange control was established barely a few weeks after the director of the Bank of Mexico had published a document arguing against such a measure. The forcible conversion of bank deposits from dollars to pesos at a rate far below the market value was another example of the policies generating panic, not just among investors but also among small savers, whose confidence in the government had supplied funds for public expenditures for decades. The bank nationalization, secretly prepared and suddenly proclaimed on September 1, 1982, also came as a total surprise to most observers (including the president's cabinet).

Economic turmoil and political reform notwithstanding, Mexico's political cycle remained unmoved. In 1982, Miguel de la Madrid Hurtado, the PRI's official presidential candidate designated by the current president (and, like his predecessor, also largely responsible for the large-scale deficit spending of the last period of the outgoing administration), was duly elected. For most organized groups, he was a dark horse, trained in the technocratic tradition of the financial sector. It was, nevertheless, beyond doubt that his main task was to "stabilize" Mexico's tottering economy—"stabilization" here, as elsewhere, being synonymous with wage restraints and budgetary austerity.

FROM BAD TO PIRE, 1982–1988

The thunderous crash of petroleum-led developmentalism was almost as sudden and frightening to those who experienced it as the seismic cataclysm that was to shake Mexico City only three years later. For most of the public, who had been lulled into believing that Mexico was successfully managing its god-sent affluence, the events that followed the end of 1982 were truly incomprehensible: capital flight of unheard-of proportions; long lines in banks to change pesos into U.S. dollars; a cascade of currency devaluations; the almost daily markups in commercial centers; the public indictment of the villains of the story ("Negro Durazo," Lopez Portillo's primary school pal appointed chief of police; Serrano, the head of PEMEX, accused of having stolen whole oil tankers; and even Lopez Portillo himself); but most of all, the bleak future outlined by the new president—the very first incoming president since the Revolution who failed to strike a note of hope and renovation. Most Mexicans, accustomed to a predictable (if rarely golden) future, were left dazed and unbelieving. Wayne Cornelius captures well the spirit of the time: "In striking contrast with the steady economic growth, sense of confidence, and political flexibility that characterized it during most of the post-1940 period, Mexico seems to have entered an era of economic instability, institutional rigidity, uncertainty (for both individuals and institutions), erosion of traditional state-society relationships, and breakdowns of the elite consensus that had buttressed the post-1940 development model" (1986:1). This statement, while it may overstate the weight of elites in Mexico's conduct of politics, faithfully reflects the fragility of the institutions and their inability to cope with the new problems on the basis of the old give-and-take methods that had regulated the slow transformation of Mexico since the 1940s.

This period saw the unfolding of a new set of pressures and counterpressures to transform the pact of domination. From 1982 to 1988, under the external pressures of international forces, the state took steps to erase every single advance in real wages made in the previous twenty-five years and to curtail welfare expenditures. The global impact of the crisis, in turn, stimulated the activation of a variety of loosely coordinated local urban movements, with little apparent mobilization on labor's part. In 1988, dissident unions joined these movements and other discontents in the biggest electoral offensive the system had sustained since 1940. After 1988, we witness the systematic dismantling of the organizational bases of this electoral offensive by the state, coupled with the extension of the welfare state to the urban (and, to a lesser extent, also rural) poor.

The dimensions of the crisis faced in 1982 and dragged out throughout the decade dwarf even the bleakest accounts of previous crises. In that year, when international bankers suspended their loans to Mexico, the country faced a yearly debt service of $US13.3 billion, equivalent to 47.5 percent of its exports (Urquidi, 1988a). Economic growth dropped from 8 percent to − 0.5 percent, and inflation soared to over 60 percent. The global deficit of the public sector rose to 18 percent of GDP, and the total external debt totalled $87.6 billion, 61 percent more than what it had been only two years previously (Urquidi, 1988a). In December 1982, when the new administration took office, the Programa Inmediato de Reordenamiento Económico (PIRE— Immediate Program of Economic Reordering), a three-year IMF-directed program of stabilization, was put into effect. The official document presenting the program identified four culprits of Mexico's misfortunes: (1) the inefficiency of the productive system, (2) the insufficient generation and irrational use of foreign currency, (3) the scarcity of internal savings, and (4) the social inequalities generated by the process of growth (Garcia Alba and Serra Puche, 1984:73). This was indeed a strong indirect indictment of an administration that had explicitly aspired to set a historical example of "good administration."[21]

In exchange for the IMF's granting the bridge loans necessary to service the debt, the government promised to reduce the public financial deficit to 8.5 percent of GDP in 1983, 5.5 percent in 1984, and 3.5 percent in 1985. This reduction could be achieved only by increasing taxes and the price of public services, which had traditionally been kept low so as to simultaneously protect low-income groups and stimulate investment. Both measures could not fail to be inflationary, at least in the short run. Given the solid tradition of tax evasion in Mexico, these increased revenues could be extracted only from captive taxpayers, (i.e., the reduced pool of those employed at above minimum wage, mainly the middle sectors) and sales taxes, whose main burden would fall on the urban poor. Both groups were to contribute heavily to the electoral opposition to the PRI throughout the 1980s but would express their discontent from different sides of the political spectrum.

Inflation, which was supposed to drop to 55 percent in 1983, reached 80 percent (even according to official sources), while economic growth fell below zero (− 5.5 percent). Popular discontent began to be felt. In May–June 1983, having initially supported austerity measures, the CTM and the CT threatened to call a general strike. The government's response was a public rebuff and an open flirtation with the now more docile CROM and CROC.[22] But labor was no longer the main stage of popular action. With the rise of unemployment and the growth of the "informal market," in which women (who increasingly contributed to family support) began to play an important role, popular demands shifted from wage increases to cheaper goods and services.

In the last year of the previous administration, Mexico had witnessed the birth of the *coordinadoras* (coordinators), umbrella organizations coordinating the actions of various popular movements. The most prominent were the CNTE, the teachers' *coordinadora*, CONAMUP, the urban *coordinadora* and the Coordinadora Nacional del Plan de Ayala (CNPA), the peasant *coordinadora*. The first had represented dissident teachers since its creation in 1979. During the Miguel de la Madrid administration, it organized the Frente Nacional de Defensa de los Salarios y contra la Carestía (FNDSCAC—National Front for the Defense of Wages and Against Austerity and the High Cost of Living). CONAMUP, which had been created in May 1980 by a coalition of neighborhood councils, mounted collective efforts to solve the most acute problems of urban dwellers: housing and basic services (water, drainage, electricity, etc.)[23]

In October 1983, the *coordinadoras* jointly mounted a gigantic *paro cívico* (civil strike), in which approximately two million people took part. This show of force emboldened the CT to renew its demands in late 1983: the suspension of the value-added tax (at a time when tax revenue was so acutely needed); a rent freeze; and the semiannual renegotiation of labor-management contracts. This time, the rebuff was not so strong. Some token concessions were made: bus fare increases were suspended, and a new law was passed to keep rents behind inflation. The immediate results of this measure were the near disappearance of formal rental contracts in Mexico City (and, therefore, also of the taxes collected from them) and the increase in the scarcity (and price) of rented housing, as landlords moved to protect themselves. The main demand—to renegotiate wage contracts every six months—which would have been highly inflationary—was not satisfied. Instead, the government opted for decreeing emergency wage raises whenever informal pressure from labor rose too high. This nearly achieved the same end but avoided legally indexing wages to the rate of inflation. In this way, wages were kept far behind inflation, in the elusive hope that a contraction in demand would slow down inflation and the not so elusive expectation that cheap labor would become Mexico's chief comparative advantage.[24]

The year 1984 also saw strong popular protests. The CTM threatened to call a general strike unless wages were raised. This threat was backed with scores of *emplazamientos*.[25] In June 1984, a second *paro cívico* was staged, mobilizing about 500 thousand people. After that date, the *coordinadoras* were unable to combine their forces to stage new civil strikes, due to internal factionalism, government repression of individual militants, and the interference of leftist parties who felt left out of the action (Middlebrook, 1989a:205). Soon, the CTM took up the offensive again, proposing an alternative to the stabilization policies undertaken: indexed wages, more profit sharing, the nationalization of food producing firms (many of which were transnational corporations), and an increased welfare package. In other words, the CTM implicitly asked the government to throw fiscal wisdom to the winds and stop paying back its debt. Contrary to his huffy attitude of 1983, de la Madrid responded by loosening up stabilization policies and making new promises. In the last quarter of 1984 and the first of 1985 (a year of state elections), a brief economic recovery was primed by increased government expenditures (Cornelius, 1986). The president went so far as to announce the end of austerity.

The immediate results of this momentary faltering were increased inflation, a new wave of capital flight, and renewed economic contraction (in addition to a rap on the president's fingers by IMF authorities). In response, the budget was further cut in August. In September, the earthquake tragedy further dimmed hopes for recovery, momentarily paralyzing the government. However, it renewed the capacity for popular collective action—this time to save lives. Despite interference by the police and the army, the population organized the rescue of victims, transported the wounded, and donated and distributed food and drugs.[26] Grass-roots organizations, such as CONAMUP, became spokesmen for the earthquake victims, actively negotiating with the government for their relocation and the reconstruction of destroyed housing.

Despite budgetary strictures, such claims received high priority on the government's agenda: they could not legitimately be

denied, nor could the *damnificados* (earthquake victims) be allowed to join forces with other discontents (Massolo, 1986). Already, they had organized as a group under the Coordinadora
Unica de Damnificados (Single Coordinator for Earthquake Victims), which presented itself to the authorities as a bargaining
agent, taking advantage of the government's disposition but also
forcing it to abandon its own renewal projects in the face of
popular mobilization and organization, and to recognize alternative projects proposed by popular movements (Foweraker,
1990).[27] As 1985 ended, inflation persisted, and the recession
deepened, as a result of the collapse of OPEC's price strategy
(World Bank, 1986).

The following years of slow reconstruction brought no appre-
ciable improvement in the lot of the popular classes. International oil prices kept going down, and inflation continued
unabated.[28] Between 1982 and 1988, per capita GDP decreased
by 15 percent (Hernández Laos, 1993). During this whole period
also, public investments decreased by over 50 percent, and private investments by 15 percent, the latter registering only a slight
increase of 3.3 percent between 1986 and 1988 (Hernández Laos,
1989, 1993). In 1986, further budget cuts were instituted, which
nevertheless did not compensate for the 57 percent loss of income from oil exports (Cornelius, 1986). Food subsidies were cut
by 80 percent: the price of tortillas increased by 140 percent, but
sugar remained subsidized, for the greatest benefit of the soft
drink industry.[29] The price of gasoline doubled, and subway
fares went up from one peso to twenty pesos, and the inflation
rate reached three digits. Despite budget cuts, the government
deficit was 12.4 percent of GDP at the end of 1986. State-owned
firms such as PEMEX, CONASUPO, and the CFE began to postpone their payments to suppliers. The public sector was in a state
of virtual bankruptcy.

The social fermentation throughout the de la Madrid administration ended in an explosion of electoral opposition in the
summer of 1988. A brief overview of the social impact of the extreme austerity measures that struck the already impoverished
classes (mainly labor, the middle sectors, the urban poor, and the
peasantry) will help to explain this unforeseen development and
the important changes that took place in the relations between
the state and subordinate classes as a result.

Aggregate figures on social conditions are unsatisfactory, because they tend to even out internal inequalities between social

categories (those between men and women; between the formally employed, the underemployed, and the openly unemployed; between town and country; etc.), which, in Mexico, have always been particularly sharp. Yet they provide an approximate measure of the depth to which the standard of living of the majority of the Mexican population was allowed to sink during the 1980s. Taking 1980 as the base year (1980 = 100), wages declined to 43 by 1987 (Brachet-Marquez and Sheradden, 1993). During the same period, the health expenditures index fell from 100 to 88.27, according to official figures.[30]

Rather than measure changes in the size of the minimum wage, as in the past, recent research has focused on changes in the purchasing power of the minimum wage with respect to the Canasta Normativa de Necesidades Esenciales (CNSE—Normative Basket of Essential Needs), a package of essential goods and services defined by COPLAMAR in the early 1980s (COPLAMAR, 1983).[31] Julio Boltvinik (1987) calculates that, from 1963 to 1977, the number of full-time minimum wage jobs necessary to purchase the CNSE for a household decreased from 3.4 to 1.6. From 1978 to 1982, the situation remained relatively stable. From 1983 on, however, this number increased steadily, reaching 3.3 in 1987. Another study shows the evolution of the "legal margination gap," representing the percentage of the population whose consumption patterns indicate that they cannot afford the CNSE. This gap dwindled from 56 percent to 3 percent between 1963 and 1977, remained relatively stable between 1977 and 1982, and grew again to 50 percent from 1983 to 1987. In other words, by 1987 the satisfaction of basic necessities had descended back to the 1963 level.[32]

Contrary to government claims, health and welfare services also suffered considerable cuts. Per capita health expenditures declined by 47.7 percent between 1980 and 1987 (Valdés Olmedo, 1991), leading to increased congestion in public health facilities. Nevertheless, the setback was less marked than that in wages.[33] Thus, it can be said that the welfare package was defended by the government, despite politically insensitive creditor pressures for more budget cuts. In 1984, for example, health was declared a constitutional right, presumably in an effort to prevent further creditor pressures on the health budget. Simultaneously, a policy of decentralization of health and education was under way. About 25 percent of the COPLAMAR clinics were incorporated into state public health departments, thereby partially relieving federal budgetary responsibility for these services. The immediate result was adminstrative chaos and increased costs to service recipients (e.g., the obligation to purchase drugs, which had been free under COPLAMAR), which could easily crystallize into social protest.[34] The reform was halted midway, leaving the potentially most contentious states (northern and southeastern) out of the reform.

On December 15, 1987, two months after Carlos Salinas de Gortari had been duly *destapado* (unveiled) as PRI's candidate for the presidency, President de la Madrid announced yet a new package of economic measures—the Pacto de Solidaridad Económica (PSE—Economic Solidarity Pact)—aimed at stopping inflation. The proposal was a combination of wage and price freezes and control over the rate of decline in the value of the peso with respect to the U.S. dollar. The president announced that through this policy, Mexico would be put back on the road to price stability and steady growth no later than December 1988 (when the new administration was to take office). This prediction depended, once again, on labor's willingness to make the necessary sacrifices. At the time that the PSE was announced, the 1988 economic forecast predicted 135 percent inflation (the highest since the Revolution) and a public deficit of 18.5 percent of GDP (Whitehead, 1989:183). Since 1982, experts in the financial sector had been disagreeing on the best remedy for the economic crisis: shock or no shock, exchange control or no exchange control, and so on. The decision to launch the PSE cut the Gordian knot dividing government elites.

No social analyst has been close enough to the chambers of power to be able to report what negotiations went on prior to this decision or what role different sectors played in its making. A price freeze was a likely issue, as it had been a steady demand of labor and urban popular organizations (the *coordinadoras*) since the onset of the crisis. In addition, the CTM had been threatening to call a general strike by January 1, 1988, unless a substantial wage hike was granted. Before a presidential election—especially with a candidate who was not labor's favorite—such demands could not be ignored. But labor and the urban masses were not the only ones who stood to benefit from this measure. It was also clear that business elites, who had been invited to sit on the commission overseeing the implementation of the pact, gained a long-awaited foothold in the government. Although several elements in that group had initially quibbled over its terms, the pact had the approval of the sector as a whole. For the government, on the other hand, the relative loss of autonomy in economic decision making, which resulted from the inclusion of business, was more than compensated by its success in disarming business opposition. In exchange for this concession, the government now could count on the bourgeoisie to actively participate in fighting inflation, instead of provoking it or investing its capital abroad.[35] For international creditors, on the other hand, the measure could only be applauded.

By March 1988, long before the election took place, the rate of inflation had been substantially reduced, and the PSE was officially declared a success. In April, the pact was consolidated as a permanent and compulsory device and renamed the Pacto de Estabilidad y Crecimiento Económico (PECE—Pact of Stability and Economic Growth). As a result, capital, which had flown to the United States, returned, taking advantage of the new monetary stability and extremely lucrative interest rates (fluctuating between 45 percent and 57 percent). At that point, the PAN ceased to be the spokesman for big business in Mexico, and the dangerous possibility of a conservative alliance of the middle sectors with big capital was forestalled.

Despite the PSE's early success, it did not bring political peace. The 1988 presidential campaign turned out (unexpectedly, for most observers of Mexican political life) to be the stormiest since 1940. Like Avila Camacho's campaign, it was blemished by electoral fraud, perpetrated in order to save a system that was no longer recognized as legitimate by vast sectors of the population—on the left, as well as on the right, of the political spectrum.[36] Whereas the state and municipal elections of 1982, 1985, and 1986 had evidenced the political mobilization of the conservative opposition led by the PAN, a new left-center political actor—the National Democratic Front (FDN)—now appeared on the political scene, born of the merger between a reformist wing of the PRI and several leftist parties.

The FDN was headed by Cuauhtemoc Cárdenas, the son of the legendary Lázaro Cárdenas, who instantly captured the enthusiasm of the crowds, which filled the entire Zócalo of Mexico City, probably for the first time for an opposition candidate. This new source of opposition was far more threatening than the PAN to the ruling party, because it represented a preemption of the official ideology of social justice by a renegade group capable of revitalizing revolutionary ideals, at a time when virtually all subordinate groups felt let down by the state. The very lack of definition by the new coalition of precise economic goals and policies achieved a conjunctural coalescence of aspirations for change of a vast sector of the Mexican population above and beyond corporatist arrangements. It brought together the new urban movements (Tamayo, 1990), dissident labor, teachers and peasants, students, professionals, and intellectuals.

The 1988 presidential election was a crucial turning point. Carlos Salinas de Gortari obtained 48.7 percent of the votes nationwide; he lost the election in the large cities (Mexico City, Guadalajara, and Monterrey); and one out of every four candidates of the official party in the Chamber of Deputies was unseated by a candidate of the opposition. Cuauhtemoc Cárdenas officially obtained 30 percent of the votes, against 16.2 percent for Manuel Clouthier, the PAN's candidate (Molinar Horcasitas and Weldon, 1990). This event openly showed the malfunctions of the corporatist mechanisms of political control over the subordinate classes: in the cities, the old electoral machine, which had been limping for some time, broke down in many places and had to be rescued by electoral fraud. The year 1988, therefore, witnessed the transmutation of the sectoral discontent that had previously flowed through corporatist channels (and received limited sector-specific solutions) into direct and massive (although divided) electoral opposition. Lastly, 1988 demonstrated the unwillingness of the party cadres to accept electoral defeat.

After endless delays in announcing the result of the election and amid protests by the opposition, Carlos Salinas de Gortari was declared the winner. The uncompromising attitude of the Electoral College, which examined fraud claims after the election, gave the defeated opposition candidates little alternative but to accept or rebel. Shortly after initial calls for civil disobedience by both candidates, political effervescence quietly subsided. Two reasons can be offered for this sudden change of mood. First, the coalitions behind the opposition parties began to lose their solidarity as soon as the election was over: the PAN, because big business, seduced by its new role in economic decision making, no longer supported it; and the FDN, because its fragile organizational basis was threatened, both from within and by the government's determination to dissolve the coalition. The second and main reason was the president elect's resolve to respond to the demands that had very nearly cost him the election.

THE NEW SYNTHESIS, 1989–1990

The Salinas administration took office in December 1988 under singularly inauspicious circumstances. Although inflation was considerably reduced by a strict implementation of the PECE, the economy was still in recession, and external debt strained to the extreme the country's fiscal capacity. The attempt (started in 1979 and continued throughout the de la Madrid period) to preserve the hegemony of the official party through limited political reform had backfired. It ushered in new political actors, potentially threatening to the regime, and strengthened old political actors beyond anything contemplated by this reform. Therefore, the PRI's majority was frittered away on both sides of the political spectrum, generating contradictory pressures for change on the new government. Out of this seemingly irreconcilable conjunction of business, middle-class, and popular demands emerged an unusual combination of political reformism, economic neoliberalism, and social welfarism during the first two years of the Salinas administration. The first contemplated the destruction of the basis for competitive politics and the transformation of the official party into a more responsive organ of the state; the second chose the regional free-trade route to economic recovery; the third rekindled the popular alliance via a revamped welfare program.

The disaggregation of the Cardenist front took place in several well-orchestrated steps. First, a series of new electoral laws (approved by the triumphant party) foreclosed the future possibility of the formation of an electoral coalition of the kind that had taken place in the 1988 election. Neo-Cardenism, if it was to survive within the relatively protective cover of an officially tolerated opposition party, had to persuade all existing leftist parties to disappear—a near impossible task, given the long tradition of intense rivalry that prevailed among the latter. It also had to obtain the unwavering loyalty of the urban masses as incorporated into the new-born urban movements. This was also a formidable task, given the known resistance of these movements to any formal party incorporation (Street, 1991). As the FDN dissolved, Cuauhtemoc Cárdenas attempted to reconstruct the alliance of the left by creating the Partido Revolucionario Democrático (PRD—Revolutionary Democratic Party). But the momentum had been lost. He succeeded only in creating another officially tolerated but politically harmless opposition party.

The second move to strengthen the new government was to remove from power ineffective or rebellious official union bosses: Joaquin Galicia, the contentious oil boss who boasted of having contributed financially to the Cardenist campaign, and Jonjitud Barrios, the ineffective and demanding SNTE boss who had been unable to uproot the teachers' democratic tendency. Following a month-long strike in April 1989, wage concessions were offered to teachers. The CTM, on the other hand, was merely further marginalized, in favor of the CROC.

The most decisive measure in the strategy to revive the tottering popular alliance was the creation of the Programa Nacional de Solidaridad (PRONASOL—National Solidarity Program) which was to distribute benefits directly to the urban and rural poor. PRONASOL's announced goals were to fight poverty, promote research on the living conditions of the poor, and find alternatives to improve their situation (Consejo Consultivo, 1990).[37] Three basic strategies were contemplated: (1) direct provision of health, education, food, housing, and urban services to the needy, (2) agricultural development and direct financial support to peasants to promote the growth of peasant agriculture and microenterprises, and (3) regional development in the most underdeveloped areas (Consejo Consultivo, 1990:141; Gonzalez Tiburcio, 1991).

PRONASOL was both a repackaged and an enlarged version of existing public programs. It provided services to urban slum areas such as water, drainage, electricity, and road building, which had been provided from the budget of the Ministry of Public Works. Primary health care centers and rural hospitals were now financed by IMSS's former COPLAMAR budget. And credit to rural communities replaced BANRURAL. To these basic programs were added a sprinkling of poorly funded but politically crucial new programs, such as scholarships to primary- and secondary-school students and financial aid to small businesses, women's groups, and so on. But PRONASOL was something more than a welfare package. The great innovation, to which no doubt it owed its resounding political success among the urban poor, was the provision for the active participation of the programs' beneficiaries—especially through cofinancing, but also in program design and implementation. At last there was a political formula exactly tailored to people's need for concrete programs and benefits. The poor were made to provide matching funds for all the projects (which relieved budgetary pressures), but they were also made to feel an active part of economic reconstruction.

By comparison, the PRD had little to offer after 1988.[38] The very demands on the basis of which it had galvanized the crowds in 1988 were being met by the government. Dissidence, therefore, had once more led to social reform. But it had also, as before, lost its political resources and the organizational framework that had made possible its threat to the political status quo. Would the old corporatist alliance, once again, benefit from his crisis? Once more, the Salinista response avoided the straight line. Inaugurating a new direct populist style, the government phased out the CNOP and elevated PRONASOL to cabinet level. The labor side of corporatism was left standing, yet the old union dinosaurs were clearly on the retreat: first, they lost their privileged representation in Congress, as machine government was gradually replaced, for the urban areas, by the direct electoral appeal of the official party, based on campaign promises. Second, they remained at the margin of labor politics, their role as intermediaries being replaced by direct bargaining between the president and individual unions: in particular, wage raises were tied to productivity increases, thereby favoring workers from the dynamic economic sectors without fanning inflation.

As for the rural population, it remained faithful to the CNC, which there was no urgency to replace, at least not until agricultural reforms proved too strong for its capacity to repress discontent. (The acid test of this vast experiment was to be the 1991 legislative election, which would see the triumph of the PRI and marginalization of the PRD and the PAN.) Mexico's authoritarianism had survived, but it had also changed. The triggering force for this process was the challenge from below, contained and transformed by social reform. How these changes would, in turn, open up new spaces and opportunities for new challenges in the future could not yet be anticipated.

CONCLUSION

In the period analyzed in this chapter, a new element— state-directed political reform—complicated the moves and countermoves of players to transform the pact of domination. Although they all aimed at reinforcing the legitimacy of the one-party system, the motives behind the reform were different in each case. They also had in common, however, the overconfidence on the part of state elites in their control of the political process, resulting in the unanticipated opening up of institutional spaces from which pressures from below could be exerted.

During the Echeverría administration, the remobilization of labor was used as a political shield to ward off business opposition to the social reforms needed to refurbish the popular alliance after the inequalities generated by the latter part of "stabilizing development." But this strategy backfired by simultaneously endangering the alliance with official labor and weakening state control over dissidence. To revive the old alliance and suffocate union independence, a major piece of social legislation—INFONAVIT—was enacted. But in this case again, the policy did not immediately achieve its goal.

From 1976 to 1982, a political reform was launched to channel and control the labor mobilization imprudently triggered by the previous administration, as well as to revive flagging electoral participation. While this reform achieved its goal of controlling labor dissidence, it led to the formation of local political organizations, which were soon to detach themselves from the official apparatus. It also stimulated the emergence of social movements pushing for democracy within the teachers' union and even within the official party itself.

In the period from 1982 to 1988, the state was unable to control the growth and coalescence of these different forces, none of which individually represented a visible threat to the status quo. The historical convergence of political liberalization, a new—yet untarnished—mouthpiece for the impoverished masses (neo-Cardenism) and widespread discontent led to the electoral challenge of 1988. The state's reaction to this unexpected threat to the regime was, again, to resort to social reform, at the same time as it fundamentally transformed the rules by which the hegemony of the official party was to be maintained in the future. In this case, again, social peace was obtained at the price of what appeared to be a major social reform, and the very forces that had made it possible was dismantled. As so many times before, the state temporarily regained control of the political process, but the changes undergone in the process were no doubt gestating new challenges.

6

Conclusion

It is now time to review the evidence gleaned from the historical record during the three periods covered and reexamine my initial postulates, analytical tool, and hypothesis in the light of these findings. Rather than a fluid narrative that selects actors and events following a broad analytical framework, we need to schematize and systematize the answers provided by the historical record. A first question is, When does one pact of domination start and the preceding one end? Although the historical process of change is continuous, the dynamics of change accelerate or slow down under the effect of specific events, actions, and contextual conditions. A second question, which complements the first, is the question of agency: Who takes the initiative in pushing for change in the pact of domination at different junctures? Finally, we must make a brief inventory of what has been gained, apart from the satisfaction of finding a reasonable fit between explanation and data, from establishing a relation between pressures from below and state reform. These questions range from what kind of problems may be clarified by these findings or what new avenues for further research they suggest to how useful the analytical approach selected may be in examining other cases.

The Pact of Domination from
1910 to 1990: A Summary

From 1910 to 1913, workers struggle to transform the Porfirian pact of domination. They are aided by the reinstatement of the 1857 Constitution in two ways: their demands now have a legal basis, and the state assists them via rudimentary implementation. The reinstatement of the 1857 Constitution, although it is not specifically aimed at benefiting labor, strengthens labor's position vis-à-vis employers. At this initial stage, renascent labor organizations individually exert pressures case by case on capitalists in order to change the pact of domination inherited from the previous period, despite capitalists' resistance.

Labor begins to acquire the capacity to exert pressure on the state gradually, over the years from 1917 to 1928, as it is incorporated into the coalition supporting the nascent postrevolutionary state. The beginning of this process can be traced to the drafting of the 1917 Constitution, interpreting Obregón's move to impose a more socially progressive text as motivated by the dependence of the revolutionary coalition on labor (and peasant) support. Most analysts argue that the concessions embodied in the Constitution were preemptive. This analysis suggests, on the contrary, that Obregón's political calculus was in no small way influenced by the proven capacity of workers (and peasants) for insurgency.

The institutionalization of this new pact is no smoother than the institutionalization of the regime itself, which it closely follows: employer resistance, labor militancy, and the vagaries of the economic cycle create constant tensions between dissatisfied workers and uncooperative employers. The state's efforts to stabilize this process begin in earnest after it has acquired external political recognition, at the price of extremely costly war damages and economic concessions to U.S. investors. One instrument of this policy is a Labor Code solidifying labor's past gains and acting as a moderator between capitalists and workers. It will achieve its objective only as long as the advantage of disciplined over independent labor can be maintained. Consequently it breaks down when the state-appointed leadership becomes too corrupt to transmit pressures from below, and the Great Depression ends the state's capacity to maintain the gains accumulated in the past by the rank and file. At this point, the state has lost the initiative and become dependent again upon support from below. In other words, the conditions have been created for the construction of a new pact of domination.

The period from 1934 to 1940 witnesses the return to direct labor pressures on capital. This change comes neither "from above" nor "from below" but represents a joint strategy: for labor, it means the possibility of renegotiating the pact of domination, at the price of incorporation into the state; for the state, it signifies renewed strength from the incorporation of a mobilizable movement, at the price of exerting pressure on capital. The explosiveness of this process is in no small part caused by Calles's repeated attempts to topple the government and by the stubborn resistance of foreign oil companies to the changes taking place in the pact of domination.

The generalized adverse reaction of capitalists to the events of this period reminds us that, if the state cannot impose the terms of exploitation on labor (the argument that occupies us), neither can it do so on capital. In 1939, the conjunction of economic downturn and continued labor pressures for more pay and more benefits spells potential disaster for the regime. Pressured by capital flight and the threat of a chaotic process of *sexenio* transition, the state takes the initiative to slow down the process of pact transformation, aided by the leadership of the labor movement.

Throughout the 1940s and until 1954, the state takes a series of initiatives (some failed, others successful) to restrict the institutional means through which labor can become an independent political actor and push for more changes in the pact of domination. From the initial, mild policies of Unidad Nacional and the failed Pacto Obrero to the suppression of union democracy in 1946–1948, Mexico enters into a spiral of ever more coercive measures. Labor leadership, as intended by the state, is reduced to responding to directives from above. In effect, the Cardenist pact of domination is destroyed, and a far less pallatable new pact is forced upon labor.

Far from taking this change passively, however, the labor leadership displaced by the new policies threatens to reconstitute an independent labor movement. This leads the state to offer and expand social security as a way to retain membership in controlled labor organizations and to limit rank-and-file attraction to independent movements. The pact of domination is changing again to labor's advantage (or rather, this reform sweetens the losses suffered) under the initiative of the state.

The year 1954 constitutes a new watershed: it marks simultaneously a currency devaluation, which further brings down the already low purchasing power of wage earners, the resurgence of labor militancy, and the adoption of deficit financing. Despite the limitations imposed by the pact of domination of the 1940s on legitimate means of labor protest, official labor leaders are either expelled or turned around by the rank and file, which threatens once again to dissolve the PRI's labor bloc. The state's conciliatory responses through wage and social policies reestablishes order, yet without altering the institutional terms of labor's subordination.

The next major disturbance in this arrangement comes from the middle class, rather than from labor: the 1968 student uprising marks the first stirrings of the aspirations for meaningful political participation by a growing, educated middle sector. Although there are no clear signs that the disturbance might reach other groups, the state acts preemptively to prevent labor mobilization by promising (although not implementing) state-sponsored housing for workers. The aftermath of the student uprising nevertheless reorients the state to offer, in the following *sexenio*, a political "opening," which, in turn, loosens up the institutional obstacles set against pact renegotiation by labor. The tensions triggered by the ensuing resurgence of demands for union democracy lead to yet another concession—INFONAVIT—and the subsequent closure of the political system, replaced by a more limited political reform.

Were it not for the fact that Mexico, in 1981, reaches the limits of debt-financed development, this pact of domination might have remained in place. From 1982 to 1988, however, the losses in jobs and wages plunge workers—along with other groups—into a rapid downward economic spiral. Encouraged by the absence of labor disturbances and the apparent waning of urban popular mobilizations after 1984, the government fails to respond to popular demands for price controls. The 1988 electoral challenge, which nearly puts Mexico on the road to political pluralism, dramatically changes the pact as well as the players. It redirects reformist state responses toward a new form of atomized populism, in the context of which corporatist actors lose their key roles as intermediaries. Although the reforms allow for the increased micropolitical participation of the popular sectors, they inhibit the crystallization of a new collective actor capable of defining and negotiating a new pact of domination.

In sum, between 1910 and 1990, Mexico went through six important transformations in the conditions determining its workers' allotment of the economic surplus through a set of institutionally sanctioned rules, which I define as the pact of domination: the first, from the Revolution to the Great Depression; the second, covering the Cardenist period, from 1934 to 1940; the third, from 1940 to 1954; the fourth, from 1954 to 1970; the fifth, from 1970 to 1982; and the last, starting after 1988.[1] Despite this broad periodization, however, transitions were generally fluid, except when economic collapse marked change more sharply, as in 1930–1934 and in 1982–1989. The notion of a continuously changing pact, marked by change-producing events, decisions, and interactions, therefore, reflects the historical record more faithfully than the assertion that there have been distinct pacts.

Whether any player preponderantly takes the initiative in pact transformation is a crucial question. In the early phase, workers took the initiative of making demands on capitalists, and the state merely tried to mediate or repress these conflicts. The ineffectiveness of these attempts (and the dangers to political stability it involved for the regime) prompted state elites to codify, centralize, and regulate labor-capital relations. Yet, this very process was an interactive one, as it incorporated the changes wrought by worker mobilizations.

Although state intervention eased labor's negotiation of change with capital, it was also intended to reduce labor to a minimal reactive role. The crux of the argument in the study is that this scheme had limits, however, as witnessed by the repeated explosions that periodically shook (and finally destroyed) corporatism in Mexico. This study shows that such explosions have occurred at crucial historical moments, when economic conditions drastically deteriorated, and officially appointed labor leaders either failed to transmit rank-and-file pressures or were ignored by state elites. This underlines the alternately repressive and mobilizing mediating role these leaders played in the process of change, contrary to their caricaturing in much of the literature as insensitive, corrupt, and rigidly bent on preventing change. Like state elites, these leaders were active agents involved in the complex interactive dynamics of change—yielding here, resisting there—but always mindful of maintaining their position. But like state elites, also, they miscalculated and occasionally lost the initiative, thereby loosening up the structure of domination. These leaders can, therefore, be considered neither as state agents (as often pictured) nor authentic leaders of the rank and file (as they would like to appear) but as alternately playing both these roles, depending on their appreciation of their interests in given situations.

If state elites have not always had the initiative in pact transformation, they have, nevertheless, followed a consistent strategy: reward the rank and file with reforms and behead the independent movements through which those demands were made, hence, the common charge that they co-opted these movements. A more accurate term would be *demobilization*, since the intent, clearly, was to prevent future mobilizations. That this strategy never worked for any length of time is testified to by the periodic reorganizations and remobilizations of labor and other repressed movements around old or new leaders and issues. The political wane of labor in the 1980s, rather than evidence of the state's final success in erasing that actor from the political scene, should be interpreted in light of the restructuring of its organizations, especially the decentralization of power, the restructuring of production (especially regionally, but also in terms of branches of industry and products), and the reorientation of the Mexican economy toward exports. This does not mean that labor will necessarily resurface as such—if the sectorially mixed urban mobilizations of the 1980s are any indication of Mexico's political future. The argument sustained in this book is not that labor alone has had the capacity or been given the historical mission to renegotiate the terms of subordination to capitalism but that it has been one of the principal and best-documented actors. Its disappearance or merger with other actors in no way invalidates this argument.

COMPETING EXPLANATIONS

My leading postulate is that pressures from below are responsible for reforms. This does not mean that state reformist responses cannot be encouraged or inhibited for other reasons. We must therefore examine competing explanations of these reforms.

Economic Factors

Against the hypothesis proposed in this study, one could argue that the likelihood that the state will offer concessions to labor demands depends on the economic cycle and the model of development adopted by the state. The Lopez Mateos administration (1958–1964), for example, because it coincided with economic prosperity, was allegedly in a better position than its predecessor to make concessions. Yet, the decision to impose profit sharing to capital was made before the economy revived. The Miguel Alemán administration (1946–1952), on the other hand, initially faced a situation of capital flight, which may be used as an argument to explain its failure to yield to labor pressures. Yet, the Korean war boom occurred during this same period without visible changes for labor. Likewise, the succeeding government (1952–1958) found itself in dire economic straits, which eventually necessitated a currency devaluation. Yet, it yielded to labor pressures for wage increases following the devaluation, which was bound to counteract the positive effects expected of that measure.

Other counterexamples to a simple cyclic explanation come to mind: Carranza granted labor's demands, much against his own inclination and in the midst of an economic debacle. Likewise, Cárdenas first carried out social reforms, in his native Michoacan, when the Great Depression was at its strongest and continued to do so as president before the economy fully recovered. It is true, however, that economically timely reforms were politically easier to carry through, whereas untimely reforms were bitterly opposed by capital (e.g., in 1939 and in 1975–1976). It is also true that the state had a greater tendency to yield to pressures from capital in times of recession by limiting or refusing to grant wage raises, unless social unrest threatened to be a greater evil than discontent from capitalists. These examples, rather than invalidate my claim, indicate that pressures from below and social reforms are more politically risky in times of recession than during economic booms, for those who agitate for change as well as for state elites who respond to these pressures. They also indicate that economic contraction postpones, rather than prevents, the implementation of welfare programs.

An alternative economicist explanation is that only limited and fiscally inexpensive reforms are adopted during times of recession, fiscally costly reforms being restricted to boom periods. Yet, social security and profit sharing adopted at economically inauspicious times were as valiantly opposed by the representatives of capital as in prosperous periods. Nevertheless, they were adopted. Public housing, on the other hand, was not heralded by an economic boom and had to be financed by further debt. Finally, when the expansion of social security to the uninsured population was decreed in 1973, the state's coffers were virtually empty and external debt was soaring to new heights. The oil boom of 1980–1982, on the other hand, did not see the expansion of labor's welfare benefits (although the rural population did receive long-awaited health services). Lastly, the constitutional right to health was declared in 1984, when the country was in the worst phase of the economic crisis of the 1980s and, therefore, least likely to be able to meet this new obligation.

In general, the process of building up the Mexican welfare system (and indeed, the Mexican economy) has been fiscally improvident. Welfare expenditures have, therefore, always been costly. Throughout postrevolutionary history, the Mexican state, no matter how apparently strong, has been endemically incapable of extracting substantial fiscal revenues from capital. Every serious attempt to increase corporate taxes (in particular, those by Cárdenas or Echeverría) has been defeated. It is surprising, under such dismal circumstances, that Mexico has been able to build up a welfare system at all. Fiscal weakness, however, has slowed down the process of implementation of welfare measures. Social security, although adopted early, took a very long time to reach more than a tiny percentage of the population. The Echeverría administration's Solidarity Program, aimed at including the whole population in social security, was never implemented except for very restricted services, such as hospital emergency service and family planning. The following administration's COPLAMAR program was formally created in the first months of 1977 but remained virtually unimplemented until the oil boom was well under way.

From the late 1950s until 1982, the only solution to Mexico's permanent fiscal impasse was debt financing. Foreign investors were enticed by cheap labor (in addition to the state-financed infrastructure, unlimited credit, non-implementation of pollution regulations, and a protected market); yet they also needed this cheap labor force to be literate, well fed, and reasonably happy about its lot. The state conciliated these contradictory requirements of economic growth and social peace by maintaining low wages while sustaining minimum living standards via welfare programs. The model of "stabilizing development" based on debt was adopted at a moment when all the institutional resources to control labor demands, short of massive brutal force, had been virtually exhausted. The adoption of a Keynesian approach to economic growth was, therefore, not just a matter of imitation but a strong internal requirement for the permanence of the form of political domination that had prevailed since the 1920s.

This model could work only as long as economic growth stayed ahead of debt. When this situation was reversed, from August 1981 on, wages regressed to levels corresponding to the 1960s. Per capita expenditures in health and education declined proportionately less, indicating the political decision to soften the decline in living standards. Nevertheless, the continuing losses in real wages and employment levels throughout the 1980s represented a permanent risk to the ruling regime, culminating in the 1988 thwarted electoral rebellion. Likewise, the reorientation of the Mexican model of development toward an economy of free exchange of goods but controlled wages, evident in the 1990s, incorporated a permanent risk of popular upheaval, to which PRONASOL provided only a temporary (and probably short-lived) answer.

In sum, it is evident that economic cycles and profound changes in the approach to development have affected the timing and the rate of change in the pact of domination. It nevertheless remains true that neither economic cycles nor the orientation of the economic policy are sufficient to explain the government concessions labor has obtained in the past by exerting pressures capable of destabilizing the regime.

External Influence

The international climate and the influence of other states on state decisions have often been cited as determinants of welfare decisions. According to this interpretation, the worldwide spread of given public policies is not merely the result of independent decisions within the confines of nation-states but the consequence of the international diffusion of innovation (Rogers and Shoemaker, 1971). David Collier and Richard Messick (1975) argue, for example, that social security adoption in Latin America was the consequence of such diffusion from developed to underdeveloped countries, manifesting the desire of leaders of developing countries to appear modern and progressive. Within this line of thinking, Roemer (1971, 1973) also notes that international organizations, by establishing norms of minimum standards of living, influenced national decisions to adopt social security legislation.

Clearly, in the case of Mexico, the action of international organizations such as the ILO and the diffusion of social security in other countries of the region (particularly in Chile and Costa Rica) served to mollify conservative opposition. In particular, the study prepared by the ILO's actuarial experts, proclaimed as a model study in international circles, demonstrated that the cost of social security adoption to Mexican employers would amount to only 6 percent of wages, which would increase their costs by only 1.5 percent. Yet the diffusion hypothesis cannot explain the timing of adoption, which, in Mexico corresponded to the policy of "national unity" aimed at reconciling labor and capital while restricting labor militancy and keeping wages low. Moreover, the diffusion theory is valid only where international debate exists regarding a particular policy, which was not the case for profit sharing or public housing.

Lastly, the diffusion hypothesis focuses almost exclusively on adoption, taking implementation for granted. In Mexico, as we noted, adoption did not establish a universal, automatic right of access to benefits. While all Mexican wage earners were theoretically to be included in social insurance coverage or public housing programs, inclusion has been carried out on a gradual basis and has never reached 100 percent. The decision of who was to be included remained a presidential prerogative, exercised at politically strategic moments as a gesture of concession to demands from below. The diffusion hypothesis, therefore, although it adds important elements to the central hypothesis of this study, cannot be considered a substitute for the explanation I propose.

The diffusion hypothesis also predicts that welfare in any one country will be phased out if the international climate is propitious to welfare cuts. Nevertheless, far from emulating southern cone dictatorships in the 1970s and 1980s or the Reagan and Bush administrations' suppression of social expenditures, Mexico retained and expanded its welfare apparatus right up to the collapse of 1982. Even after that date, welfare expenditures did not decline as fast as other indicators of living standards, and at no point did the official discourse use antiwelfare neoliberal slogans. In fact, the Miguel de la Madrid administration was at pains to demonstrate (with the use of incomplete and misleading statistics) that the welfare net had expanded. The declaration of the constitutional right to health in 1984 and continued efforts to maintain and expand the COPLAMAR network also flies in the face of the diffusion hypothesis.

Another version of the external influence hypothesis concerns the direct or indirect political interference of another power into internal decisions. It has been argued, for example, that the Cárdenas reforms were viable because their timing corresponded to the Roosevelt administration in the United States, which adopted similar reformist policies. It has also been suggested that the anti-labor policies of the 1940s coincided with the worst period of the Cold War, which unleashed anticommunist zeal all over Latin America, allegedly dictated by the United States. Likewise, the reforms undertaken in the 1960s can be seen as the result of the climate of reformism actively promoted in the region by the United States following the Cuban Revolution, when the Alliance for Progress briefly flourished. Conversely, when the U.S. zeal for reforms to prevent revolution waned in the midsixties, social programs should also have declined.

As in the case of the economicist approach, the actions of the United States, when favorable to social reforms, have undeniably helped make internal reform initiatives more palatable to those opposed, especially when international funds were available to finance them, as in the 1960s. Yet, it would be a mistake to portray Mexican presidents as mere political weather vanes, following the direction set by the United States. When Lopez Mateos promised in 1958 that his government would be of the extreme left within the Constitution, the Cuban Revolution had not yet triumphed, and the Punta del Este Conference not yet been convened. Likewise, Cárdenas did not wait for the New Deal to define his political profile. And both Diaz Ordaz (1964–1970) and Alemán (1940–1946) had antecedents of dealing violently with political conflict and, therefore, had no need to find new models to follow.

Above and beyond macroeconomic or international currents explanations is the fact that very few economic gains have been achieved by the Mexican working class without struggle, regardless of the allies or enemies found along the way.

Interelite Competition

It has been suggested that the dynamics of change in Mexico have been prompted more by interelite rivalries than by tensions between the state and subordinate groups. Ruth Collier (1982), for example, argues that the incorporation of the popular sectors into the revolutionary regime was due to the crucial role they played in the hegemonic struggles within the revolutionary elite. This should mean that the balance of power between caudillos in the early phase of the Revolution was precarious enough that labor's defection from one faction could spell its political defeat and its opponent's victory.

Let us briefly go back to 1917 to reexamine the evidence in the light of this hypothesis. It leads us to expect that if Carranza had resisted Obregón's reformist proposal (Article 123 of the Constitution), Obregón could have opted for mobilizing workers and peasants against the Primer Jefe, who would have then been swept aside. When closely matched to the political situation of the time, however, this interpretation appears highly implausible. Such a "competitive" strategy would have been so uncertain for the victorious faction as to be foolhardy. The debates that took place at the Aguascalientes Convention three years earlier, when the constitutionalist coalition met to define its agenda, laid bare the internal ideological divisions inside the victorious camp. Obregón's followers were moderates who were shocked by Zapata's radical demands and outraged by Villa's banditism. Obregón was, therefore, not free to simply take his followers with him and choose Zapata and Villa against Carranza. Instead, he continued to support Carranza for three more years and helped him suppress both Villa and Zapata, using the worker batallions to rout them militarily. To mobilize peasants and workers against Carranza in 1917 was not a real political option: it would have revived these grass-roots movements and the war would probably have been resumed. Article 123, on the contrary, was meant to demonstrate to the peasant and worker delegates who met in Querétaro that they did not need extremist leaders, such as Zapata or Villa, to be included in the new regime.

In short, open competition for popular support within the revolutionary coalition could only endanger the new regime. That Obregón was the driving force behind the reforms incorporated into the Constitution testifies to his political acumen more than to a rivalry with Carranza. Such rivalry, by all accounts, only developed two years later, when Carranza tried to prevent Obregón from succeeding him as president.

The interrivalry hypothesis would seem most clearly sustained in the succession from Carranza to Obregón. Yet in this case again, it is unlikely that CROM or the demoblizied peasantry would have been able to ensure Obregón's victory. Obregón succeeded in removing Carranza from power by military means. Thereafter, popular support (ascertained by an election) helped him consolidate his government. The social peace earned by reforms also facilitated the delicate task of obtaining the backing of the United States, an indispensable step to ensure military defense against potential military coups.

The interelite rivalry explanation fares even less well after the caudillo era ended in 1924 with the orderly designation of the fairly conservative Plutarco Elías Calles as Obregón's successor. Adolfo de la Huerta's attempt to engineer a coup in 1924 by seeking support from labor's more radical elements failed, not for the obvious reason that these groups were too weak to confront the government but mainly because Obregón's government had sufficiently benefited rank-and-file labor to prevent their radicalization by anarchist-syndicalist elements. In other words, these unions had lost their mobilizing capacity, thanks in great part to Obregón's conciliatory policies toward nonanarchist unions, especially CROM.

Finally, if by interelite competition is meant simply the notion that the state is always divided between competing reformists and nonreformists—true of any state with any degree of internal political differentiation—it cannot mean that they compete for popular support in the pluralist sense of the term, given the ritual character of elections in Mexico. But it can mean that an internally plural state is in a better position than a monolithic one to be sensitive to pressures from below and their possible consequences for state stability. This explanation therefore reinforces, rather than invalidates, the position that reforms are triggered by pressures from below. It also prompts the question of why, and especially *when*, the Mexican state is likely to recruit and heed the advice of reformist elites, despite the often starkly antidemocratic principles that govern this process. If the Cárdenas and Lopez Mateos appointments are any indication, it would seem that elite recruitment also follows the dynamics of pressures from below. It would seem, therefore, that the famed Mexican political culture of give-and-take is not the cause, but the consequence, of a reformist and "inclusionary" tendency. This tendency has been historically learned and periodically reinforced by pressures for pact renegotiation.

The End of Contentious Labor

This argument might take the following form: granted that, in the past, labor played a central role in pushing for reforms, it has now lost this role (through attrition, economic restructuring, the dismantling of corporatism, etc.), and thus no more pressures from below can be expected in the future. This argument must be confronted, not because this study relies exclusively on labor as a force from below but because some remnants of the Marxist faith in the special mission of workers for radical political change still linger. The demise of the labor movement in the postindustrial age, therefore, may also presage the end of progressive change.

To begin with, it bears repeating that I have nowhere in this study pretended that labor organizations have single-handedly forced reforms upon the state. I do contend that labor's potential for mobilizing other sectors has repeatedly threatened to break down the vertical character of Mexico's political organization. Although this analysis centers on labor, due to the necessity of showing relevant historical evidence, I also describe mobilizations of the "popular" sector of the PRI (doctors, teachers, and students) and show the impact of these parallel mobilizations on the state's response to labor. It was the exemplary capacity of labor that posed a threat to the regime (as I have asserted from the beginning), not its strength as measured in numbers or militancy. Precisely because this threat was always more potential than real (as power always is), it is impossible to isolate objective criteria to define how serious a threat it was at any one moment. The major error committed by contemporary analysts has been to minimize the importance of such pressures by interpreting events retrospectively rather than prospectively. It is easy for us to laugh at Lombardo Toledano's attempts to form an independent party in the 1940s, but neither Avila Camacho nor Alemán were smiling at the time. By reconstituting the political situations without benefit of hindsight, which the actors themselves could not possess, this analysis tries to show that it was impossible *not* to take seriously the threats of insurgency from below.

Even though labor was not the sole political actor, doesn't its destruction inexorably change the capacity of subordinate classes to press for changes? This question is in response to the undeniable wane of labor protest and union activism in Mexico since the 1980s. The events of two historical periods—1946–1948 and

1988–1990—address this important question. In the first period, the state essentially attempted to eliminate labor as a political actor. Far from heralding a golden age for capitalists, however, the suppression of union democracy merely postponed union insurgency. The age of the "Mexican Miracle" came after the 1954–1959 reforms reestablished peace. In this first example, therefore, the labor movement was able to reconstitute itself as a political actor despite state repression.

What of the labor movement in 1990? It is a profoundly eroded and delegitimated movement, weighed down by a cynical and corrupt gerontocracy better known as "dinosaurs." It has seen its ranks diminished by the destruction of small and medium-sized enterprises during the "lost decade" and by the growth of assembly plants where labor laws are at best poorly implemented. It has also seen its rights further restricted by amendments to the 1943 Labor Code allowing for more "flexible" labor contracts that permit employers to fire their labor force without the previously stipulated "just cause". At the end of the 1980s, who could have taken seriously the threat from labor or from the popular sectors? Probably no one. Yet, the threat was carried out and was effective precisely because it was unexpected (not unlike Madero's threat to Porfirism). The interesting fact, for this argument, is that none of the component parts of the popular coalition against the PRI was of any significance by itself, hence the difficulty of predicting (and even perceiving) something that was not present until very late in the decade. What was present was a collection of separate foci of organized discontent, which were equally ready for a unique and, therefore, highly contingent convergence of actors and strategies or for a continuation of their separate trajectories of limited individual actions.

In 1993, as the writing of this book is being completed, it is difficult to visualize on what basis pressures from below may be exerted in the future. Once again, the actors capable of mounting a challenge to the established order seem to have declined in numbers or to have disappeared altogether. Yet, the analytical model proposed here still offers possibilities for the constitution of new actors and the resurrection of old ones. Will PRONASOL continue to placate urban protest when the urban poor discover (as the rural poor already have) that they have no place in the "modernization" of the economy? What will happen to the millions of landless and jobless peasants now that Article 27 of the Constitution, which gave them limited protection, has been modified (UNAM, 1992)? How will their immigration to the over-crowded cities change the political economy of the urban areas? Last but not least, what will happen when Fidel Velazquez dies, at long last? All these questions point to the transformation of actors and political processes in the future.

Although it is difficult to visualize in 1993 a democracy prematurely announced almost a decade earlier, it is undeniable that our eyes should be set on the pluralization of the Mexican political process. If the past holds any lessons, this pluralization, rather than an electoral "big bang," should follow a push-and-pull process fraught with setbacks and unexpected leaps forward. What it probably won't be, if this analysis is correct, is either a package wholly manufactured from above or a heroic conquest from below.

Mexican Exceptionalism

Of all the possible rebuttals to the thesis presented in this book, the hardest one to confront is the argument that it does not apply to other national realities. In essence, my imaginary opponent would say: yes, this scheme works for Mexico, but it does not really matter. Mexico's record of government and regime stability is an anomaly. To reconstruct its genesis as a history of partial confrontations and limited concessions, although it provides an alternative to the more structurally determinist "view from above," runs the risk, of adding one more stone to the already imposing edifice of analytical constructions that have isolated Mexico from general theorizing on the political process.

What is truly exceptional and undeniably specific to Mexico is the unique concatenation between presidential power and official party dominance, and the assurance of this dominance by the popular sectors incorporated into the party. The tight coupling of these elements has ensured the smooth succession of power for nearly seventy years. As if this were not exceptional enough, Mexico holds (with Costa Rica, which nevertheless has a wholly different political regime) a record of resolving its internal political conflicts without the help of military violence.[2] This means that the coercive power of the state can be effectively exercised only against relatively small and easily identifiable groups (e.g., student protesters in 1968 and localized peasant uprisings throughout the 1980s) but not against a very large coalition of forces, as in countless other Latin American countries. Domination in Mexico, therefore, appears to be basically an organizational affair.

Yet corporatism is no panacea for stability, as the history of Argentina and Brazil testify. Rules can be violated, as they repeatedly have been in Mexico. Despite the restrictions imposed by corporatism, the official party has been in danger, more than once, of being massively abandoned through the actions of minorities that escaped the logic of the system and yet unwittingly renewed this system by forcing its defenders to carry out limited change. The erosion of these mechanisms in the 1980s, far from changing general dynamics of change, set the Mexican political system on a new path, attempting to maintain the state's flexible formula for domination without corporatism.

In the rest of Latin America, rebellion among popular groups has more often triggered crises of governability followed by implacable military rule than this kind of flexible reformism. As several countries of the region have reverted to civilian rule based on popular elections in the midst of economic debacle, the problem of peaceful tension management and limited concessions to demands from below becomes paramount again, especially in view of recent returns to state absolutism (e.g., Peru after Alberto Fujimori's self-coup). In some cases, this problem is preemptively resolved by the potential resort to military force: in Chile, tanks and soldiers can be produced at the slightest intimation of public disorder. Such regimes, sometimes labeled "pacted democracies" (Malloy and Seligson, 1987), should be analyzed as military regimes managed by civilians. But if we visualize a democratic regime unaided by the potential resort to state terror, we must face the basic difficulty of defining the conditions under which such a regime can respond to demands from below, especially in the context of neoliberal economic policies that virtually exclude the masses.

In the Mexico of the past, this imperative was dealt with via a triangular relation between the state, independent forces, and official popular leadership, which reduced direct friction between capital and labor. We must now ask, Is this experience in any way repeatable? And if not, is the pact of domination approach condemned to intellectual parochialism?

To begin with the most obvious disclaimer, history is never repeatable. To be persuasive, my thesis had to be solidly grounded on Mexican soil. Any transplanting of the insights derived from it must be done with care—and probably in small packages.

Let us start with the most general lessons to be learned from the study. Perhaps the most important one, which by itself makes the whole enterprise worthwhile, is the conclusion—certainly transferable to other societies—that we should judge the solidity of a political regime not by the assumed virtues of its organizational features (be they corporatism or anything else) but instead, judge the solidity of these features by how well they balance the contradictory demands of accumulation and social justice. If corporatism has been successful in that respect in Mexico (at least until recently), it was not, as social scientists used to think, by virtue of its organizing principles (verticality, centralization, clientelism, presidentialism, etc.) but because Mexico's particular brand of corporatism, until 1980, managed—despite the formal rules imposed upon its players—to balance (imperfectly and with dire fiscal consequences) demands from below for social justice with economic growth.

This conclusion holds many lessons for the contemporary study of democracy, which too often reverts to definitional formalism. Democracies, especially new ones born in the wake of painful monetary stabilizations, should be studied with an eye to how well—how acceptably for the majority of the population—they can moderate and postpone the progressive aspirations they have awakened: the question, in other words, is, How do they propitiate the successful renegotiation of domination. The requirements for success are difficult to satisfy, because they depend on political traditions most new democracies lack, specifically a political culture of tolerance and bargaining.

Another general lesson has to do with the codification of the pact of domination. The incorporation of subordinate groups into the postrevolutionary regime was marked by the slow incorporation of the aspirations of these groups into the constitutional and legal texts that form the basis of government discourse. As Michael Fowley remarks (1991), these texts and the legitimizing government discourses derived from them have led to the historical construction by subordinate groups of "constitutive agendas," which state elites have had to deal with, even if they were not always willing to respect them.

If we compare, for example, Argentina, Chile, and Mexico, it is striking that, of these three, only Argentina still lacked a labor code by 1930, and only in Argentina did the wave of popular (mostly labor) demands which exploded from 1946 to 1956 under Peron produce long-lasting exclusionary conservative reactions. While Mexico and Chile were managing their pacts of domination with popular front policies in the 1930s, Argentina was going through the "infamous decade" of military-oligarchic repression of workers, from which the players emerged without any sense that the game was played according to certain rules. Military preference for "order" (even among progressive military leaders) seems to preclude the kind of conflictive give-and-take process that governs the transformation of the pact of domination. Military rule, therefore, may well be a recipe for disaster: it prepares society for the alternation between weak proto-democratic civilian regimes incapable of moderating demands from below and order-imposing military regimes that repress these demands altogether. Any society steeped in that tradition is bound to have more difficulty negotiating a stable pact of domination than one, like Chile, whose democratic past has helped to gradually ease the country out of military rule.

Is manageable domination such a great achievement that we should try to persuade other countries that this is a goal worth striving for? After all, Mexico's working class has little to boast of after seventy years of struggle. What it has obtained and the political upheavals it has spared Mexico have been very costly. Admittedly, this does not offer a very attractive utopia for the future. But is unbridled faith in the market to solve all problems a better formula? On the eve of the twenty-first century, poor countries do not have many alternatives. The lesson to be learned from Mexico's history is that, no matter what democratic or nondemocratic political formulas are historically produced in the future, they must create the mediating institutional links that limit capitalist exploitation through the dynamic management of a pact of domination. This is the condition under which they can be even minimally progressive and stop the infernal cycle of repression and ungovernability.

Such links may be created by political parties, insofar as these bodies are capable of satisfying these requirements. That is especially difficult in the age of mass political marketing and mass culture. Democracy is, therefore, no panacea, if by democracy we mean the right to vote but not to choose. This analysis of the Mexican case indicates that, unless the conflicts generated among subordinate groups by unequal development—the only kind contemplated in the economic policies of most poor countries—are effectively transmitted to the top and negotiated through solidly institutionalized mechanisms, social protest will likely trigger a repressive, rather than reformist, response. In most cases, this response will bring these countries full circle back to military or totalitarian limbo.

For Mexico, the main problem for the future is not simply how to build democracy, but how to replace the eroded institutional mechanisms of the past with new ones capable of withstanding and moderating the starker inequalities looming ahead. Although present and future administrations and intellectuals will no doubt produce a variety of blueprints for Mexico's political future, the formulas that will eventually manage the dynamics of domination will be historically constructed. If Mexico's long political tradition is anything by which to predict the future, subordinate classes will have their say in the making of this future. But they will most probably not make it just as they please.

Appendixes
Notes
Bibliography
Index

Appendix 1
General Chronology

	National Events	Labor and Social Laws	International Events
1906–08	Strike at the Cananea mine and Rio Blanco textile works		
1908		Insurance against work-related accidents in the states of Mexico and Nuevo Leon	
1910	Rigged election, F. Madero jailed		
	Armed rebellion declared by Madero (nov20)		
1911	F. Madero's Election		
	Reinstatement of the 1857 Constitution	Freedom of association for workers (unions); freedom to enter labor management agreements	

	National Events	Labor and Social Laws	International Events
		Creation of "Conciliation and Arbitration" mechanism for industrial conflicts	
1913	Madero's assassination		
1913–14	Victoriano Huerta takes power by coup		
1914–15	Emiliano Zapata & Francisco Villa unseat Huerta		Onset of WWI
1915	Aguascalientes Convention: Constitutionalists define their agenda		
1917–20	Venustiano Carranza president		Russian Revolution
1917	1917 Constitution	Art. 123 of the 1917 Constitution	
1918			Versailles Treaty
1920	Alvaro Obregon's coup against Carranza; Adolfo de la Huerta interim president (May–Dec.); Obregon elected (Dec.)		
1920–24	Alvaro Obregon president		
1923	Adolfo de la Huerta's aborted coup		
1924	Bucarelli Agreement		
1924–28	Plutarco Elías Calles president		

	National Events	Labor and Social Laws	International Events
1925	Foundation of the Bank of Mexico	Limited Social Security scheme for civil servants and armed forces	Foundation of International Labor Organization
1927		Federalization of Conciliation and Arbitration	
1928	Obregon's second election and assassination	Limited Social Security scheme for teachers	
	Foundation of the Partido Nacional Revolucionario		
1929			Onset of World Depression
1928–30	Emilio Portes Gil president		
1930–32	Pascual Ortiz Rubio president	Federal Labor Code enacted	
1932–34	Abelardo Rodriguez president		
1934		Bach-Zamora proposal for Social Security	
1934–40	Lázaro Cárdenas president		
1938	Foundation of the Partido Revolucionario Mexicano		
	Nationalization of Oil	Social Security for oil & railroad workers	
	Founding of the Partido Acción Nacional		
1939			Outbreak of WWII

	National Events	Labor and Social Laws	International Events
1940–46	Manuel Avila Camacho president		
1941	Exclusion of the Military from CTM		
1942		Workers Pact	
1943	Creation of CNOP	Social security for workers: creation of IMSS	
		Revision of the Labor Code restricts strike rights	
1945			End of WWII
1946	Founding of the Partido Revolucionario Institucional		
1946–52	Miguel Alemán president		
1948	Currency devaluation		
	Founding of the Partido Popular		
1950–53			Korean War
1952–58	Adolfo Ruiz Cortinez president		
1954	Currency devaluation	Creation of CEIMSA	
1958–64	Adolfo Lopez Mateos president		
1959		Social security for civil servants: creation of ISSSTE	Cuban Revolution

	National Events	Labor and Social Laws	International Events
1961–62		Adoption of profit sharing	Bay of Pigs Invasion & Missile Crisis
1963			Alliance for Progress
1964–70	Gustavo Díaz Ordaz president		
1968	Tlatelolco massacre of students	Amendment of Art.111 of the Labor Code to provide worker housing	Olympics Games in Mexico, French student movement
1970–76	Luis Echeverría president		
1972		Housing for workers (INFONAVIT); for civil servants (FOVISSSTE); for the poor (INDECO)	
1973			Oil Shock
1974		Population Law	
1976	Currency devaluation		
1976–82	José Lopéz Portillo president		
1977	Political Reform	Creation of COPLAMAR	
1980		Creation of Mexican Food System (SAM)	
1981	Debt payment moratorium		
1982	Bank Nationalization		

	National Events	Labor and Social Laws	International Events
1982–88	Miguel de la Madrid president	Discontinuation of Mexican Food System	
1984		Right to health declared constitutional	
1985	Earthquake	desubsidization of food and transport	
1987	Economic Solidarity Pact		
1988–94	Carlos Salinas de Gortari president		
1989	Jailing of oil union leader: Joaquin Galicia	Creation of National Solidarity Program (PRONASOL) Discontinuation of food distribution by CONASUPO	Falling down of Berlin Wall. Disintegration of the Soviet Union
1990	Phasing out of CNOP		

Appendix 2
List of Abbreviations

BANRURAL	Banco Rural (Rural Bank)
BID	Banco Internacional para el Desarrollo (International Bank for Reconstruction and Development)
BUO	Bloque Unidad Obrera (Worker Unity Bloc)
CANACINTRA	Cámara Nacional de las Industrias de Transformación (National Chamber of Transformation Industries)
CEIMSA	Compañía de Exportaciones e Importaciones Mexicanas Sociedad Anónima (Import Export Mexican Company)
CFE	Comisión Federal de Electricidad (Federal Electricity Commission)
CGOCM	Confederación General de Obreros y Campesinos de México (General Confederation of the Workers and Peasants of México)
CGT	Confederación General de Trabajadores (General Confederation of Workers)
CNC	Confederación Nacional de Campesinos (National Confederation of Peasants)
CNOP	Confederación Nacional de Organizaciones Populares (National Confederation of Popular Organizations)
CNPA	Coordinadora Nacional del Plan de Ayala (National Coordinator of the Ayala Plan)

CNSE	Canasta Normativa de Satisfactores Escenciales (Normative Basket of Essential Needs)
CNTE	Coordinadora Nacional de Trabajadores de la Educación (National Coordinator of Education Workers)
COCM	Confederación de Obreros y Campesinos de México (Mexican Confederation of Workers and Peasants)
COM	Casa del Obrero Mundial (House of the World's Worker)
CONAMUP	Coordinadora Nacional de los Movimientos Urbanos Populares (National Coordinator of Popular Urban Movements)
CONASUPO	Compañía Nacional de Subsistencias Populares (National Company of Popular Subsistence)
CONCAMIN	Confederación de Cámaras Industriales (Confederation of Industrial Chambers)
CONCANACO	Confederación de Cámaras Nacionales de Comercio (Confederation of National Chambers of Commerce)
COPARMEX	Confederación Patronal de la República Mexicana (Employers' Confederation of the Mexican Republic)
COPLAMAR	Coordinadora General del Plan Nacional de Zonas Deprimidas y Grupos Marginados (General Coordinator of the National Plan for Depressed Zones and Marginalized Groups)
CORETT	Comisión para la Regularización de la Tenencia de la Tierra (Commision for the Regulation of Land Tenure)
CROC	Confederación Revolucionaria de Obreros y Campesinos (Revolutionary Confederation of Workers and Peasants)
CROM	Confederación Regional Obrera Mexicana (Mexican Regional Confederation of Mexican Workers)
CSF	Confederación de Sociedades de Ferrocarriles (Confederation of Railroad Societies)
CT	Congreso del Trabajo (Congress of Labor)
CTAL	Confederación de Trabajadores de América Latina (Workers Confederation of Latin America)
CTM	Confederación de Trabajadores de México (Confederation of Mexico's Workers)
CTRM	Confederación del Trabajo de la Región Mexicana (Workers Confederation of the Mexican Region)

CUT	Central Unica de Trabajadores (Workers' Single Central)
FDN	Frente Democrático Nacional (National Democratic Front)
FEP	Frente Electoral del Pueblo (People's Electoral Front)
FMI	Fondo Monetario Internacional (International Monetary Fund)
FNDSCAC	Frente Nacional en Defensa del Salario y Contra la Carestia, Asociación Civil (National Front for the Defense of Wages and Against Austerity and the High Cost of Living)
FOCM	Federación de Obreros y Campesinos de México (Workers' and Peasants' Federation of Mexico)
FOVISSSTE	Fondo de Vivienda del Instituto de Seguridad y Servicios Sociales de los Trabajadores del Estado (Housing Fund of the Institute of Social Security and Services for State Workers)
FSODF	Federación de los Sindicatos Obreros del Distrito Federal (Federation of Workers Unions of the Federal District)
FSTSE	Federación de Sindicatos de Trabajadores del Estado (Federation of State Workers' Unions)
IMSS	Instituto Mexicano del Seguro Social (Mexican Institute of Social Security)
INDECO	Instituto Nacional para el Desarrollo de la Comunidad (National Institute for Community Development)
INFONAVIT	Instituto del Fondo Nacional de Vivienda para los Trabajadores (The Institute of National Housing Fund for Workers)
INV	Instituto Nacional de la Vivienda (National Housing Institute)
ISSSTE	Instituto de Seguridad y Servicios Sociales de los Trabajadores del Estado (Institute of Social Security and Services for State Workers)
MLN	Movimiento de Liberación Nacional (National Liberation Movement)
MSF	Movimiento Sindical Ferrocarrilero (Railroad Worker's Movement)
MUR	Movimiento de Unión Revolucionaria (Revolutionary Union Movement)
PAN	Partido de Acción Nacional (National Action Party)
PCM	Partido Comunista Mexicano (Mexican Communist Party)

PECE	Pacto de Estabilización y Crecimiento Económico (Pact of Stabilization and Economic Growth)
PEMEX	Petroleos Mexicanos (Mexican Petroleum)
PIRE	Programa Inmediato de Reordenamiento Económico (Immediate Program of Economic Reordering)
PLM	Partido Laborista Mexicano (Mexicano Labor Party)
PNR	Partido Nacional Revolucionario (National Revolutionary Party)
PP	Partido Popular (Popular Party)
PPS	Partido Popular Socialista (Popular Socialist Party)
PRD	Partido Revolucionario Democrático (Revolutionary Democratic Party)
PRI	Partido Revolucionario Institucional (Institutional Revolutionary Party)
PRM	Partido de la Revolución Mexicana (Mexican Revolution Party)
PRONASOL	Programa Nacional de Solidaridad (National Program of Solidarity)
PSE	Pacto de Solidaridad Económica (Economic Solidarity Pact)
PSUM	Partido Socialista Unificado de México (Single Socialist Party of Mexico)
SAM	Sistema Alimentario Mexicano (Mexican Food System)
SME	Sindicato Mexicano de Electricistas (Mexican Union of Electricity Workers)
SNESCRM	Sindicato Nacional de Electricistas, Similares y Conexos de la República Mexicana (National Electricians and Related Workers' Union for the Mexican Republic)
SNTE	Sindicato Nacional de los Trabajadores de la Educación—National Education Workers Union
STERM	Sindicato de Trabajadores del Estado de la República Mexicana (State Workers' Union of the Mexican Republic)
STERM	Sindicato de Trabajadores Electricistas de la República Mexicana (Electricity Workers' Union of Mexico)
STFRM	Sindicato de Trabajadores Ferrocarrileros de la República Mexicana (Railroad Workers' Union of Mexico)
STPRM	Sindicato de Trabajadores Petroleros de la República Mexicana (Petroleum Worker's Union of Mexico)

STUNAM	Sindicato de Trabajadores de la Universidad Nacional de México (Workers' Union of the National University of Mexico)
SUTERM	Sindicato Unico de Trabajadores Electricistas de la República Mexicana (Single Electricity Workers' Union of Mexico)
UGOCM	Unión General de Obreros y Campesinos de México (General Union of Workers and Peasants of Mexico)
UNAM	Universidad Nacional Autónoma de México (National Autonomous University of Mexico)
UPN	Universidad Pedagógica Nacional (National Pedagogical University)

Appendix 3
Historical Statistics

TABLE A.1.
Mexican Population, 1900–1990
(Thousands)

Year	Population
1900	13,607,272
1905	14,331,188
1910	15,160,369
1921	14,334,780
1930	16,552,722
1940	19,653,552
1950	25,791,017
1960	34,923,129
1970	48,225,238
1975	60,153,387
1980	69,392,835
1985	78,524,158
1990	85,124,000

Sources: 1900–1985: *Estadísticas Históricas* (México, D. F.: INEGI); 1990: *Anuario Estadístico 1991* (México, D. F.: CEPAL, 1991).

TABLE A.2.
Index of Workers' Real Wages,
Federal District, 1938–1982

Year	Index	Year	Index
1938	100.0	1961	66.4
1939	92.0	1962	70.9
1940	83.2	1963	75.7
1941	79.1	1964	74.2
1942	66.1	1965	79.9
1943	66.8	1966	84.6
1944	53.0	1967	90.7
1945	50.3	1968	91.4
1946	45.8	1969	99.8
1947	46.4	1970	96.9
1948	52.4	1971	99.5
1949	52.1	1972	107.5
1950	66.1	1973	116.6
1951	50.9	1974	125.7
1952	49.7	1975	117.6
1953	53.3	1976	143.5
1954	57.0	1977	125.7
1955	57.1	1978	123.6
1956	60.2	1979	122.6
1957	59.9	1980	116.8
1958	63.5	1981	122.6
1959	64.2	1982	100.2
1960	64.7		

Source: Bortz, 1986:45.

TABLE A.3.
Mexican Gross National Product, 1900–1991

Date	Index (1980 = 100)	GNP (millions of pesos) Current	1980
1900	0.74	1,316.80	176,799
1901	0.94	1,774.10	188,574
1902	0.94	1,672.30	177,753
1903	0.94	1,859.00	197,598
1904	0.92	1,835.70	199,273
1905	1.02	2,272.80	222,998
1906	1.02	2,216.60	217,484
1907	1.02	2,346.00	230,181
1908	1.04	2,407.60	231,767
1909	1.12	2,643.10	236,583
1910	1.29	3,100.50	239,680

TABLE A.3. (continued)

Date	Index (1980 = 100)	GNP (millions of pesos) Current	1980
1921	2.12	5,455.00	257,700
1922	1.74	4,590.20	263,139
1923	1.84	5,013.60	272,123
1924	1.72	4,632.60	268,588
1925	1.84	5,468.80	296,830
1926	1.80	5,468.80	303,283
1927	1.72	4,987.00	289,135
1928	1.72	5,017.80	290,921
1929	1.74	4,862.90	278,772
1930	1.78	4,667.70	261,701
1931	1.55	4,218.80	272,462
1932	1.39	3,205.50	230,346
1933	1.47	3,781.70	257,259
1934	1.51	4,150.90	275,040
1935	1.55	4,540.30	293,225
1936	1.69	5,345.70	317,139
1937	2.08	6,800.40	327,320
1938	2.18	7,281.10	334,671
1939	2.21	7,785.10	351,504
1940	2.31	8,248.80	356,659
1941	2.35	9,232.40	392,534
1942	2.59	10,680.80	412,832
1943	3.04	13,035.30	429,075
1944	4.06	18,801.20	463,403
1945	4.29	20,565.70	479,119
1946	5.49	27,929.60	508,921
1947	5.88	31,022.60	527,595
1948	6.04	33,101.20	548,324
1949	6.29	36,411.80	578,737
1950	6.62	42,162.80	636,439
1951	7.94	54,374.70	684,992
1952	8.55	60,992.60	713,731
1953	8.49	60,663.70	714,801
1954	9.41	73,935.60	785,880
1955	10.54	90,053.30	854,007
1956	11.29	102,919.90	911,635
1957	12.05	118,205.70	980,635
1958	12.72	131,376.80	1,032,804
1959	13.23	140,771.50	1,064,033
1960	13.88	159,703.20	1,150,865
1961	14.35	173,236.10	1,207,456
1962	14.78	186,780.70	1,263,876
1963	15.25	207,952.30	1,363,729
1964	16.11	245,500.50	1,523,788
1965	16.48	267,420.20	1,622,341

TABLE A.3. (continued)

Date	Index (1980 = 100)	GNP (millions of pesos) Current	1980
1966	17.13	297,196.00	1,734,904
1967	17.62	325,024.80	1,844,594
1968	18.05	359,857.70	1,993,495
1969	18.76	397,796.40	2,120,766
1970	19.60	444,271.40	2,266,691
1971	20.76	490,011.00	2,360,771
1972	22.05	564,726.50	2,561,118
1973	24.87	690,891.30	2,777,743
1974	30.54	899,706.80	2,946,303
1975	35.34	1,100,049.80	3,112,867
1976	42.26	1,370,968.30	3,244,312
1977	55.12	1,849,262.70	3,355,268
1978	64.35	2,337,397.90	3,632,501
1979	77.36	3,067,526.40	3,965,200
1980	100.00	4,470,077.00	4,470,077
1981	126.00	6,127,632.00	4,863,200
1982	202.80	9,797,791.00	4,831,258
1983	386.10	17,878,720.00	4,630,593
1984	614.40	29,471,575.00	4,796,806
1985	962.90	47,391,702.00	4,921,768
1986	1672.90	79,191,347.00	4,733,776
1987	4001.10	192,801,935.00	4,818,723
1988	7981.80	389,258,523.00	4,876,826
1989	10006.70	503,667,765.00	5,033,305
1990	12915.10	678,923,486.00	5,256,819
1991	15650.20	852,783,201.00	5,449,024

Source: Banco de México, unpublished document.
Note: 1980 GNP = Current GNP × 100/1980 index.

TABLE A.4.
Mexican Public (pesos) Debt, 1913–1946

Year	External	Internal	Total
1913	463,500,000	136,500,00	600,000,000
1922	1,037,116,145	113,475,388	1,150,591,533
1925	669,467,826	108,015,902	777,483,728
1929	656,500,000	116,000,000	772,500,000
1942	2,589,382,874	523,050,000	3,112,432,847
1946	485,341,343	1,068,143,000	1,553,484,343

Source: Ian Bazant, *Historia de la deuda exterior de México 1823–1946*
(México, D.F.: El Colegio de Mexico, 1968.), 227.

TABLE A.5.
Service Costs, Mexico's External Public Debt,
and Export Earnings, 1960–1973
(millions of dollars)

Year	Earnings from Exports	Debt Service Cost	Debt Service Cost as Percentage of Exports
1960	1,457.2	219.0	15.0
1961	1,545.8	218.9	14.2
1962	1,664.0	321.5	19.3
1963	1,767.9	288.2	16.3
1964	1,907.7	433.5	22.7
1965	2,112.5	483.8	22.9
1966	2,265.6	456.5	20.1
1967	2,324.5	469.8	20.2
1969	2,588.4	622.3	24.0
1970	2,868.0	493.5	24.2
1971	3,106.9	724.7	23.3
1972	3,736.1	851.2	22.8
1973	4,665.2	747.5	17.2

Source: Green, 1976:147.

TABLE A.6.
Service Costs, Mexico's External
Public Debt, 1980–1990
(millions of dollars)

Year	Balance at End of Year
1980	50,700
1981	74,900
1982	87,600
1983	93,800
1984	96,700
1985	97,800
1986	100,500
1987	102,400
1988	100,900
1989	95,100
1990	98,200

Source: *Statistical Yearbook for Latin America and the Caribbean* (ECLA, 1991), 491–92.

Notes

Chapter 1. Introduction

1. Marx assumed that the going rate for labor was determined by the market. This assumption is valid only in a laissez-faire economy in which the labor force is totally atomized, i.e., lacks any means of collectively affecting political decisions regarding wage levels. Clearly, these assumptions are no longer valid in late capitalism.

2. Exceptions to this rule are Roxborough, 1984; Bergquist, 1985; Collier and Collier, 1991; and Rueschemeyer, Stephens, and Stephens, 1992.

3. I am here referring exclusively to Third World formations in which capitalism has expanded beyond the commodity export form usually associated with the oligarchic state. This excludes state forms such as that which existed in Nicaragua until 1981, in Haiti until 1985 (and recently again in 1991), or in Paraguay until the fall of Stroessner. In such countries, the state, often under the control of one single family, is literally the property of the capitalist class.

4. I am not disputing the claims of world system theorists that the hacienda system, which started in the sixteenth century, was capitalist (Wallerstein, 1974; Cockroft, 1972); I am merely marking the onset of industrial capitalism.

5. For a critical discussion of the analysis of political change in Mexico in the 1980s, see Brachet-Marquez (1992). On changes in central-local relations, see Gonzalez Block (1989); Leyva Flores (1990).

6. Teachers who belong to the Sindicato Nacional de Trabajadores de la Educación (SNTE—National Union of Education Workers) also belong to the CT, although they form part of the Federación de Sindicatos de Traba-

jadores al Servicio del Estado (FSTSE—Federation of State Workers' Unions), an umbrella organization grouping all state employees. Nevertheless, although this study includes several episodes of teacher protests as background to potential or real labor mobilizations, it does not focus on teachers who would have to be linked to a different set of policy outputs as dependent variables. UNE is not an acronym, but is the spanish word *une* itself, meaning "unite" or "join up"; the short-lived organization was subtitled Ciudadanos en movimiento (Citizens in Motion).

7. Mutualism refers to the societies for mutual aid formed by workers since the end of the nineteenth century, emulating the European model. Through these mutual societies, workers pooled their resources to face the contingencies of death and illness against which employers offered no protection.

8. For IWW's influence on Mexican labor, see Hart (1978).

9. For the concept of policy currents, see Kaztenstein (1978) and Joseph (1981). See also Maxfield (1990).

10. The most important examples of union insurgency since the beginning of the Salinas administration have been the strikes at the state-owned steel plant of SICARTSA, the state-owned copper mine of Cananea, and the Modelo Brewery Company. All three ended in mass firings.

11. The most prominent representative of that approach for Latin America is Sloan (1984).

12. Few students of public policy in Latin America pay much attention to what happens after a policy has been adopted. In the case of Mexico, this lacuna greatly reinforces the belief in the omnipotence of the state, as the process from presidential proposal to legislative endorsement is largely guaranteed by the majority of the official party. Important exceptions are Grindle (1977a, 1981, and 1984), regarding rural development policies and Bennett and Sharpe (1985), regarding the automobile industry. These studies show that the real political process starts after, rather than before, adoption. It determines whether or not a policy will be implemented or will remain on the books as (1) a mere symbolic gesture of no consequence (e.g., antipollution policy) or (2) an established principle of the legitimacy of state intervention which can be taken up later when the political conjuncture is more favorable (e.g., social security before 1943).

CHAPTER 2. POPULAR STRUGGLES AND SOCIAL REFORMS

1. See, for example, Cosio Villegas (1965); Womack (1969); Gilly (1971); Hart (1978); Tutino (1986); Knight (1986).

2. This term is a translation from the Spanish *clases populares* which includes a wider spectrum of the subordinate classes (from peasants to street vendors, from the employed to the underemployed and unemployed) than the concept of *proletariat* as defined in classical Marxism. I use this term to convey the fact that all members of the popular classes participate in one way or another in the process of capital accumulation, regardless of their location in the labor process.

3. As depicted in O'Donnell (1973, 1977b, 1983, 1988); Malloy (1977); Collier (1979); Stepan (1978); Remmer and Merckx (1982).

4. This eponymous movement sought to elect Enrique Guzman president over Adolfo Ruiz Cortinez, the PRI's designated candidate. Analysts generally agree that Guzman won in his own state but that electoral results were falsified to make it appear that he had failed. Although acknowledging his victory there could not have altered the results of the national election, it would probably have created pressures to elect him as governor. The possibility of a governor in partisan opposition to the president was not a political option in Mexico (and still is not, excepting one token PAN governor elected after 1988.)

5. The lack of scholarly interest in the broad implications of social reform has not been limited to Mexico and finds few exceptions in studies of other Latin American countries. Apart from Malloy's (1979) seminal study of the politics of social security in Brazil and Mesa Lago's (1978) comparative study of social security in Latin America, the importance of social reforms for shedding light upon the role of society—especially organized popular forces—in modifying state action in that area has remained underrated to this day.

6. On the transition from authoritarianism, see in particular O'Donnell, Schmitter, and Whitehead (1986); O'Brien and Cammack (1985); Malloy and Seligson (1987). Discussions of recent electoral politics in Mexico can be found in Middlebrook (1986); Alvarado (1987); Gomez-Tagle (1987, 1988a, 1988b, 1990); Peschard (1988); Molinar Horcasitas (1987a, 1987b, 1992); Molinar Horcasitas and Weldon (1990); Torres Mejía (1987); Tamayo (1990); and Loaeza (1990).

7. The direct influence of U.S. Latin Americanists in this respect should not be discounted. When the first reader on redemocratization in Latin America appeared in print in the mid-1980s (O'Donnell, Schmitter, and Whitehead, 1986), it did not fail to contain an article on liberalization in Mexico, with little to go on but the relatively modest gains of the conservative National Action Party (PAN) in 1982. Similarly, the hottest center of debate on whether Mexico was bound on a democratic course in the 1980s was centered in the United States, specifically, in San Diego, California.

8. See Loaeza (1987, 1989, 1990); Molinar Horcasitas (1987a, 1987b); Maxfield and Anzaldua Montoya (1987); Story (1987); and Arriola (1987).

9. For a review of literature on the capacity of social movements in the 1980s to effect political change in Mexico, see Street (1991).

10. O'Donnell (1973) initially characterized Mexico as "bureaucratic-authoritarian" (BA), but later retracted himself (1977b); Cardoso (1979) restricted the BA label to military regimes, thereby excluding Mexico; Reyna (1977) chose "populism" as the correct characterization of the regime; Córdova (1985) labeled it "paternalist"; Cotler (1979) argued that Mexico was moving toward bureaucratic authoritarianism due to increasing economic pressures to cut back on redistribution. More generally, Mexican authoritarianism was qualified as "inclusionary" (Stepan, 1978; Reyna and Weinert, 1977), although the exact meaning of the term was rarely defined as any-

thing more precise than the "presence" of the popular sectors in the regime or their incorporation into the official party.

11. Linz defines *authoritarianism* in the following way: "Authoritarian regimes are political systems with limited, not responsible, political pluralism; without elaborate and guiding ideology (but with distinctive mentalities); without intensive nor extensive political mobilization (except at some point in their development); and in which a leader (or occasionally a small group) exercises power with formally ill-defined limits but actually quite predictable ones" (Linz, 1970:255). *Corporatism,* on the other hand, is defined by Schmitter as "a system of interest representation in which the constituent units are organized into a limited number of singular, compulsory, noncompetitive, hierarchically ordered and functionally differentiated categories, recognized or licensed (if not created) by the state and granted a deliberate representational monopoly within their respective categories in exchange for observing certain controls on their election of leaders and articulation of demands and supports" (Schmitter, 1974:93). Although the two concepts are clearly different, they have tended to be merged in the case of Mexico.

12. The historical origin of these institutional mechanisms is detailed in chapter 4.

13. In this line of thinking, see, for example, Coleman and Davis (1983) and Stevens (1974).

14. The Mexican Revolution is characterized as "bourgeois" in most Marxist analyses, not because the bourgeoisie fought for it but because it eventually benefited from it (Córdova, 1985). Historically, the bourgeoisie postdates the revolution and may therefore be considered its main heir. Contrary to this orthodoxy, Gilly (1971) and Cockroft (1983) hold that the Revolution was an aborted proletarian revolution ("interrupted" for the first, and "defeated" for the second).

15. Although the literature on the increasing "technocratization" of the Mexican state makes a questionable argument regarding the differentiation between technocrats and politicians and the superior professionalism of the former (Lerner de Sheinbaum, 1983), its measurement of the increasingly high academic standards of high-level bureaucrats is unimpeachable. See, for example, Smith (1979, 1986); and Ai Camp (1983, 1986).

16. In Uruguay, for example, there has existed since the redemocratization of the 1980s a formal pact that specifies the conditions under which the military is willing to stay out of politics. In Chile, the situation is similar.

17. The term *class* is used here merely to signify a group sharing a common economic position. In this very limited sense, it envisages not one but a large variety of subordinate classes, often with little in common but their propinquity on an imagined scale of the distribution of economic resources in society.

18. The term *agreement* signifies not the notion of normative consensus but simply assent, i.e., acceptance. Whether such assent and acceptance are emotionally and normatively internalized is not a problem considered here.

In the urban areas, where the political culture among popular classes is highly sophisticated, the assumption that government discourse is taken at face value is simply not a reasonable one any more, as the 1988 presidential election showed.

19. The efforts to link regime to policy outputs follow a long and fruitless tradition in the study of Latin America, as Remmer (1978, 1986) tirelessly reminds us.

CHAPTER 3. FROM REVOLUTION TO INSTITUTIONALIZATION, 1910–1940

1. In 1891, for example, Mexico owed foreign investors 56.7 million pesos for subsidies granted for the construction of 5,930 kilometers of railroads; this represented 30 percent of the value of exports for that year. See Arnaud (1981).

2. The principal legal device for such actions was the fraudulent implementation of the *Ley de Terrenos Baldíos,* or Law of Unoccupied Land, initially created under the Reform (1848–1876) to develop small agricultural property. It allowed special "surveying companies" to appropriate all unoccupied land and sell it to the highest bidder. By 1906, almost 25 percent of the national territory (49 million hectares) had been "surveyed." A more apt description of this process is that land was forcefully taken away from Indian communities, whose members now found themselves without any independent means of livelihood.

3. In the state of Chihuahua alone, 7 million hectares belonged to a single owner, the Terrazas-Creel family.

4. Womack (1969) contends that this dissolution was started earlier by Porfirio Díaz himself, through his contradictory tactics of alternately announcing his political retirement and eliminating would-be successors.

5. Victoriano Huerta is the archvillain of modern Mexican history. His name is associated with atrocities committed against peasants, particularly in Morelos, the birthplace of the movement that followed Zapata (Womack, 1969). Why Madero chose him as one of his closest aides and disregarded repeated warnings about his impending treachery remains a mystery. His name should not be confused with Adolfo de la Huerta's, a committed constitutionalist and close associate of Obregón and Carranza in the campaign against Victoriano Huerta.

6. The rate of literacy of the working class was around 70 percent, as against 30–35 percent in the rural areas.

7. Mutual aid societies, copied from the European model, pooled the meager resources of their members to defend them against illness and death. They provided limited funds for the sick, the disabled, widows, and orphans. They were politically uninvolved, although many of them adhered to a doctrine of gradual revolution achieved through the organization of these societies, followed by the restructuration of work on a cooperative basis.

8. Knight (1987a) recalls that thousands of copies of the Constitution were sold at ten centavos apiece to the working class, an amount that rep-

resented a substantial expenditure, given that the daily wage rarely went beyond one peso and frequently was as low as thirty centavos.

9. Letter to C. Villareal Márquez, cited in Hernández Laos (1980:154–56, n. 100).

10. During this presidential campaign, he spoke favorably about worker organization in Orizaba and Veracruz, urging employers to accept unionization and refrain from firing unionizing workers. But in Metepec, during the same campaign, he also warned that his presidency would be based on order and progress and "could not be interrupted by any strike movement." See Meyer (1971:5); Cumberland (1972:22); and Ruiz (1976:192).

11. The church had gathered new strength thanks to the state's nonimplementation of the laws of the Reform of 1867, which forbade the Catholic church to control either education or the registration of vital statistics.

12. Most of the armed insurrections that postrevolutionary governments had to contend with—three during the fifteen-month administration of Madero, ending with the victory of the fourth; four under Carranza; three under Obregón; three under Calles—were fomented by coalitions of traditional landowners, foreign companies, the Catholic church, and unsatisfied adventurous caudillos.

13. For example, in Veracruz, male textile workers earned between fifty-six centavos and two pesos daily, while women earned between fifty and eighty centavos and children, from thirty to sixty centavos, for the same amount of work (Ramos-Escandón, 1987:25).

14. Walker (1981) calculates that workers lost 57 percent of their purchasing power by the end of the Porfiriato.

15. A manager of the Compañía Industrial de Orizaba, a corporation controlled by foreign interests, told a reporter that he "had nothing to fear, because the federal government zealously safeguarded the interests of foreign investors. He defended as sensible and wise Madero's policy of giving foreign corporations a voice in determining formulas for capital and labor" (Ruiz, 1976:191).

16. Inspectors of the department reported that in many textile mills, workers were still paid as little as thirty centavos a day (Ruiz, 1976:200).

17. The United States had at first sealed its border from arms and supply traffic, which hampered the constitutionalist war effort, while leaving Huerta free to receive supplies from Great Britain through Veracruz. Only after World War I erupted and Huerta was suspected of a strong inclination toward becoming an ally of Germany, did the United States move to occupy Veracruz.

18. See Ulloa (1979:15–25) for the measures adopted in Veracruz.

19. U.S. hostility was due to Villa's murderous incursions into U.S. territory, leading to the "punitive expedition" led by General Pershing, which turned out to be a humiliating defeat for the giant of the north. After Huerta's defeat, Carranza, whose anti–United States feeling were no secret, experienced serious difficulties convincing the United States to pull its marines out of the port of Veracruz.

20. For example, the *infalsificables*, issued in 1914, by far the most "solid" Carranista paper money, had lost 25 percent of their value the same year, nearly 70 percent the following year, and 91 percent in 1916 (Basurto, 1975:177).

21. Several countries claimed considerable damages for losses incurred during the period of armed rebellion. Among these, only the United States was eventually to receive any compensation.

22. Ironically, he chose as his envoy for this mission of goodwill Luis Morones himself, the head of the CROM.

23. *Pliegos petitorios* are the lists of demands presented by the unions to management prior to bargaining.

24. There is usually a considerable gap between recognized and actual striking activities in Mexico. In those days, however, the Juntas de Conciliación y Arbitraje (conciliation and arbitration courts) had not yet acquired the right to pronounce strikes legal or illegal, which makes these statistics relatively more reliable than those that were to follow. However, they do exclude strikes that were threatened but not carried out because the conflicts were settled. There is little doubt that many firms must have preferred settlement to the risk of a crippling strike; as well, the example of other strikes settled in favor of labor must have presented a strong disincentive to adopt uncompromising attitudes. Strikes are only the tip of the iceberg of the whole process of demand and response, as influenced by the history of past settlements and those in the immediate environment of the firm. For this, we need careful comparative case studies of single companies based on company archives and chronicles of the time.

25. Complaints against verbal and physical violence on the part of foremen, including the rape of women workers, were frequent at the time.

26. Calles had retired as many as sixty generals during his administration. To soften this bitter pill, many had been given gubernatorial posts. Solving the military problem had therefore worsened the centrifugal forces of federalism and also of corruption, as these generals would use land reform laws to become landowners themselves.

27. A brief examination of the presidential succession from Portes Gil (1928–1930) to Ortiz Rubio (1930–1932) illustrates the nature of the political process during the Maximato. In 1929, while the presidency was temporarily filled by Portes Gil, the PNR was entrusted with finding a suitable presidential candidate. The most popular candidates were Aaron Saenz, supported by peasant organizations, and José Vasconcelos, an ideologue of the left (Liss, 1984). Calles nevertheless decided to have the obscure Ortiz Rubio nominated. Prior to the party convention, he sent emissaries to each party member to obtain from each of them a personal pledge of support for Ortiz Rubio. Any delegate who failed to make this pledge was simply not "recognized" by the Organization Committee of the party as a bona fide delegate and was denied entrance to the convention hall. This information is given by Garrido (1985), who in 1976 personally interviewed the head of the committee, who had received those instructions.

28. Information on the ILO's proselytizing in favor of social insurance and examples of early adoptions in Latin America can be found in Spalding (1978); Mesa Lago (1978); and Malloy (1979).

29. For declarations regarding labor, see Cárdenas's Electoral Speech of May 11, 1934; the Inaugural Presidential Speech of Nov. 30, 1934; the Presidential Speech to the Workers of Monterrey, Feb. 9, 1936; and the Presidential Allocution to the Employers' Center of Monterrey, Feb. 11, 1936 (Cárdenas, 1984).

30. The amount of credit available through this channel was grossly insufficient in relation to the number of peasants who received land, so that only 15 percent, according to Hamilton (1982), benefited from it.

31. For more details on the organization of rural health centers and their subsequent fate in other administrations, see Gonzalez Block (1989).

32. As we have seen, Adolfo de la Huerta failed to attract labor support against Obregón.

CHAPTER 4. FROM ALLIANCE TO CONFRONTATION, 1940–1970

1. Almazán's legitimacy as a revolutionary caudillo stems from the fact that he was subsequently pardoned by Obregón.

2. Militias of ninety thousand men taken from the CTM ranks were organized by the Ministry of Defense in order to offset the possibility of a military sedition during the Cárdenas administration. In 1938, a right-wing military coup headed by General Cedillo was attempted, but failed.

3. The inclusion of the military as a separate sector had been on shaky constitutional grounds in the first place and had been dictated by the immediate necessity of protecting the regime against the menace of Callism in the 1930s. After this decision, the military could still participate in the party, but had to join the ranks of the "popular" wing which still lacked a precise legal status in the PRM.

4. The argument for postponement was based on the notion emphasized in the Third International that capitalism must first develop to its fullest extent before a socialist revolution can take place.

5. The governor of Veracruz was the successor and protégé of Miguel Alemán, who was the most prominent supporter of Avila Camacho and was responsible for rallying congressional support for his candidacy. He would also be his campaign organizer. Alemán later became head of the CNOP. These actions should have been a warning to the CTM not to support Alemán's candidacy, but the warning went unheeded.

6. According to Rivero (1990), who bases her assertions on Kevin Middlebrook's (1981) study of that period, if 1940 is used as the base year, the index of the urban minimum wage declined to 63.53 percent in 1943 and 58.96 percent in 1945. During the same period, prices went from 100 percent in 1940 to 158.5 percent in 1943 and 213.5 percent in 1945.

7. Among major labor opponents of social security were Confederación Proletaria Nacional, Sindicato de Empleados de Periódicos, Alianza de

Uniones y Sindicatos de Empleados de Artes Gráficas, Unión Lino-tipográfica de la República Mexicana, Unión de Trabajadores de Periódicos, Sindicato de Redactores, Sindicato de Dibujantes, and Frente Nacional Proletario. The latter, by far the most vocal, was both anti-Lombardo Toledano and anti-Velazquez and united various dissident unions, including telephone workers and the Federación de Obreros y Campesinos del Distrito Federal (the local branch of the FOCM). It claimed that social security protected the 3 percent of wage earners who died accidentally, while throwing into poverty the 97 percent who died of natural causes (Pozas Horcasitas, 1990:129).

8. Following several secret meetings with U.S. representatives, Miguel Alemán was later deemed acceptable to the United States.

9. Collier and Collier (1991) go so far as to assert that the period of social reforms ended after 1940, precisely when it was in fact, beginning.

10. See appendix 3.

11. Even though Lombardo Toledano had never been a member of the PCM, he chose not to repudiate it, thereby setting himself up as a target for anticommunist feeling and making it nearly impossible for the bourgeoisie to side with him.

12. This figure agrees with a government census of union membership (Talavera and Leal, 1977).

13. According to Gomez Zepeda's defenders, as reported by Basurto (1984), this amount of money had been withdrawn from union funds with the due authorization of the directorate and with the purpose of financing the CUT.

14. These expelled members (e.g., Valentin Campa, also an STFRM member) were, nevertheless, still publicly branded as communists.

15. The Alianza was later known as the General Union of Workers and Peasants of Mexico (UGOCM).

16. The 1940 amendment to the 1930 labor law required unions to announce a strike two weeks ahead of schedule. This time interval could be used by management and labor to come to an agreement, based on previous guidelines established by the government. As a result, there were many fewer strikes than strike announcements.

17. Pellicer de Brody and Reyna (1978:80) assert that the CROC was formed by the government's initiative. But Alonso (1972:10) reports that it was born from a coalition of independent forces. Both assertions are made without citing sources. Middlebrook (1981) takes his cue from Pellicer de Brody and Reyna. He cites as evidence the attendance of the minister of labor and social welfare at the CROC's founding ceremony and the fact that from then on the CROC was affiliated with the PRI, despite the continuation of its factional rivalries with the CTM (1981:90–91).

18. CEIMSA would later become the National Company for Popular Subsistence (CONASUPO).

19. "Railroad deputies" were railroad union officials rewarded for their docility to state directives with seats in the Chamber of Deputies, thanks to

the nondemocratic system of candidate nomination known as the *dedazo* (finger-pointing) system.

20. This contrasts with Reyna's assertion in another publication that "since the foundation of the official party in 1929, there has not been one single opposition movement that has endangered [the state's] internal cohesion" (Reyna and Trejo Delabre, 1981:34).

21. "Mi gobierno es, dentro de la constitución, de extrema izquierda." Extract from a July 1, 1960, speech delivered in Guaymas, Mexico.

22. Among the groups most enthusiastic about showing their active support of Castro's government were dissident teachers (Movimiento Revolucionario del Magisterio); what was left of opposition in the railroad union (Consejo Nacional Ferrocarrilero); and student organizations from UNAM and the Escuela Normal (the teachers' school). Given the experience of the late 1950s, it is no wonder that the government was in no mood to provide these groups with a new forum to air their demands.

23. Lombardo Toledano made clear his party's unconditional support of the government since the beginning of the Ruiz Cortinez administration, stating that "[it] had not changed" but that the Ruiz Cortinez administration had adopted its program (Hofstader, 1974:56)

24. This tendency was manifested once more during the Lopez Mateos administration, which failed to carry out a promised fiscal reform.

25. "Social dissolution" was an old law inherited from 1916, which allowed Carranza to crush his former allies from the COM. According to this law, any disturbance could be defined as "social dissolution," an offense technically punishable by death.

26. Between 1960 and 1965, direct foreign investment rose from $1,080 million to $1,745 million, $1,465 million of which belonged to U.S. firms. By 1967, Mexico had the highest number of Transnational Corporation (TNC) branches in all Latin America, ranking 5th in the world (Wionzcek, 1986).

27. These data are drawn from Rosario Green's analysis of external debt under Diaz Ordaz, particularly table 14, (1976:158–63), which details lenders, amounts loaned, and the purpose of each loan. This table is reproduced in appendix 3.

28. For example, a single loan to the Cia San Cristobal, an old national paper-making company that found itself forced to sell a large portion of its stock to Scott, represented over 30 percent of the totality of all foreign loans destined to education during the whole 1964–70 period. See Green (1976:158–63).

29. The *aguinaldo* is not a Christmas bonus but a forced savings withdrawn from paychecks throughout the year.

30. There has been no subsequent amnesty for this decision. As a result, hundreds of doctors had to leave Mexico permanently.

31. These same buildings were to become the tombs of hundreds of medical students in the 1985 earthquake, due to the fraudulent handling

of building materials. The higher functionary responsible for the fraud was merely asked to step down from the cabinet position he occupied at the time.

32. In those days, all but a small majority of the faculty were in fact practitioners who gave one occasional course. Many lacked advanced professional training and were not up to date on the latest research and teaching methods in their respective fields. Teaching at UNAM gave prestige and connections to such professionals, although little or no money. The university, on the other hand, was able to save on its budget by paying only token compensations to hundreds of these practitioners. This tendency was reversed in the mid-1970s, when UNAM began to hire a larger number of full-time faculty with academic credentials. Yet to this day, it still relies heavily on such well-intentioned but basically undertrained teachers for a large proportion of the classes taught and, in some cases, even uses third- or fourth-year undergraduates to teach freshmen and sophomores.

33. The last three years of the secondary-school cycle in Mexico is called the *preparatoria*. It is considered higher education, particularly by its participants. An important proportion of the student population of the National University (UNAM) are, therefore, high school students between the ages of fifteen and eighteen.

The nature of the fights between high schools is not clearly indicated by existing analyses, which implicitly trivialize them. Stevens denies the political nature of student demands when she asserts that "most of the concerns that had moved Mexican students to active protest had been parochial in nature. . . . There was rarely an involvement with the wider national scene" (1974:195). Leftist writers, on the other hand, emphasize the ideological nature of student demands (Hellman, 1983; Cockroft, 1983; Zermeño, 1978; Mabry, 1982). For the point of view of the participants, see Revueltas (1978).

34. Official estimates put the number of dead at forty-nine, but these could hardly have filled the three hundred coffins displayed at UNAM the following day or account for the large number of people who simply got caught in the cross fires within the cordoned-off area, among them children. More realistic estimates are five hundred dead, twenty-five hundred wounded, and fifteen hundred arrested (Cockroft, 1983:241).

35. CT grouped all major industrial unions as well as SNTE, the Teachers' Union.

36. Real wages nearly doubled during the 1960s, while prices increased by only 31.4 percent (Looney, 1982:87).

Chapter 5. From Riches to Rags, 1970–1990

1. Government expenditures for agriculture in the 1960s dwindled to 9 percent of the federal budget, while expenditures for industrialization increased to 34 percent (Fitzgerald, 1978:30).

2. As early as 1964, the population issue was very much alive among Mexican intellectuals. Following the creation in El Colegio de México of the Center for Economic and Demographic Studies, a new journal, *Economía y Demografía*, was inaugurated. In its preamble, Victor Urquidi declared that the regulation of fertility "appeared more necessary everyday." The weekly magazine *Siempre* also advocated family planning during the same period. Between 1964 and 1971, many publications spoke to the necessity of integrating population and economic policies. (For more details on the circumstances of adoption of this policy, see Brachet-Marquez, 1984a, 1984b.)

3. Not all observers of the Mexican scene share this view. To underline the gap between presidential decisions and their realization, Cosio Villegas goes so far as to assert that, rather than an absolute decision maker, the president of Mexico is a *predicador*, i.e., one who preaches what the future should bring rather than decides what it will be (1972).

4. Bravo Ahuja (1982) shows a division among state-owned productive firms between those whose main objective is to provide subsidies to private capital (electricity, petroleum, water, etc.) and those destined to generate state revenues. In a matched sample of nationalized versus private firms, the author demonstrates that the productivity and profitability of nationalized firms is comparable to that obtaining in the private sector. It is, therefore, false to assume, as neoliberal ideologues usually do, that state-owned firms are invariably wasteful.

5. Examples are the Unidad Obrera Independiente (Independent Worker Unit) in the automotive industry; the Frente Auténtico del Trabajo (Authentic Work Front) in the Christian Democratic line; the Frente Sindical Independiente (Independent Union Front) of communist leanings, and the Confederación Obrera Revolucionaira.

6. Gomez Zepeda was the founder of the CUT, the independent splinter organization that separated from CTM in the early 1940s. See above, chap. 4.

7. In other words, it followed the tripartite structure introduced by the Avila Camacho administration. Although this scheme failed as an overall organizational scheme for labor-state-capital relations, it retained this limited application. Echeverría also set up a National Tripartite Commission (Molina, 1977), but it served merely as a channel of communications, soon to be blocked by the growing conflict between the state and private enterprise during this period.

8. Following this unsolicited and unearned reform, Fidel Velazquez, the CTM's boss, mounted a campaign to obtain the same for workers, but to no avail (Molina, 1977:71).

9. These figures refer to the population included in the geographical areas defined by the Ministry of Health as served by its clinics and hospitals. Therefore, this definition has nothing to do with actual use or the functioning of these services. In some regions, the areas are too large for the available transportation (by foot or by donkey); in others, the figures adequately represent the availability of services. A portion of rural clinics may remain

unmanned for months and still count as covered. For the IMSS, on the other hand, coverage figures represent the number of affiliates and their dependents, also regardless of actual use.

10. For example, strikes by mine and metal workers, in 1975, and telephone workers, in 1976, eventually ousted their *charro* leadership by an 85 percent vote.

11. This event gave birth to a still more radical newspaper, the weekly *Proceso*, created by *Excelsior's* ousted editor, which to this day is the harshest critic of any administration. But its high price prevents a wide distribution, making it more politically tolerable than a more affordable daily.

12. Whitehead and Saldivar assert respectively that this strategy may not even have existed (Whitehead, 1980:501; Saldivar, 1985:112).

13. An estimated US $4 billion left Mexico in 1976 (Reyna, 1979; Pellicer de Brody, 1977).

14. During his term, Echeverría tried once to make a formal visit to the university. He was booed, and tomatoes were thrown at him.

15. These were contradictory objectives, given that productivity increases were easier to achieve via subsidized mechanization and automation than through troublesome labor-intensive technologies.

16. COPLAMAR's first activity was to gather information on the satisfaction of minimum needs (a term put in vogue, at the, time by the World Bank) in housing, nutrition, health, and education, which yielded in 1982 a collection of four volumes, edited by Julio Boltvinik (1982), summarizing the current state of affairs regarding these needs.

17. The following information on the UPN is based on Kovacs (1989).

18. Throughout its existence (1980–1988), COPLAMAR was a financial agency subcontracting other government agencies to offer services to the marginalized. The health portion of COPLAMAR was subcontracted to the IMSS, the social security institute. Yet services to the rural population cost approximately one-tenth of those offered to workers through the IMSS's central budget. Commercialization was entrusted to CONASUPO. The health services were called IMSS-COPLAMAR, and commercialization services CONASUPO-COPLAMAR. In 1988, IMSS-COPLAMAR was rebaptized IMSS-SOLIDARIDAD and CONASUPO-COPLAMAR has simply disappeared. For more details on health policies during the 1980s, see Brachet-Marquez and Sheradden (1993). For details see Fox, 1993.

19. Mexico City, to this date, does not have home rule. It is governed by a "regent" or head of the Department of the Federal District appointed directly by the president.

20. Bizberg reports the following figures of change in purchasing power during the Lopez Portillo years: 0.2 percent in 1977, 0.5 percent in 1978, −6.8 percent in 1981 (despite the oil boom), and 1.8 percent in 1981 (Bizberg, 1984). If we compare these figures with those of the following administration (−9.4 percent in 1982 and −28.6 percent in 1983, according to the same author) we can appreciate the difference between real and relative deprivation. Bortz presents a similar picture regarding changes in the index

of real wages in the Federal District. Taking 1938 as the base, the index was 125.7 in 1977, 123.6 in 1978, 122.8 in 1979, 116.8 in 1980, and 122.6 in 1981; the downward plunge started in 1982, with 100.2 (Bortz, 1986:45).

21. During the Lopez Portillo administration, an extensive administrative reform had been carried out, consisting mostly of alternately splicing and merging divisive ministries in order to lower the level of interbureaucratic conflict, as, for example, the division between the Secretaría de Hacienda in charge of collecting taxes and the Secretaría de Programación y Presupuesto in charge of controlling public expenditures; or the merger between the Ministries of Agriculture and Hydraulic Resources. Lopez Portillo also took the first steps toward the decentralization of education and health services.

22. This flirtation was reflected in repeated public praise of these organizations and government help in their recruiting efforts.

23. For more details on the *coordinadoras,* see Prieto (1986). A consumer defense organization more closely linked to the official left than the FNDSCAC was the *Comité Nacional para la Defensa de la Economía Popular* CNDEP—(National Committee for the Defense of the Popular Economy). These two rival organizations merged in June 1983 under the name of *Asociación Nacional Obrero Campesino Popular* (ANOCP—National Worker, Peasant, and People's Association (Carr, 1986:13).

24. According to Alvarez (1986), who uses the figures published by the Banco Nacional de México (BANAMEX) as its source, the average per hour cost of labor in July 1983 was U.S. $0.91. This can be compared with $1.75 in Singapore, $1.45 in Hong Kong, and $8–$13 in the United States. The only country "cheaper" than Mexico in this respect was Malaysia ($0.49), which cannot be compared with Mexico regarding industrial experience of the labor force or propinquity to the U.S. market.

25. *Emplazamiento* is the legal procedure for announcing a strike. See chap. 4, n. 16.

26. The first three days following the earthquake witnessed the near-total paralysis of the government and its bureaucracy. Citizens, and later foreign teams, organized rescue squads and food distribution throughout Mexico City, only to find their task made more difficult after the government took over. Several foreign teams left in disgust. I was part of a group from El Colegio de México that attempted, in vain, to save the dying seamstresses in an illegal factory in San Antonio Abad. Even some doctors sent by the health authorities to care for the victims were stopped by the soldiers. For a saga of the first week that followed the earthquake, see Arreola et al. (1986).

27. For an analysis of the role of popular movements in the response to the 1985 earthquake, see also Ramirez Saiz (1986, 1989); Aguilar Zinser (1986); Azuela (1987); and Connolly (1987).

28. The average rate of inflation between 1982 and 1988 was 83.5 percent, according to Hernandez Laos (1989).

29. After 1986, women could obtain tortilla coupons (*tortibonos*) and special cards for subsidized milk, provided they could spare the time to stand in

long lines, sometimes as early as 5 a.m. Such policies, designed to "target" the poor, in fact excluded those among the working poor who could not find the transportation or spare the time to obtain these goods.

30. The data that follow are based on the research and discussions carried out by Boltvinik (1987); Bronfman and Gomez de León (1989); CIEMEX-WEFA (1989); Gonzalez Block (1989); Hernandez Laos (1989, 1993); Lustig (1987); Stern et al. (1990); and Urquidi (1988). They are summarized in Brachet-Marquez (1988, 1990).

31. The CNSE includes essential family expenditures for food, housing, drugs, education, clothes, shoes, transportation, recreation, and culture. This methodology, although far better than previous attempts to estimate family income by means of surveys, nevertheless has a basic methodological limitation: it takes the household as the unit of analysis, without any estimation of variations in the number of people or wage earners in each household. Calculations are based on an average of 3.6 people per household.

32. In fact, however, since the average wage earners per household has always been above 1 (the mean being 1.77), the margination gap became negative in the 1970s, meaning that somewhat more than the bare necessities were being met. It became positive again after 1982.

33. The loss of real wages by health personnel during this period also created some budgetary savings.

34. For details on the decentralization of health services during the de la Madrid administration and their negative impact on the equitable distribution of health services, see Gonzalez Block (1989).

35. Interestingly, price restraints by large chain stores after 1987 gave the big retail business a competitive edge over the small stores, which continued to change price stickers as if nothing had happened.

36. This assertion is based on three incontrovertible facts: (1) the long delay in giving the final results of the election, despite the highly sophisticated computerized system installed, (2) the unrealistic figure of 50 percent of electoral absenteeism, despite eyewitness evidence of a high degree of political mobilization of the population, especially in urban centers, and (3) the refusal of the government to open for inspection the original vote "packages" on the basis of which results had supposedly been calculated. Molinar Horcasitas and Weldon (1990) argue that the PRI would have won the presidential election anyway, although by a much slimmer margin, but would have lost its legislative majority. Although a hurriedly enacted law of "governability" would have made it possible to reestablish such a majority, it was unlikely to be popular.

37. Many of the reformers from COPLAMAR were involved in planning the PRONASOL program. For a description, see Sheradden (1989).

38. The association of PRONASOL with the PRI was unabashed. For example, the symbol for PRONASOL in television programs was three entwining cordons, each with one of the colors of the national flag. All Mexicans associated these colors with the official party, which had preempted the national flag as its exclusive symbol.

CHAPTER 6. CONCLUSION

1. I leave 1982–1988 as a no-man's-land, in which actors are overcome by the economic catastrophe, although they all try to extricate themselves from it.

2. Unlike Costa Rica, Mexico has a military. The fact that it spends more of its budget on education than on the military is an indication of the relative weight of education in Mexico's political arrangements.

Bibliography

Aguilar Zinser, Adolf. 1986. *Aún Tiembla*. México, D.F.: Gijalbo.

————. 1989. "Desconcertante Aceptación del Nuevo Presidencialismo." *Excelsior*, July 23.

Aldrete Haas, José Antonio. 1989. "The Decline of the Mexican State? The Case of State Housing Intervention (1917–1988)." Ph.D. diss., Massachussetts Institute of Technology.

————. 1991. *La Desconstrucción del Estado Mexicano. Políticas de Vivienda 1917–1988*. México, D.F.: Nueva Imagen.

Alonso, Antonio. 1972. *El Movimiento Ferrocarrilero en México 1958–1959*. México, D.F.: ERA.

Alonso, Jorge. 1985. *La Tendencia al Enmascaramiento de los Movimientos Políticos*. México, D.F.: SEP.

————. 1986. *Los Movimientos Sociales en el Valle de México*. México, D.F.: SEP.

————. 1988. "El Papel de las Convergencias de los Movimientos Sociales en los Cambios del Sistema Político Mexicano." La Jolla: Center for US-Mexican Studies, University of California, San Diego. Photocopy.

Alvarado, Arturo, ed. 1987. *Electoral Patterns and Perspectives in Mexico*. Monograph Series No. 22. La Jolla: Center for US-Mexican Studies, University of California, San Diego.

Alvarez, Arturo. 1986. "Crisis in Mexico: Impact on the Working Class and the Labor Movement." In *The Mexican Left, the Popular Movements, and the Politics of Austerity, 1982–1985*, ed. Barry Carr and Ricardo Anzaldúa, pp. 47–58. Research Monograph Series No. 18. La Jolla: Center for US Mexican Studies, University of California, San Diego.

Anguiano, Arturo. 1986. *El Estado y la Política Obrera del Cardenismo.* México, D.F.: ERA.

———, ed. 1988. *La Transición Democrática.* México, D.F.: UNAM.

Arnaud, Pascal. 1981. *Estado y Capitalismo en América Latina, Casos de México y Argentina.* México, D.F.: Siglo XXI.

Arreola, Alvaro; Gerardo José; Matilde Luna; and Ricardo Tirado. 1986. "Memoria: los Primeros Ocho Días." *Revista Mexicana de Sociología* 48(2);105–20.

Arriola, Carlos. 1987. "De la Pérdida de Confianza en el Buen Gobierno, 1970–1982." In *La Vida Política en la Crisis,* ed. Soledad Loaeza and Rafael Segovia, pp. 41–60. México, D.F.: El Colegio de México.

Arteaga, Javier. 1985. "El Sistema Alimentario Mexicano (SAM): Una Perspectiva Política." *Estudios Sociológicos* 3(8):297–314.

———. 1990. "Vivienda y Descentralización: Necesidades Sociales Frente a Demandas Económicas." México, D.F.: El Colegio de México. Photocopy.

Austin, James E,. and Gustavo Esteva, eds. 1987. *Food Policy in Mexico: The Search for Self-Sufficiency.* Ithaca, N.Y.: Cornell University Press.

Aziz Nassif. 1989. "Modernización Presidencialista." *La Jornada,* October 17.

———. 1990. *Incertidumbre y Democracia en México.* Cuadernos Chata No. 177. México, D.F.: CIESAS.

Azuela, Antonio. 1987. "Derecho y Política en el Programa de Renovación Habitacional Popular." *Estudios Demográficos y Urbanos* 2(1):53–73.

Barkin, David, and Gustavo Esteva. 1982. "Social Conflict and Inflation in Mexico." *Latin American Perspectives* 9(1):48–64.

Basurto, Jorge. 1985. *El Proletariado Industrial en México (1850–1930).* México D.F.: Universidad Nacional Autónoma de México.

———. 1983. *En el Régimen de Echeverría: Rebelión e Independencia.* Colección la Clase Obrera en la Historia de México. México, D.F.: Siglo XXI/UNAM.

———. 1984. *Del Avilacamachismo al Alemanismo 1940–1952.* Colección la Clase Obrera en la Historia de México. México, D.F.: Instituto de Investigaciones Sociales, UNAM.

Bataillon, Claude. 1968. "Le Mexique du Président Diaz Ordaz." Monograph No. 3520. *Notes et Etudes Documentaires.*

Bennett, Douglas C., and Kenneth E. Sharpe. 1980. "Agenda Setting and Bargaining Power: The Mexican State versus Transnational Automobile Corporations." *World Politics* 32:57–89.

———. 1985. *Transnational Corporations vs. the State.* Princeton, N.J.: Princeton University Press.

Bergquist, Charles. 1986. *Labor in Latin America.* Stanford, Calif.: Stanford University Press.

Bizberg, Ilan. 1983. "Las Perspectivas de la Oposición Sindical en México." *Foro Internacional* 23 (April–June):331–58.

———. 1984. "Política Laboral y Acción Sindical en México (1976–1982)." *Foro Internacional* 25 (Oct.–Dec.):166–89.

————. 1990. *Estado y Sindicalismo en México.* México, D.F.: El Colegio de México.

Boltvínik, Julio. 1987. "Ciudadanos de la Pobreza y la Marginación." *El Cotidiano* 19 (Sept.–Oct.):305–26.

Bortz, Jeffrey. 1984. *La Estructura de los Salarios en México.* México, D.F.: El Caballito.

————. 1986. "Wages and Economic Crisis in Mexico." In *The Mexican Left, the Popular Movements and the Politics of Austerity 1982–1985,* ed. Barry Carr and Ricardo Anzaldúa. Monograph Series No. 18. La Jolla: Center for US-Mexican Studies, University of California, San Diego.

Brachet-Marquez, Viviane. 1976. *La Población de los Estados de México en el Siglo XIX.* México, D.F.: SEP-INHA.

————. 1984a. "El proceso Social en la Formación de Políticas Públicas: el Caso de la Planificación Familiar." *Estudios Sociológicos* 2(5–6):51–70.

————. 1984b. "La Politica de Planificación Familiar en México: ¿Un Proceso institucionalizado?" *Revista Mexicana de Sociología* 46 (2):285–310.

————. 1988. "Poverty and Social Programs in Mexico (1970–1980): The Legacy of a Decade." *Latin American Research Review* 23(1):220–29.

————. 1990. "Crisis Económica, Impacto Social y Respuesta Estatal: el Caso de México." *Estudios Sociológicos* 8(22):163–71.

————. 1992. "Explaining Sociopolitical Change in Latin America: The Case of Mexico." *Latin American Research Review* 27(3): 91–122.

Brachet-Marquez, Viviane, and Margaret Sherraden. 1993. "Austérité Fiscale, Etat Providence et la Changement Politique au Mexique." *Les Cahiers de l'Amérique Latine.* Forthcoming.

Brandenburg, Frank Ralph. 1964. *The Making of Modern Mexico.* Englewood Cliffs, N.J.: Prentice Hall.

Bravo Ahuja, Victor. 1982. *La Empresa Pública en México.* México. D.F.: INAP.

Bravo Mena, Luis Felipe. 1987. "COPARMEX and Mexican Politics." In *Government and Private Sector in Contemporary Mexico,* ed. Sylvia Maxfield and Ricardo Anzaldua Montoya. Monograph Series No. 20. La Jolla: Center for US-Mexican Studies, University of California, San Diego.

Bronfman, Mario, and J. Gomez de León, eds. 1989. *La Mortalidad en México: Niveles, Tendencias y Determinantes.* México, D.F.: El Colegio de México.

Calderón, G. Fernando. 1986. "Los Movimientos Sociales Frente a la Crisis." In *Los Movimientos Sociales ante la Crisis,* ed. Fernando Calderon, pp. 327–86. Buenos Aires: Universidad de Naciones Unidas, CLACSO, Instituto de Investigaciones Sociales de UNAM.

Camp, Roderick A. 1983. "El Tecnócrata en México." *Revista Mexicana de Sociologia* 45(2): 579–600.

————. 1986. *Mexico's Political Stability: The Next Five Years.* Austin: University of Texas Press.

Cárdenas, Lázaro. 1984. *Ideario Político.* Selección y Presentación de Leonel Durán. México: ERA.

Cárdenas, Enrique. 1987. *La Industrialización durante la Gran Depresión.* México, D.F.: El Colegio de México.

Cardoso, Fernando Henrique. 1977a. "Estado Capitalista e Marxismo." *Estudios Cebrap* No. 21. São Paulo, Brazil.

————. 1977b. "The Consumption of Dependency Theory in the United States." *Latin American Research Review* 12(3):7–24.

————. 1979. "On the Characterization of Authoritarian Regimes in Latin America." In *The New Authoritarianism in Latin America*, ed. David Collier, pp. 33–60. Princeton, N.J.: Princeton University Press.

————. 1987. "Democracy in Latin America." *Politics and Society* 15 (1):23–42.

Carr, Barry. 1976. *El Movimiento Obrero y la Política en México 1910–1929.* México, D.F.: ERA.

————. 1983. "The Mexican Economic Debacle and the Labor Movement: A New Era or More of the Same?" In *Mexico's Economic Crisis: Challenges and Opportunities*, ed. Donald L. Wyman, pp. 91–116. Monograph Series No. 12. La Jolla: Center for US-Mexican Studies, University of California, San Diego.

————. 1986. "Introduction." In *The Mexican Left, the Popular Movements, and the Politics of Austerity 1982–1985*, ed. Barry Carr and Ricardo Anzaldúa, pp. 1–18. Monograph Series No. 18. La Jolla: Center for US-Mexican Studies, University of California, San Diego.

CIEMEX-WEFA. 1989. *Perspectivas económicas de México.* 21 (July):95–186.

Clark, Marjorie Ruth. 1932. *Organized Labor in Mexico.* Chapel Hill: University of North Carolina Press.

Coatsworth, John Henry. 1975 "Los Orígenes del Autoritarismo Moderno en México." *Foro Internacional* 16(2):205–32.

Cockroft, James. 1972. "Coercion and Ideology in Mexican Politics." In *Dependence and Underdevelopment in Latin America's Political Economy*, James Cockroft, André Gunder Frank, and Dales L. Johnson. New York: Anchor.

————. 1983. *Mexico: Class Formation, Capital Accumulation and the State.* New York: Monthly Review.

Coleman, Kenneth M., and Charles L. Davis. 1983. "Preemptive Reform and the Mexican Working Class." *Latin American Research Review* 18(1):3–32.

Collier, David, ed. 1979. *The New Authoritarianism in Latin America.* Princeton, N.J.: Princeton University Press.

Collier, David, and Richard E. Messick. 1975. "Prerequisites vs. Diffusion: Testing Alternative Explanations of Social Security Adoption." *American Political Science Review* 69 (4):1299–1315.

Collier, Ruth Berins. 1982. "Popular Sector Incorporation and Political Supremacy: Regime Evolution in Brazil and Mexico." In *Brazil and Mexico. Patterns in Late Development*, ed. Sylvia Ann Hewlett and Richard Weinert, pp. 57–110. Philadelphia, Pa.: Institute for the Study of Human Issues.

Collier, Ruth Berins, and David Collier. 1979. "Inducements versus Constraints: Disaggregating "Corporatism"," *American Political Science Review* 73 (4):967–86.

———. 1991. *Shaping the Political Arena*. Princeton, N.J.: Princeton University Press.

Connolly, Priscilla. 1987. "La Política Habitacional después de los Sismos." *Estudios Demográficos y Urbanos* 2(1):101–20.

Consejo Consultivo del Programa Nacional de Solidaridad. 1990. *El combate a la pobreza: Lineamientos programáticos*. México, D.F.: El Nacional.

Contreras, Ariel José. 1985. *Industrialización y Crisis Política*. México, D.F.: Siglo XXI.

Cook, María Elena. 1990. "Organizing Opposition in the Teachers' Movement in Oaxaca." In *Popular Movements and Political Change in Mexico*, ed. Joe Foweraker and Ann L. Craig, pp. 199–212. Boulder and London: Lynne Rienner.

COPLAMAR. 1983. 2d ed. *Macroeconomía de las Necesidades Esenciales en México. Situación Actual y Perspectivas al Año 2000*. México, D.E.: Siglo XXI.

Cordera, Rolando, and Carlos Tello. 1981. *México: La Disputa por la Nación. Perspectivas y Opciones del Desarrollo*. México, D.F.: Siglo XXI.

Córdova, Arnaldo. 1985. 2d ed. *La Ideología de la Revolución Mexicana*. México: ISUNAM/ERA.

Cornelius, Wayne. 1973. "Nation Building Participation and Distribution: The Politics of Social Reform Under Cárdenas." In *Crisis, Choice, and Change: Historical Studies of Political Development*, ed. Gabriel A. Almond, Scott C. Flanagan, and Robert J. Mundt, pp. 392–498. Boston: Little Brown.

———. 1975. *Politics and the Migrant Poor in Mexico City*. Stanford, Calif.: Stanford University Press.

———. 1986. *The Political Economy of Mexico under de la Madrid: The Crisis Deepens, 1985–1986*. Research Report Series No. 43. La Jolla: Center for US-Mexican Studies, University of California, San Diego.

———. 1987. "Political Liberalization in an Authoritarian Regime: México, 1976–1985." In *Mexican Politics in Transition*, ed. Judith Gentleman, pp. 15–40. Boulder, Colo.: Westview Special Studies on Latin America and the Caribbean.

Cornelius, Wayne; Judith Gentleman; and Peter H. Smith, eds. 1989a. *Mexico's Alternative Political Futures*. Monograph Series No. 30. La Jolla: Center for US-Mexican Studies, University of California, San Diego.

————. 1989b. "The Dynamics of Political Change in Mexico." In *Mexico's Alternative Political Futures*, ed. Cornelius Wayne, Judith Gentleman, and Peter H. Smith, pp. 1–54. Monograph Series No. 30. La Jolla: Center for US-Mexican Studies, University of California, San Diego.

Cornelius, Wayne, and Ann L. Craig. 1988. 2d ed. *Politics in Mexico: An Introduction and Overview*. La Jolla: Center for US-Mexican Studies, University of California, San Diego.

Cosio Villegas, Daniel, ed. 1965. *Historia Moderna de México*. México, D.F.: Editorial Hermes.

Cotler, Julio. 1979. "State and Regime: Comparative Notes on the Southern Cone and the 'Enclave' Societies." In *The New Authoritarianism in Latin America*, ed. David Collier, pp. 255–84. Princeton, N.J.: Princeton University Press.

Crozier, Michel, and Erhart Friedberg. 1977. *L'Acteur et le Système*. Paris: Le Seuil.

Cumberland, Charles C. 1972. *Mexican Revolution: The Constitutionalist Years*. Austin: University of Texas Press.

————. 1974. *Mexican Revolution: Genesis under Madero*. Austin: University of Texas Press.

Davis, Diane E. 1989a. "Debts, Doubts and Disciplines." *Sociological Forum* 4(4): 439–46.

————. 1989b. "Divided Over Democracy: Social Movements, State Conflicts, and Obstacles to Democratic Change in Contemporary Mexico." *Politics and Society* 17(3): 247–80.

————. 1990. "Social Movements and Mexico's Crisis." *Journal of International Affairs* 43(2): 343–67.

Domitra, Michael. 1983. "Arbeitsmarkt und Gewerkschaften." In *Mexiko: der Weg in die Krise*, ed. Albrecht von Geich, Rainer Godau, and Michael Ehre, pp. 76–91. Hamburg: Verlag Ruegger.

Durand, Victor Manuel. 1986. *La Ruptura de la Nación. Historia del Movimiento Obrero Mexicano desde 1938 hasta 1952*. México, D.F.: UNAM.

————. 1990. "La Descomposición Politica del Lombardismo." In *Entre la Guerra y la Estabilidad Política. El México de los 40*, ed. Rafael Loyo, pp. 163–194. México, D.F.: Grigalbo.

Eckstein, Susan. 1977. *The Poverty of Revolution*. Princeton, N.J.: Princeton University Press.

Esping Andersen, Gosta. 1985. *Politics Against Markets: The Social Democratic Road to Power*. Princeton, N.J.: Princeton University Press.

Esping Andersen, Gosta; Roger Friedland; and Erik Olin Wright. 1976. "Modes of Class Struggle and the Capitalist State." *Kapitalstate* 4–5.

Fitzgerald, E.V.K. 1979. "Stabilization Policy in Mexico: The Fiscal Deficit and Macroeconomic Equilibrium, 1960–1977." In *Inflation and Stabilization in Latin America*, ed. Rosemary Thorp and Lawrence Whitehead. New York and London: Holmes & Meier.

Flores de la Peña, Horacio. 1971. "México: una Economía en Desarrollo." *Comercio Exterior,* 21.

Foweraker, Joe. 1989. "Popular Movements and the Transformation of the System." In *Mexico's Alternative Political Futures,* ed. Wayne Cornelius, Judith Gentleman, and Peter H. Smith, pp. 3–22. Research Monograph Series No. 30. La Jolla: Center for US-Mexican Studies, University of California, San Diego.

———. 1990. "Popular Movements and Political Change in Mexico." In *Popular Movements and Political Change in Mexico,* ed. Joe Foweraker and Ann L. Craig, pp. 3–22. Boulder and London: Lynne Rienner.

Foweraker, Joe, and Ann L. Craig, eds. 1990. *Popular Movements and Political Change in Mexico.* Boulder and London: Lynne Rienner.

Fowley, Michael W. 1991. "Agenda for Mobilization: The Agrarian Question and Popular Mobilization in Contemporary Mexico." *Latin American Research Review* 26(2): 439–74.

Fox, Jonathan. 1993. *The Politics of Food in Mexico.* Ithaca: Cornell University Press.

Fox, Jonathan, and Gustavo Gordillo. 1989. "Between State and Market: The Campesinos' Quest for Autonomy." In *Mexico's Alternative Political Futures,* ed. Cornelius Wayne, Judith Gentleman, and Peter H. Smith, pp. 131–72. Research Monograph Series No. 30. La Jolla: Center for US-Mexican Studies, University of California, San Diego.

Gamboa Ojeda Leticia. 1991. "La Huelga Textil de 1906–1907 en Atlixco." *Historia Mexicana* 41(1):135–61.

Garcia Alba, Pascual, and Jaime Serra Puche. 1984. *Causas y Efectos de la Crisis Económica en México.* Jornada No. 104. México, D.F.: El Colegio de México.

García Cruz, Miguel. 1972. *La Seguridad Social en México, (1906–1953).* Vol. 1. México, D.F.: B. Acosta-Amic Editor.

García Tellez, Manuel. 1942. "Presentación de la Iniciativa al Sr. Presidente de la República." In *Memoria.* México, D.F.: Secretaría del Trabajo y Previsión Social.

Garrido, Luis Javier. 1985. *El Partido de la Revolución Institucionalizada, Medio Siglo de Poder Político en México. La Formación del Nuevo Estado 1928–1945.* México, D.F.: SEP.

———. 1987. "Un Partido sin Militantes." In *La Vida Política Mexicana en la Crisis,* ed. Loaeza Soledad and Rafael Segovia, pp. 61–76. México, D.F.: El Colegio de México.

Gentleman, Judith, 1987. "Political Change in Authoritarian Systems." In *Mexican Politics in Transition,* ed. Judith Gentleman, pp. 3–14. Boulder, Colo.: Westview Special Studies on Latin America and the Caribbean.

Gilly, Adolfo. 1971. *La Revolución Interrumpida.* México, D.F.: El Caballito.

Gomez Tagle, Silvia. 1987. "Democracy and Power in Mexico: The Meaning of Conflict in the 1979, 1982 and 1985 Federal Elections." In *Mex-*

ican Politics in Transition, ed. Judith Gentleman, pp. 153–80. Boulder and London: Westview.

———. 1988a. "Conflictos y Contradicciones en el Sistema Electoral Mexicano." *Estudios Sociológicos* 6(16):3–38.

———. 1990. *Las Estadísticas Electorales de la reforma México*. Cuadernos del CES No. 34. México, D.F.: El Colegio de México.

Gomez Tagle, Silvia, and Marcello Miquet. 1976. "Integración y Democracia Sindical: el Caso de los Electricistas." In *Tres Estudios sobre el Movimiento Obrero en México*, ed. José Luis Reyna, Francisco Zapata, Marcello Miquet, and Silvia Gomez Tagle. Jornada No. 80. México, D.F.: El Colegio de México.

Gonzalez Block, Miguel Angel. 1989. "Economía Política de las Relaciones Centro-Locales de las Instituciones de Salud." Ph.D. diss., El Colegio de México.

Gonzalez Casanova, Pablo. 1970a. *Democracy in Mexico*. New York: Oxford University Press.

———, ed. 1970b. *México ante la Crisis: el Impacto Social/Cultural, las Alternativas*. México, D.F.: Siglo XXI.

———. 1980. *El Primer Gobierno Constitucional (1917–1929)*. Colección la Clase Obrera en la Historia de México. México, D.F.: Siglo XXI.

Gonzalez Díaz Lombardo, Francisco. 1973. *El Derecho Social y la Seguridad Social Integral*. México, D.F.: Textos Universitarios.

Gonzalez Tiburcio, Enrique. 1991. "PRONASOL: hacia la nueva síntesis." *Cuadernos de Nexos*, October: X–XIII.

Green, Rosario. 1976. *El Endeudamiento Público Externo de México 1940–1973*. México, D.F.: El Colegio de México.

Grindle, Merilee S. 1977a. *Bureaucrats, Politicians and Peasants in Mexico*. Berkeley and Los Angeles: University of California Press.

———. 1977b. "Policy Change in an Authoritarian Regime: Mexico under Echevarria." *Journal of Interamerican Studies and World Affairs* 19(4):523–56.

———, ed. 1981. *Politics and Policy Implementation in the Third World*. Princeton, N.J.: Princeton University Press.

———. 1984. "Rural Underdevelopment and Public Policy in Mexico." In *Politics and Public Policy in Latin America*, ed. Steven W. Hughes and Kenneth J. Mijeski, pp. 148–62. Boulder and London: Westview.

Hamilton, Nora. 1982. *The Limits of State Autonomy: Postrevolutionary México*. Princeton, N.J.: Princeton University Press.

Handleman, Howard. 1976. "The Politics of Labor Protest in Mexico: Two Case Studies." *Journal of Interamerican Studies and World Affairs* 18(3):267–94.

Hart, John. 1978. *Anarchism and the Mexican Working Class, 1860–1931*. Austin: University of Texas Press.

Harvey, Neil. "Peasant Strategies and Corporatism in Chiapas." In *Popular Movements and Political Change in Mexico*, ed. Joe Foweraker and Ann L. Craig, pp. 183–98. Boulder and London: Lynne Rienner.

Hellman, Judith A. 1983. 2d ed. *Mexico in Crisis.* New York and London: Holmes and Meier.

Hernández, Luis. 1986. "The SNTE and Teachers' Movement, 1982–1984." In *The Mexican Left, the Popular Movements, and the Politics of Austerity,* ed. Barry Carr and Ricardo Anzaldúa, pp. 59–74. Research Monograph Series No. 18. La Jolla: Center for US-Mexican Studies, University of California, San Diego.

Hernández, Salvador. 1971. *El PRI y el Movimiento Estudiantil de 1968.* México, D.F.: El Caballito.

———. 1980. "Tiempos Libertarios. El Magonismo en México: Cananea, Rio Blanco y Baja California." In *De la Dictadura Porfirista a los Tiempos Libertarios,* Colección La Clase Obrera en la Historia de México, ed. Ciro F. S. Cardoso, Francisco G. Hermosillo, and Salvador Hernandez, pp. 101–231. México, D.F.: Siglo XXI.

Hernández Laos, Enrique. 1989. "Efectos del Crecimiento Económico y la Distribución del Ingreso sobre la Pobreza Extrema en México (1960–1988)." Document prepared for the United Nations Development Program (UNDP). Universidad Autónoma Metropolitana, México D.F. Photocopy.

———. 1993. *Crecimiento Económico y Pobreza en México: Una Agenda para Investigación.* México, D.F.: UNAM.

Hernández S., Ricardo. 1987. *La Coordinadora Nacional del Movimiento Urbano Popular (CONAMUP): su Historia 1980–1986.* México, D.F.: Equipo Pueblo.

Hodges, Donald, and Ross Gandy. 1979. *Mexico 1910–1976: Reform or Revolution?* London: Zed Books.

Hofstadter, Dan, ed. 1974. *Mexico 1946–73.* New York: Facts on File.

Huntington, Samuel. 1968. *Political Order in Changing Societies.* New Haven, Conn.: Yale University Press.

Joseph, Paul. 1981. *Cracks in the Empire.* Boston: South End Press.

Karl, Terry Lynn. 1986. "Petroleum and Political Pacts: The Transition to Democracy in Venezuela." In *Transitions from Authoritarian Rule: Latin America,* ed. Guillermo O'Donnell, Philippe C. Schmitter, and Laurence Whitehead, pp. 196–220. Baltimore: Johns Hopkins University Press.

Katz, Frank. 1976. "Peasants in the Mexican Revolution of 1910." In *Forging Nations: A Comparative View of Rural Ferment and Revolt,* ed. Spielbey and Scott Whiteford, pp. 3–44. East Lansing: Michigan State University Press.

Katznelson, Ira. 1986. "Working Class Formation in Western Europe and the United States." In *Working Class Formation in Western Europe and the United States,* ed. Ira Katznelson and Aristide R. Zolby, pp. 3–44. Princeton, N.J.: Princeton University Press.

Katzenstein, Peter J. 1978. *Between Power and Plenty.* Madison: University of Wisconsin Press.

Kaufman, Susan. 1973. "Decision Making in an Authoritarian Regime:

Theoretical Implications from a Case Study." *World Politics* 25(1):28–54.

———. 1975. *The Mexican Profit-Sharing Decision: Politics in an Authoritarian Regime.* Princeton, N.J.: Princeton University Press.

King, Timothy. 1970. *Mexico: Industrialization and Trade Policies Since 1940.* London: Oxford University Press.

Knight Alan. 1986. *The Mexican Revolution.* Cambridge: Cambridge University Press.

———. 1987a. "The Working Class and the Mexican Revolution." In *Latin America,* ed. Eduardo P. Archetti, Paul Cammack, and Bryan Roberts, pp. 97–108. London and New York: Monthly Review.

———. 1987b. *US-Mexican Relations, 1910–1940: An Interpretation.* La Jolla: Center for US-Mexican Studies, University of California, San Diego.

———. 1990. "Historical Continuities in Social Movements." In *Popular Movements and Political Change in Mexico,* ed. Joe Foweraker and Ann L. Craig, pp. 78–104. Boulder, Colo.: Lynne Rienner.

Kovacs, Karen. 1989. "Intervención Estatal y Transformación del Régimen Político: El Caso de la Universidad Pedagógica Nacional." Ph.D. diss., El Colegio de México.

Krause, Enrique. 1987a. *Francisco I. Madero: Místico de la Libertad.* México D.F.: Fondo de Cultura Económica.

———. 1987b. 2d ed. *Por una Democracia sin Adjetivos.* México, D.F.: El Caballito.

Labastida M. del Campo, Julio. 1974. "Algunas hipotesis sobre el modelo politico mexicano y sus perspectivas." *Revista Mexicana de Sociología* 36(3):629–42.

Leal, Juan Felipe. 1975. 2d ed. *La Burguesia y el Estado Mexicano.* México: El Caballito.

———. 1986. "The Mexican State, 1915–1973: A Historical Interpretation." In *Modern Mexico: State, Economy and Social Conflict,* ed. Nora Hamilton and Timothy F. Harding, pp. 21–42. Beverly Hills: Sage.

Lerner de Sheinbaum, Bertha. 1983. "La Tecnocracia en México: ni Embrión ni Garantia de Profesionalismo." *Revista Mexicana de Sociología* 45(3):1051–66.

Levy, Daniel, and Gabriel Szekely. 1985. *Estabilidad y cambio. Paradojas del sistema politico mexicano.* México, D.F.: El Colegio de México.

Leyva Flores, René. 1990. "Descentralización Municipal de los Servicios de Salud en México. Estudio de caso en el Estado de Guerrero, 1984–1987." Master's thesis, Universidad Metropolitana Autónoma, Xochimilco.

Liss, Sheldon B. 1984. *Marxist Thought in Latin America.* Berkeley and Los Angeles: University of California Press.

Loaeza, Soledad. 1977. "La Política del Rumor: México, Noviembre–Diciembre 1976." In *Las Crisis en el Sistema Político Mexicano (1928–*

1977), ed. Centro de Estudios Internacionales. México, D.F.: El Colegio de México.

———. 1987. "El Partido Acción Nacional: de la Oposición Leal a la Impaciencia Electoral." In *La Vida Política Mexicana en la Crisis,* ed. Soledad Loaeza and Rafael Segovia, pp. 77–106. México, D.F.: El Colegio de México.

———. 1989. "The Emergence and Legitimation of the Modern Right, 1970–1988." In *Mexico's Alternative Political Futures,* ed. Cornelius Wayne, Judith Gentleman, and Peter H. Smith, pp. 351–66. La Jolla: Center for US-Mexican Studies, University of California, San Diego.

———. 1990. "Derecha y Democracia en el Cambio Político Mexicano 1982–1988." *Foro Internacional* 30(4):631–58.

Linz, Juan. 1970. "Totalitarian and Authoritarian Regimes." In *Handbook of Political Science,* ed. Fred Greenstein and Nelson Polsby. Reading, Mass.: Addison-Wesley.

Lomnitz, Larissa. 1974. "The Social and Economic Organization of a Mexican Shantytown." In *Anthropological Perspectives on Latin American Urbanization,* ed. Wayne Cornelius and Felicity M. Trueblood. Beverly Hills: Sage.

———. 1975. *Como Sobreviven los Marginados.* México, D.F.: Siglo XXI.

———. 1977. "Conflict and Mediation in a Latin American University." *Journal of Interamerican Studies and World Affairs* 19(3):315–38.

———. 1979. "The Latin American University: Breeding Ground of the New State Elites." Paper presented at the American Anthropological Association Congress in Houston, Texas, January 3–6.

Looney, Robert. 1978. *Mexico's Economy: A Policy Analysis with Forecasts to 1990.* Boulder, Colo.: Praeger, Westview Special Studies on Latin America.

———. 1982. *Development Alternatives of Mexico.* New York: Praeger.

Loyo, Aurora. 1990. "La Confederación Proletaria Nacional: un Primer Intento de Quebrar la Hegemonia de la CTM." In *Entre la Querra y la Estabilidad Política. El México de los 40,* ed. Rafael Loyo, pp. 85–108. México, D.F.: Grigalbo.

Lozoya, Jorge Alberto. 1970. *El Ejercito Mexicano.* México, D.F.: El Colegio de México, Jornada.

Luiselli, Casio. 1985. *The Route to Food Self-Sufficiency in Mexico: Interaction with the U.S. Food System.* Monograph Series No. 17. La Jolla: Center for US-Mexican Studies, University of California, San Diego.

Luna, Matilde; Ricardo Tirado; and Francisco Valdes. "Businessmen and Politics in Mexico, 1982–1986." In *Government and Private Sector in Contemporary Mexico,* ed. Sylvia Maxfield and Ricardo Anzaldua Montoya. Monograph Series No. 20. La Jolla: Center for US-Mexican Studies, University of California, San Diego.

Lustig, Nora. 1987. "Crisis Economica y Niveles de Vida en México 1982–1985." *Estudios Económicos* 2(2).

Mabry, Donald J. 1982. *The Mexican University and the State: Student Conflicts, 1910–1971.* College Station: Texas A&M University Press.

Maldonado, Edelmiro. 1981. *Breve Historia del Movimiento Obrero.* Mazatlán: Universidad Autonoma de Sinaloa.

Malloy, James, ed. 1977. *Authoritarianism and Corporatism in Latin America.* Pittsburgh: University of Pittsburgh Press.

———. 1979. *The Politics of Social Security in Brazil.* Pittsburgh: University of Pittsburgh Press.

Malloy, James, and Mitchell A. Seligson, eds. 1987. *Authoritarians and Democrats: Regime Transition in Latin America.* Pittsburgh: University of Pittsburgh Press.

Martin del Campo, Antonio C. 1989. "Notas sobre la Revolución Reciente de los Subsidios a Productos Básicos Alimenticios." Paper presented at the Seminar on the Effects of the Crisis on the Poorest Sectors, Centro Tepoztlán, Tepoztlán Morelos, June 12.

Martinez Nava, Juan Manuel. 1982. "El Conflicto Estado-Empresarios en los Gobiernos de Cárdenas, Lopez Mateos y Echeverría." Ph.D. diss., El Colegio de México, México D.F.

Massolo, Alejandra. 1986. "¡Que el Gobierno Entienda, lo Primero es la Vivienda!" *Revista Mexicana de Sociología* 48(2):195–238.

Maxfield, Sylvia. 1990. *Governing Capital: International Finance and Mexican Politics.* Ithaca, N.Y.: Cornell University Press.

Maxfield, Sylvia, and Ricardo Anzaldua Montoya, eds. 1987. *Government and Private Sector in Contemporary Mexico.* La Jolla: Center for US-Mexican Studies, University of California, San Diego.

Medina, Luis. 1974. "Origen y Circunstancias de la Idea de Unidad Nacional." *Foro Internacional* 14(3):265–90.

———. 1978. *Historia de la Revolución Mexicana 1940–1952. Del Cardenismo al Avilacamachismo.* México, D.F.: El Colegio de México.

———. 1979. *Historia de la Revolución Mexicana 1940–1952. Civilismo y Modernización del Autoritarismo.* México, D.F.: El Colegio de México, 1979.

Mesa Lago, Carmelo. 1978. *Social Security in Latin America: Pressure Groups, Stratification, and Inequality.* Pittsburgh: University of Pittsburgh Press.

Meyer, Jean. 1971. "Los Obreros en la Revolución Mexicana: los Batallones Rojos." *Historia Mexicana* 21(1):1–37.

Meyer, Lorenzo. 1977. "Historical Roots of the Authoritarian State in Mexico." In *Authoritarianism in Mexico,* ed. José Luis Reyna and Richard S. Weinert. Philadelphia, Pa.: Institute for the Study of Human Issues.

———. 1989. "Democratization of the PRI: Mission Impossible?" In *Mexico's Alternative Political Futures,* ed. Wayne Cornelius, Judith Gentleman, and Peter H. Smith, pp. 325–50. Center for US-Mexican Studies, University of California, San Diego.

Middlebrook, Kevin. 1981. "The Political Economy of Organized Labor, 1940–1978." Ph.D. diss., Harvard University.

———. 1982. "International Implications of Labor Change: The Automobile Industry." In *Mexico's Political Economy: Challenges at Home and Abroad*, ed. Jorge I. Dominguez, pp. 133–70. Beverly Hills: Sage.

———. 1986. "Political Liberalization in an Authoritarian Regime: The Case of Mexico." In *Transitions from Authoritarian Rule*, ed. O'Donnell Guillermo, Philip Schmitter, and Laurence Whitehead, pp. 123–47. Baltimore, Md.: Johns Hopkins University Press.

———. 1989a. "The CTM and the Future of State-Labor Relations." In *Mexico's Alternative Political Futures*, ed. Wayne Cornelius, Judith Gentleman, and Peter H. Smith, pp. 291–306. La Jolla: Center for US-Mexican Studies, University of California, San Diego.

———. 1989b. "The Sounds of Silence: Organised Labour's Response to Economic Crisis in Mexico." *Journal of Latin American Studies* 21(2):195–220.

Miller, Richard. 1966. "The Role of Labor Organizations in a Developing Country." Ph.D. diss., Cornell University.

Molina, Daniel. 1977. "La Política Laboral y el Movimiento Obrero (1970–1976)." *Cuadernos Políticos* 12 (April–June): 69–88.

Molina Pineiro, Luis. 1988. *Estructura del Poder y Reglas del Juego Político en México*. México, D.F.: UNAM.

Molinar Horcasitas, Juan. 1987a. "The 1985 Federal Elections in Mexico: The Product of a System." In *Electoral Patterns and Perspectives in Mexico*, ed. A. Alvarado, pp. 17–32. Monograph Series No. 22. Center for US-Mexican Studies, University of California, San Diego.

———. 1987b. "Vicisitudes de una Reforma Electoral." In *La Vida Política Mexicana en la Crisis*, ed. Soledad Loaeza and Rafael Segovia, pp. 25–40. México, D.F.: El Colegio de México.

———. 1992. *Elecciones, Autoritarismo y Democracia en México*. México DF: Cal y Arena.

Molinar Horcasitas, Juan, and John Weldon. 1990. "Elecciones de 1988 en México: Crisis del Autoritarismo." *Revista Mexicana de Sociología* 52(4): 229–62.

Montaño, Jorge. *Los Pobres de la Ciudad en los Asentamientos Espontáneos*. México, D.F.: Siglo XXI.

Mosk Sanford, Alexander. 1950. *Industrial Revolution in México*. Berkeley and Los Angeles: University of California Press.

Munck, Ronaldo, with Ricardo Falcón and Bernardo Galitelli. 1987. *Argentina from Anarchism to Peronism: Workers, Unions and Politics, 1855–1985*. London: Zed Books.

Nadal Egea J., Alejandro. 1977. *Instrumentos de Política Científica y Tecnológica en México*. México, D.F.: El Colegio de México.

Navarro, Bernardo, and Pedro Moteczuma. 1989. *La Urbanización Popular en la Ciudad de México*. México, D.F.: Instituto de Investigaciones Económicas, UNAM.

Needler, Martin. 1987. "The Significance of Recent Events for the Mexican Political System." In *Mexican Politics in Transition*, ed. Judith Gentleman, pp. 201–16. Boulder and London: Westview.

O'Brien, Philip, and Paul Cammack. 1985. *Generals in Retreat*. Manchester: Manchester University Press.

O'Donnell, Guillermo. 1973. *Modernization and Bureaucratic Authoritarianism: Studies in South American Politics*. Berkeley and Los Angeles: University of California Press.

———. 1977a. "Apuntes para una Teoría del Estado." Documento CEDES/ G.E. CLACSO/No. 9.

———. 1977b. "Corporatism and the Question of the State." In *Authoritarianism and Corporatism in Latin America*, ed. James M. Malloy. Pittsburgh: University of Pittsburgh Press.

———. 1983. *El Estado Burocrático Autoritario 1966–1973*. Buenos Aires. Editorial Belgrano.

———. 1988. *Bureaucratic Authoritarianism: Argentina (1966–1973) in Comparative Perspective*. Berkeley and Los Angeles: University of California Press.

O'Donnell, Guillermo, and Philippe C. Schmitter. 1986. *Tentative Conclusions about Uncertain Democracies*. Baltimore: Johns Hopkins University Press.

O'Donnell, Guillermo; Philippe C. Schmitter; and Laurence Whitehead, eds. 1986. *Transitions from Authoritarian Rule: Latin America*. Baltimore, Md.: Johns Hopkins University Press.

Offe, Claus. 1985. "New Social Movements: Challenging the Boundaries of Institutional Politics." *Social Research* 52(4):817–68.

Otero, Gerardo. 1989. "The New Agrarian Movement: Self-managed Democratic Production." *Latin American Perspectives* 18(Fall):28–59.

Pastor, Robert. 1989. *Democracy in the Americas: Stopping the Pendulum*. New York: Holmes & Meier.

Pellicer de Brody, Olga. 1974. *México y la Revolución Cubana*. México, D.F.: El Colegio de México.

———. 1977. "La Crisis Mexicana: Hacia una Nueva Dependencia." *Cuadernos Políticos* 14(Oct.–Dec.):45–56.

Pellicer de Brody, Olga, and José Luis Reyna. 1978. *Historia de la Revolución Mexicana 1952–1960. El Afianciamiento de la Establidad Política*. México, D.F.: El Colegio de México.

Peschard, Jacqueline. 1988. "Las Elecciones en el Distrito Federal entre 1964 y 1985." *Estudios Sociológicos* 6(16):67–102.

Pozas Horcasitas, Ricardo. 1990. "De lo Duro a lo Seguro: la Fundación del Seguro Social Mexicano." In *Entre la Guerra y la Estabilidad Política. El México de los 40*, ed. Rafael Loyo, pp. 109–36. México, D.F.: Grigalbo.

Prieto, Ana. 1986. "Mexico's National Coordinadoras in a Context of Economic Crisis." In *The Mexican Left, the Popular Movements, and the Politics of Austerity*, ed. Barry Carr and Ricardo Anzualdúa, pp. 75–94. Monograph Series No. 18. La Jolla: Center for U.S.-Mexican Studies, University of California, San Diego.

Purcell, Susan K., and John F. H. Purcell. 1980. "State and Society in Mexico: Must a Stable Polity Be Institutionalized?" *World Politics* 32(2):194–227.

Ramirez Saiz, Juan Manuel. 1986. *El Movimiento Urbano Popular en México.* México, D.F.: Siglo XXI.

Ramirez Saiz, Juan Manuel. 1989. "Efectos Políticos de la Proposición y Puesta en Práctica del Programa del Movimiento Urbano Popular (MUP)." Paper presented at the workshop on Popular Movements and the Transformation of the Mexican Political System. La Jolla: Center for US-Mexican Studies, University of California, San Diego.

———. 1990. "Urban Struggles and Their Political Consequences." In *Popular Movements and Political Change in Mexico,* ed. Joe Foweraker and Ann L. Craig, pp. 234–46. Boulder and London: Lynne Rienner.

Ramos-Escandón, Carmen. 1987. "La Política Obrera del Estado Mexicano: De Diaz a Madero. El Caso de los Trabajadores Textiles." *Mexican Studies* 3(1): 19–48.

Redclift, Michael R. 1981. "Development Policy-Making in Mexico: The Sistema Alimentario Mexicano." Working paper in US-Mexican Studies No. 24. La Jolla: Center for US-Mexican Studies, University of California, San Diego.

Remmer, Karen. 1978. "Evaluating the Impact of Military Regimes in Latin America." *Latin American Research Review* 13: 39–54.

———. 1986. "Exclusionary Democracy." *Studies in Comparative International Development* Winter:64–85.

Remmer, Karen, and Gilbert Merckx. 1982. "Bureaucratic Authoritarianism Revisited." *Latin American Research Review* 17(2):3–40.

Revel-Mouroz, Jean. 1980. "La politique économique mexicaine (1976–1980)." *Problèmes d'Amérique Latine* 57.

Revista Mexicana del Trabajo. 1971. "Conferencia Sustentada por el C. General Alvaro Obregón, Candidato a la Presidencia de la República, la Noche del Domingo 8 de Agosto de 1927 en el Teatro de la República de la Ciudad de Morelia, Michoacán." 1 (Jan.–July).

Revueltas, José. 1978. *México 68: Juventud y Revolución.* México, D.F.: ERA.

Reyna, José Luis. 1974. *Control Político, Estabilidad y Desarrollo en México.* Cuadernos del CES No. 3. México, D.F.: El Colegio de México.

———. 1977. "Redefining the Authoritarian Regime." In *Authoritarianism in Mexico,* ed. José Luis Reyna and Richard S. Weinert, pp. 155–72. Philadelphia: Institute for the Study of Human Issues.

———. 1979. "El Movimiento Obrero en una Situación de Crisis: México 1976–1978." *Foro Internacional* 19(3):155–72.

Reyna, José Luis, and Raul Trejo Delabre. 1981. *La Clase Obrera en la Historia de México. De Adolfo Ruiz Cortinez a Adolfo Lopez Mateos (1952–1964).* México, D.F.: UNAM-Siglo XXI.

Reyna, José Luis, Francisco Zapata; Marcelo Miquet Fleury; and Silvia Gomez-Tagle. *Tres Estudios sobre el Movimiento Obrero en México.* México, D.F.: El Colegio de México, Jornada 80.

Reynolds, Clark. 1974. *La Economía Mexicana: su Estructura y Crecimiento en el Siglo XX*. México, D.F.: Fondo de Cultura Económica.

———. 1977. "Why Mexico's 'Stabilizing Development' Was Actually Destabilizing (with Some Implications for the Future)." Hearings before the Subcommittee on Interamerican Economic Relationships. Washington, D.C.: U.S. Government Printing Office.

Rivera Urrutia, Eugenio, and Ana Sojo. 1985. "Movimiento Popular, Conflicto Social y Democracia." *Revista Mexicana de Sociología* 47(4):17–34.

Rivero, Martha. 1990. "La Política Economica durante la Guerra." In *Entre la Guerra y la Estabilidad Política: el México de los 40*, ed. Rafael Loyo, pp. 13–48. México, D.F.: Grigalbo.

Roemer, Milton J. 1971. "Social Security for Medical Care: Is it Justified in Developing Countries?" *International Journal of Health Services* 1(Nov.):354–61.

———. 1973. "Development of Medical Services Under Social Security in Latin America." *International Labour Review* 108(6):1–23.

Rogers, Everett M., and Floyd Shoemaker. 1971. 2d ed. *Communication of Innovation: A Cross-Cultural Approach*. New York: Free Press.

Rosenzweig, Fernando. 1960. "Las Exportaciones Mexicanas de 1877 a 1911." *Historia Mexicana* 9(3):394–413.

Roxborough, Ian. 1984. *Unions and Politics in Mexico: The Case of the Automobile Industry*. New York: Cambridge University Press, 1984.

Rueschemeyer, Dietrich; Evelyn H. Stevens; and John D. Stephens. 1992. *Capitalist Development and Democracy*. Chicago: University of Chicago Press.

Ruiz Ramón, Eduardo. 1976. "Madero's Administration and Mexican Labor." In *Contemporary Mexico*, ed. James Wilkie, Michael C. Meyer, and Edna Monzón de Wilkie. Berkeley and Los Angeles: University of California Press.

Saldívar, Américo. 1985. 2d ed. *Ideologia y Política del Estado Mexicano (1970–1976)*. México, D.F.: Siglo XXI.

Schmitter, Phillip. 1974. "Still the Century of Corporatism." *The Review of Politics* 36(1): 85–131.

Segovia, Rafael. 1987. "El Fastidio Electoral." In *La Vida Política en la Crisis*, ed. Loaeza Soledad and Rafael Segovia. México, D.F.: El Colegio de México.

Semo, Enrique. 1985. 2d ed. *Historia Mexicana. Economia y Lucha de Clases*. México, D.F.: ERA.

———. 1986. "The Mexican Left and the Economic Crisis." In *The Mexican Left, the Popular Movements, and the Politics of Austerity, 1982–85*, ed. B. Carr and Ricardo Anzaldúa, pp. 19–32. La Jolla: Center for US-Mexican Studies, University of California, San Diego.

———. 1988. *Entre Crisis te Veas*. México, D.F.: Nueva Imagen.

Sherraden, Margaret. 1989. "Social Policy Reform in Mexico: Rural Primary Health Services." Ph.D. diss., Washington University.

Skidmore, Thomas E., and Peter H. Smith. 1984. *Modern Latin America.* Cambridge: Cambridge University Press.

Skocpol, Theda. 1985. "Bringing the State Back In: Strategies of Analysis in Current Research." In *Bringing the State Back In,* ed. Peter B. Evans, D. Rueschemeyer, and Theda Skocpol, pp. 3–43. Cambridge: Cambridge University Press.

Sloan, John W. 1984. *Public Policy in Latin America: A Comparative Survey.* Pittsburgh: University of Pittsburgh Press.

Smith, Peter H. 1979. *Labyrinths of Power: Political Recruitment in Twentieth Century Mexico.* Princeton, N.J.: Princeton University Press.

———. 1986. "Leadership and Change, Intellectuals and Technocrats." In *Mexico's Political Stability: The Next Five Years,* ed. Roderick Ai Camp, pp. 101–18. Boulder and London: Westview.

Solis, Leopoldo. 1970. *La Realidad Económica Mexicana: Retrovisión y Perspectivas.* México, D.F.: Siglo XXI.

———. 1977a. "A Monetary Will-o'-the-Wisp: Pursuit of Equity Through Deficit Spending." Discussion Paper No. 77. Princeton, N.J.: Princeton University.

———. 1977b. "El Desarrollo Estabilizador: la Economía Mexicana durante los Sesentas." Paper delivered at a conference at the Colegio Nacional. Photocopy.

———. 1980. *Alternativas para el Desarrollo.* México, D.F.: Joaquin Mortiz.

Spalding, Rose, 1978. "Social Security Policy Making: The Formation and Evolution of the Mexican Social Security Institute." Ph.D. diss., University of North Carolina.

———. 1980. "Welfare Policymaking: Theoretical Implications of a Mexican Case Study." *Comparative Politics* 12(4): 414–38.

———. 1981. "State Power and Its Limits: Corporatism in Mexico." *Comparative Political Studies* 14(2):315–50.

———. 1985. "El Sistema Alimentario Mexicano: Ascenso y Decadencia." *Estudios Sociológicos* 3(8): 414–38.

Stepan, Alfred. 1978. *The State and Society: Peru in a Comparative Perspective.* Princeton, N.J.: Princeton University Press.

Stern, Claudio; R. M. Nuñez; K. Tolbert; Victor Cárdenas; and M. Goodwin. 1990. "Cambio en las condiciones de Sobrevivencia infantil en México y estrategias para el futuro." *Salud Pública de México* 32 (5):532–42.

Stevens, Evelyn. 1974. *Protest and Response in Mexico.* Cambridge, Mass: MIT Press.

Story, Dale. 1986. *Industry, the State and Public Policy in Mexico.* Austin: University of Texas Press.

———. 1987. "The PAN, the Private Sector and the Future of the Mexican Opposition." In *Mexican Politics in Transition,* ed. Judith Gentleman. Boulder and London: Westview.

Street, Susan. 1989. "The Role of Social Movements in the Analysis of Sociopolitical Change in Mexico." Paper presented at the Latin American Studies Association Fifteenth International Congress, Sept. 21–23.

———. 1991. "El Papel de los Movimientos Sociales en el Análisis del Cambio Social en México." *Revista Mexicana de Sociología* 53(2): 142–58.

———. 1992. *Maestros en Movimiento. Transformaciones en la Burocracia Estatal.* Colección Miguel Othón de Mendizábal. México, D.F.: SEP.

Talavera, Fernando, and Juan Felipe Leal. 1977. "Organizaciones Sindicales Obreras de México, 1948–1970: Enfoque Estadístico." *Revista Mexicana de Sociología* 39(4): 1251–86.

Tamayo, Jaime. 1990. "Neoliberalism Encounters Neocardenismo." In *Popular Movements and Political Change in Mexico,* ed. Joe Foweraker and Ann L. Craig, pp. 121–36. Boulder and London: Lynne Rienner.

Tarrés, Maria Luisa. 1990. "Middle-Class Associations and Electoral Opposition." In *Popular Movements and Political Change in Mexico,* ed. Joe Foweraker and Ann L. Craig, pp. 137–49. Boulder and London: Lynne Rienner.

Teichman, Judith A. 1988. *Policymaking in Mexico: From Boom to Crisis.* Boston: Allen and Unwin.

Therborn, Góran. 1977. "The Rule of Capital and the Rise of Democracy." *New Left Review* 103 (May–June):3–42.

Thomas, Clyve Y. 1984. *The Rise of the Authoritarian State in Peripheral Societies.* New York: Monthly Review.

Tilly, Charles. 1978. *From Mobilization to Revolution.* New York: Random House.

Topete, Jesus. 1961. *Terror en el Riel: de "El Charro" a Vallejo.* México, D.F.: Editorial Cosmonauta.

Torres Mejía, David. 1987. *Politica y Partidos en las Elecciones Federales de 1985.* México: UNAM.

Torres R., Blanca, ed. 1986. *Descentralización y Democracia en México.* México: El Colegio de México.

Trejo Delarbre, Raul. 1976. "The Mexican Labor Movement: 1917–1975." *Latin American Perspectives* 3(1): 133–53.

———. 1979. "El Movimiento Obrero: Situación y Perspectivas." In *México Hoy,* ed. P. Gonzalez Casanova and E. Florescano, pp. 121–51. México, D.F.: Siglo XXI Editores.

Tuñón, Esperanza. 1982. *Huerta y el Movimiento Obrero.* México: El Caballito.

Tutino, John Mark. 1986. *From Insurrection to Revolution in México: Social Bases of Agrarian Violence, 1750–1940.* Princeton, N.J.: Princeton University Press.

Ulloa, Berta. 1979. *Historia de la Revolución Mexicana 1914–1917: La Encrucijada de 1915.* México, D.F.: El Colegio de México.

———. 1983. *Historia de la Revolución Mexicana 1914–1917: La Constitución de 1917.* México, D.F.: El Colegio de México.

UNAM. 1992. *Constitución Política de los Estados Mexicanos Comentada*. 3rd. ed. México, D.F.: UNAM, Instituto de Investigaciones Jurídicas. Serie Textos y Estudios Legislativos 59.

Urquidi, Victor. 1988a. "Perspectivas de la Economía Mexicana, con Especial Referencia a la Deuda Externa." *Revista de El Colegio de Sonora*, Año I(1):70–85.

———. 1988b. "Structural Constraints and Strategic Choices in Mexican Development." Paper presented at the conference "Overcoming Constraints on Mexican Development" at the Center for Latin American Studies, Brown University, Providence, R.I., November 3–5, 1988.

Valdés Olmedo, Cuauhtémoc. 1991. *Bonanza, crisis . . . recuperación? Financiamiento de la salud: 1970–1990, una perspectiva hacia el año 2000*. México, D.F.: Fundación Mexicana para la Salud.

Vallejo, Demetrio. 1957. *Las Luchas Ferrocarrileras que Conmovierón a México*. México, D.F.: Liberación Nacional.

Vernon, Raymond. 1963. *The Dilemmas of Mexico's Development: The Roles of the Private and Public Sectors*. Cambridge, Mass: Harvard University Press.

Walker, David. 1981. "Porfirian Labor Politics: Working Class Organizations in Mexico City and Porfirio Diaz, 1876–1902." *The Americas* 37(3):257–89.

Whitehead, Laurence. 1980. "La Política Economica del Sexenio de Echevarría: Que salió mal y por qué?" *Foro Internacionl* 20(3): 484–513.

———. 1987. "La Perspectiva Económica de México: Sus Implicaciones para las Relaciones entre el Estado y los Trabajadores." *Foro Internacional* 28(Oct.–Dec.):165–95.

———. 1989. "Political Change and Economic Stabilization: The 'Economic Solidarity Pact'." In *Mexico's Alternative Political Futures*, ed. Wayne Cornelius, Judith Gentleman, and Philip H. Smith, pp. 181–214. La Jolla: Center for US-Mexican Studies, University of California, San Diego.

Wildavsky, Aaron. 1987. *Speaking Truth to Power*. New Brunswick, N.J.: Transaction Pubs.

Wilkie, James. 1970. *The Mexican Revolution: Federal Expenditures and Social Change Since 1910*. Berkeley and Los Angeles: University of California Press.

Wilson, Richard. 1981. "The Corporatist Welfare State, Social Security and Development in Mexico." Ph.D. diss., Yale University.

Wionzcek, Miguel. 1986. "Industrialización, Capital Extranjero y Transferencia de Tecnologia: la Experiencia Mexicana, 1930–1985." *Foro Internacional* 26(2):550–66.

Wolf, Eric. 1969. *Peasant Wars of the Twentieth Century*. New York: Harper-Torch.

Womack, John, Jr. 1969. *Zapata and the Mexican Revolution.* New York: Knopf.

World Bank. 1986. *Poverty in Latin America. The Impact of Depression.* Washington, D.C.: The World Bank.

Zermeño, Sergio. 1978. *México: una Democracia Utópica, el Movimiento Estudiantil del 68.* México, D.F.: Siglo XXI.

Zertuche Muños, Fernando, et al. 1980. *Historia del IMSS: los Primeros Años.* México, D.F.: Instituto Mexicano del Seguro Social.

Index

122–23; under Echeverría administration, 138–39, 172; foreign influence in adoption of, 173–74; labor
opponents of, 210n7; under Lopez
Mateos administration, 118–19;
1954 expansion of, 106; proposals
for, 12, 56, 60, 62–63, 68–69, 70–
71. *See also* Instituto Mexicano del
Seguro Social
Social Medicine, Department of, 75
Social order, 5, 40
Social reform, 8, 14–15, 29, 52; analyses of popular struggles and, 18–
21, 205n5; under de la Madrid
administration, 157–58, 174–75; as
incentives, 23, 38–39; and introduction of welfare state, 83–84,
87–88; under Lopez Mateos administration, 118–20; magnanimous
state view of, 22–25; PRONASOL,
17, 28, 162–63, 173, 179, 217n38;
as response to economic factors,
171–72; responsive state view of,
25–28; as tool for social peace, 31,
32, 96; types of, 9–10. *See also*
Health services; Housing; Profit
sharing; Social insurance
Social Security Institute. *See* Instituto
Mexicano del Seguro Social (IMSS)
Social Security Party, 68
Social Solidarity program (Echeverría
administration), 27, 138–39, 172
Socialist Mexican League, 92, 95, 102
Socialists, 92, 95, 102–03, 109, 116,
145–46. *See also* Popular Party
Society, defined, 40
Solis, Leopoldo, 106
Sonorans. *See* Calles, Plutarco Elias;
Obregón, Alvaro; Ortiz Rubio,
Pascual; Portes Gil, Emilio;
Rodriguez, Abelardo
Spalding, Rose, 27, 106
Speaking Truth to Power (Wildavsky), 15
Stabilizing development, 84, 111–13,
121, 133, 164, 172
State: defined, 40; and industrializa-
tion, 6; legitimacy need of, 30–31;
magnanimous, 22–25; mediating
role of, 4, 7, 10; post-debt morato-
rium, 28–30; relation of, to labor

1910–1940, 78–80, 166–67;
relation of, to labor 1940–1970,
83–84, 167–68; response to dissidence, 31–32, 61; responsiveness
of, 25–28, 204n12
State corporatism. *See* Corporatism
State elites, 27, 39, 127, 132; and need
for social reform, 31, 43, 171, 182;
rivalry among, 25, 26, 57–58, 175–
77; role of, in labor demobilization,
169–70
State revenues. *See* Taxes
State Workers' Union of the Mexican
Republic (STERM), 87, 94
Stephen, Alfred Linz, 22
Strikes, 46, 72, 99–100, 114, 209n24;
announcement of, 104, 211n16;
during Avila Camacho administration, 89–90, 91, 94; civil, 154, 155;
during constitutionalist decade, 48,
50, 54–55, 56; by doctors and students, 122, 123–24; during Echeverría administration, 136, 139–40;
to eliminate *charro* leadership,
215n10; during Ruiz Cortinez administration, 109, 110; during
Salinas administration, 204n10;
during Sonoran period, 60–62,
65, 66, 67, 68; by teachers, 68,
146–48, 162
Structural determinism, 19
Student uprising of 1968, 30, 38, 123–
24, 133, 213nn 33, 34; and mobilization of other groups, 121, 125–
26, 128, 168

Tapia, Sanchez, 86, 88
Taxes, 43, 132, 149, 153, 172
Teachers' unions, 107, 150–51, 203n6,
213n35; democratization of, 134,
146, 147–48, 149, 150; strikes by,
68, 146–48, 162
Technocratization, 147, 206n15
Ten-hour workday, 50, 53
Tlatelolco massacre, 16, 30, 84, 121,
126; casualties of, 124, 213n34
Transnational corporations,
116, 212n26
Tripartidismo (tripartite decision mak-
ing), 56, 90, 93, 137

Pitt Latin American Series
James M. Malloy, Editor

ARGENTINA

Argentina Between the Great Powers, 1936–1946
Guido di Tella and D. Cameron Watt, Editors

Argentina in the Twentieth Century
David Rock, Editor

Argentina: Political Culture and Instability
Susan Calvert and Peter Calvert

Argentine Workers: Peronism and Contemporary Class Consciousness
Peter Ranis

Discreet Partners: Argentina and the USSR Since 1917
Aldo César Vacs

The Franco-Perón Alliance: Relations Between Spain and Argentina, 1946–1955
Raanan Rein, translated by Martha Grenzeback

The Life, Music, and Times of Carlos Gardel
Simon Collier

Institutions, Parties, and Coalitions in Argentine Politics
Luigi Manzetti

The Political Economy of Argentina, 1946–1983
Guido di Tella and Rudiger Dornbusch, Editors

BOLIVIA

Unsettling Statecraft: Democracy and Neoliberalism in the Central Andes
Catherine M. Conaghan and James M. Malloy

BRAZIL

Capital Markets in the Development Process: The Case of Brazil
John H. Welch

External Constraints on Economic Policy in Brazil, 1899–1930
Winston Fritsch

The Film Industry in Brazil: Culture and the State
Randal Johnson

Kingdoms Come: Religion and Politics in Brazil
Rowan Ireland

The Manipulation of Consent: The State and Working-Class Consciousness in Brazil
Youssef Cohen

The Politics of Social Security in Brazil
James M. Malloy

Politics Within the State: Elite Bureaucrats and Industrial Policy in
Authoritarian Brazil
Ben Ross Schneider

The Meaning of Freedom: Economics, Politics and Culture After Slavery
Frank McGlynn and Seymour Drescher, Editors

CENTRAL AMERICA

At the Fall of Somoza
Lawrence Pezzullo and Ralph Pezzullo

Black Labor on a White Canal: Panama, 1904–1981
Michael L. Conniff

The Catholic Church and Politics in Nicaragua and Costa Rica
Philip J. Williams

Perspectives on the Agro-Export Economy in Central America
Wim Pelupessy, Editor

OTHER NATIONAL STUDIES

Chile: The Political Economy of Development and Democracy in the 1990s
David E. Hojman

The Overthrow of Allende and the Politics of Chile, 1964–1976
Paul E. Sigmund

Primary Medical Care in Chile: Accessibility Under Military Rule
Joseph L. Scarpaci

Rebirth of the Paraguayan Republic: The First Colorado Era, 1878–1904
Harris G. Warren

US POLICIES

The Hovering Giant: U.S. Responses to Revolutionary Change in Latin America
Cole Blasier

Illusions of Conflict: Anglo-American Diplomacy Toward Latin America
Joseph Smith

Images and Intervention: U.S. Policies in Latin America
Martha L. Cottam

The United States and Latin America in the 1980s: Contending Perspectives on a Decade of Crisis
Kevin J. Middlebrook and Carlos Rico, Editors

SOCIAL SECURITY

Ascent to Bankruptcy: Financing Social Security in Latin America
Carmelo Mesa-Lago

The Politics of Social Security in Brazil
James M. Malloy

OTHER STUDIES

Adventurers and Proletarians: The Story of Migrants in Latin America
Magnus Mörner, with the collaboration of Harold Sims

Authoritarianism and Corporatism in Latin America
James M. Malloy, Editor

Authoritarians and Democrats: Regime Transition in Latin America
James M. Malloy and Mitchell A. Seligson, Editors

The Constitution of Tyranny: Regimes of Exception in Spanish America
Brian Loveman

Female and Male in Latin America: Essays
Ann Pescatello, Editor

The Giant's Rival: The USSR and Latin America
Cole Blasier

Latin American Debt and the Adjustment Crisis
Rosemary Thorp and Laurence Whitehead, Editors

Public Policy in Latin America: A Comparative Survey
John W. Sloan

Selected Latin American One-Act Plays
Francesca Colecchia and Julio Matas, Editors and Translators

The Social Documentary in Latin America
Julianne Burton, Editor

The State and Capital Accumulation in Latin America. Vol. 1:
Brazil, Chile, Mexico. Vol. 2: Argentina, Bolivia, Colombia, Ecuador, Peru, Uruguay,
Venezuela
Christian Anglade and Carlos Fortin, Editors

Transnational Corporations and the Latin American Automobile Industry
Rhys Jenkins